MW00646915

BUSINESS TRENDS IN PRACTICE

BUSINESS TRENDS IN PRACTICE

THE 25+ TRENDS THAT ARE REDEFINING ORGANIZATIONS

BERNARD MARR

WILEY

This edition first published 2022
© 2022 by Bernard Marr

Registered office
John Wiley & Sons Ltd, The Atrium, Southern Gate, Chichester, West Sussex, PO19 8SQ, United Kingdom

For details of our global editorial offices, for customer services and for information about how to apply for permission to reuse the copyright material in this book please see our website at www.wiley.com.

All rights reserved. No part of this publication may be reproduced, stored in a retrieval system, or transmitted, in any form or by any means, electronic, mechanical, photocopying, recording or otherwise, except as permitted by the UK Copyright, Designs and Patents Act 1988, without the prior permission of the publisher.

Wiley publishes in a variety of print and electronic formats and by print-on-demand. Some material included with standard print versions of this book may not be included in e-books or in print-on-demand. If this book refers to media such as a CD or DVD that is not included in the version you purchased, you may download this material at http://booksupport.wiley.com. For more information about Wiley products, visit www.wiley.com.

Designations used by companies to distinguish their products are often claimed as trademarks. All brand names and product names used in this book are trade names, service marks, trademarks or registered trademarks of their respective owners. The publisher is not associated with any product or vendor mentioned in this book.

Limit of Liability/Disclaimer of Warranty: While the publisher and author have used their best efforts in preparing this book, they make no representations or warranties with respect to the accuracy or completeness of the contents of this book and specifically disclaim any implied warranties of merchantability or fitness for a particular purpose. It is sold on the understanding that the publisher is not engaged in rendering professional services and neither the publisher nor the author shall be liable for damages arising herefrom. If professional advice or other expert assistance is required, the services of a competent professional should be sought.

Library of Congress Cataloging-in-Publication Data

Names: Marr, Bernard, author.
Title: Business trends in practice : the 25+ trends that are redefining organizations / Bernard Marr.
Description: [Hoboken, NJ] : Wiley, 2022. | Includes index.
Identifiers: LCCN 2021033030 (print) | LCCN 2021033031 (ebook) | ISBN 9781119795575 (cloth) | ISBN 9781119795599 (adobe pdf) | ISBN 9781119795582 (epub)
Subjects: LCSH: Business forecasting. | Business—21st century.
Classification: LCC HD30.27 .M353 2022 (print) | LCC HD30.27 (ebook) | DDC 658.4/0355—dc23
LC record available at https://lccn.loc.gov/2021033030
LC ebook record available at https://lccn.loc.gov/2021033031

Cover Design: Wiley
Cover Image: © rvika/Getty Images

Set in 10.5/13pt Minion Pro by Straive, Chennai, India

SKY34C7E41B-517E-4981-809B-6A25D303EA10_101921

To my wife, Claire; my children, Sophia, James, and Oliver;
And everyone who will be inspired by these trends to make the world a
better place

CONTENTS

PART I   Introduction: Riding the Wave of Transformation   1

Chapter 1   The Five Global Shifts That Will Shape the
Organizations of the Future   3

Chapter 2   The Ten Tech Mega-Trends Every Business
Leader Should Know About   21

PART II   Rethinking Key Sectors   45

Chapter 3   How We Generate Energy: The Three Trends
Transforming the Energy Sector   47

Chapter 4   How We Stay Healthy: The Seven Trends Shaping
Healthcare   59

Chapter 5   How We Learn: The Two Main Shifts in Education   73

Chapter 6   How We Feed Ourselves: The Two Key Innovations
Needed to Transform Agriculture   85

Chapter 7   How We Make and Build Things: Eleven Trends
to Watch Across Manufacturing and Construction   99

Chapter 8   How We Move People and Goods: The Three Trends
Revolutionizing Transportation   111

Chapter 9   How We Look After Our Money: The Four Shifts
That Will Shape the Financial Sector   121

PART III   Rethinking What Businesses Offer   131

Chapter 10   Channel Digitization and Expansion: The Move
from Physical to Digital/Hybrid Products
and Channels   133

CONTENTS

Chapter 11   Cognifying Products and Services: Smarter
Products, Smarter Services   145

Chapter 12   Right Time, Right Place, Right for You: The Rise
of Micro-Moments and Personalization   155

Chapter 13   Subscription and Servitization: The As-a-Service
Revolution   165

Chapter 14   Cutting Out the Middlemen: How Brands Are
Going Direct to the Consumer   177

Chapter 15   From B2C to "All to All": The Rise of Platforms,
the Sharing Economy, and Crowdsourcing   189

Chapter 16   More Immersive Experiences: How Brands Are
Wowing Customers with Memorable Experiences   199

Chapter 17   Conscious Consumption: Consumer Demand
for Sustainable, Responsible Products   209

PART IV   Rethinking How Businesses Are Run   221

Chapter 18   Sustainable and Resilient Operations: Building
a Stronger, More Responsible Company   223

Chapter 19   Finding the Balance Between Humans and
Intelligent Cobots: The Blended Workforces
of the Future   237

Chapter 20   Finding and Keeping Talent: The Shifting Talent
Pool and Employee Experience   249

Chapter 21   Organizing to Win: Flatter, More Agile
Organizations   259

Chapter 22   Authenticity: Why Brands and Leaders Need
to Keep It Real   271

Chapter 23   Purposeful Business: Why Does Your
Business Exist?   281

Chapter 24   Co-Opetition and Integration: A New Age
of Integrated Collaboration   291

Chapter 25   New Forms of Funding: The Democratization
of Business Funding   301

CONTENTS

PART V   Where to Go from Here   309

Chapter 26   Final Words: Four Key Takeaways for Business
Leaders   311

Acknowledgments   *317*
About the Author   *319*
Index   *321*

PART I
INTRODUCTION: RIDING THE WAVE OF TRANSFORMATION

Our world is rapidly changing and the pace of change has been accelerating. Business leaders tell me all the time how challenging it is to keep up with the pace and extent of change, and I couldn't agree more. I'm frequently staggered by the pace of change, particularly (although not exclusively) in technology advancements – and I say that as someone whose job title is futurist!

That, in a nutshell, is what sparked the idea for this book. I wanted to provide business leaders with an accessible overview of the key trends that are transforming the way we do business. In my advisory work with companies and government organizations, I noticed that the same transformative forces seem to be coming up again and again, irrespective of the size of the organization or the industry in which they operate. This book pulls those insights together in one place. My goal is to give business leaders a chance to learn from other industries and build a business that is more successful, more resilient, and better equipped for the changes coming our way. In short, this book is designed to help you ride the wave of transformation.

I believe the role of any futurist is to be practical. So, far from describing some sort of futuristic business utopia, I cut through the hype and distill each of the business trends into practical insights – insights that business leaders can translate into action.

1

To help with this, I include plenty of real-world examples to show how other organizations are adapting and responding to change. There are use cases from all kinds of businesses, big and small, from startup eco toilet tissue makers to traditional manufacturers to tech giants, and a whole lot in between. I'm keen to demonstrate that the trends in this book apply to all organizations, regardless of size and industry.

Here's what else to expect from this book:

- In Part I, we'll start by exploring the forces – both societal and technological – that are driving the massive changes taking place.

- Then, in Part II, we'll look at the impact of these trends on key industries to illustrate just how transformative their collective impact is. (I must stress that I had to stick to just the most important industries here. But if your industry isn't featured, please don't skip this part – many of the insights will no doubt be relevant to your own industry.)

- Part III focuses on the key consumer trends that are emerging today – trends that will likely prompt a rethink of your products and services, and how to deliver them.

- Building on the consumer trends, Part IV is all about key trends that impact how businesses operate internally. In other words, as well as rethinking your products and services, you'll also have to rethink how your business is run.

- And in the final chapter, I'll pull these (often interlinked, some-times disparate, even contradictory) trends together into some broader key lessons and takeaways. These are the things I want to leave you with as you look to the future.

As well as helping business leaders ride the wave of transformation, there is also a loftier goal at the heart of this book. As you'll see in the next chapter, it's not just businesses that are being impacted by these trans-formational forces; society as a whole is facing enormous changes and challenges. By building better businesses, we can collectively tackle the issues facing our world and create the future we want to live in. If this book plays a small role in that very big task, I'll be happy.

CHAPTER 1
THE FIVE GLOBAL SHIFTS THAT WILL SHAPE THE ORGANIZATIONS OF THE FUTURE

This is a book about business trends. But no business operates in a vacuum. Organizations are constantly shaped by the world around them. And that's why we start our journey here, with some of the biggest trends emerging in politics, economics, and society.

In this chapter, I outline five major global shifts that business leaders must take into consideration as they plan for the future. This is not just a "nice to know" chapter; these trends have very real business implications (you'll find some practical lessons at the end of the chapter). Each global shift outlined in this chapter indicates where future business opportunities may lie, meaning the most successful organizations of the future will be those that address and move with these shifts. The flip side, of course, is that these global shifts also pose risks for businesses, particularly the risk of being left behind. As a result, many businesses will end up sidelined, overtaken by their more forward-thinking competitors.

What struck me as I was writing this chapter is that many of these trends are contrasting. For example, we're seeing a trend toward cultural convergence at the same time as growing divergence, which, on the surface, is a bit of a head-scratcher. Perhaps one feeds into the other. Or maybe it's simply a sign of the confusing, uncertain world we live in these days. One thing is sure: businesses will have to contend with some trends that are seemingly pulling in different directions. Adapting to this new age of uncertainty may mean rethinking what your business offers and how it is run (more on this in Parts III and IV of this book). For now, let's immerse ourselves in five of the biggest global shifts that are emerging, starting with our relationship with our planet.

Trend 1: Our Changing Relationship with Our Planet

To put it mildly, we've not had the best relationship with our planet. We've chopped down forests, burnt carbon, dug mines, polluted waterways – all in the name of growing prosperity. For Western countries at least, this has paid off. Using our natural resources has led to greater prosperity. But it has also led to climate change, the collapse of ecosystems and loss of biodiversity, chemical and plastic pollution, and the decline of our natural resources (particularly water). As a result, our planet is under immense pressure and showing the strain through abnormal weather patterns and natural disasters, which, in turn, create pressures around crop production, food security, migration, and more.

Some food for thought on the emerging climate crisis:

- Climate change is happening so quickly, many species are struggling to adapt. The Intergovernmental Panel on Climate Change says that a 1.5°C average rise in global average surface temperature may put up to 30 percent of species at risk of extinction. Push that up to 2°C and most ecosystems will struggle.[1] For context, the temperature has already increased by 0.9°C since 1906 (the figure is even higher in polar regions).[2]

- By the end of this century, 150–200 million people could be forced to migrate from land that will be underwater.[3]

- Some of the biggest sectors in terms of greenhouse gas emissions include agriculture and forestry (responsible for 18.4 percent of global emissions), energy use in industry (24.2 percent), energy use in buildings (17.5 percent), and transportation (16.2 percent).[4]

- Our precious resources are under enormous pressure. Fresh water makes up just 2.5 percent of the world's total volume of water (and half of that is ice). So it's perhaps no wonder that 1.8 billion people are already living with water scarcity. Even more worryingly, 5.2 billion people are expected to face water stress by 2025.[5]

- Competition for land (particularly land for agriculture) is also growing, and many countries such as China and Saudi Arabia are already pursuing land in Africa. Global competition for finite resources, including land and water, is only going to increase as the population grows.

- There may also be a global fight for rare earths, some of the most important minerals and metals found in the ground, which are used in everything from lithium-ion batteries to electric cars. The US is 80 percent reliant on China (the world's biggest rare earths producer) for rare earth imports, and this could lead to further strains on political relationships in future.[6]

- To keep pace with the growing population (I talk more about global demographics later in the chapter), an often-quoted statistic is that we'll have to double crop and animal production by 2050. More conservative estimates suggest that, as food production has already increased in recent years, we may only need to increase production by between 26 percent and 68 percent by 2050.[7] But that's still a significant increase to accommodate on an already struggling planet.

- Plastic pollution is another pressing concern. Single-use plastics account for 40 percent of the plastic produced every year, meaning something that may be used for mere minutes ends up hanging around for hundreds of years. Every year, around 8 million tons of plastic waste finds its way into the oceans (the equivalent of five garbage bags of trash being placed on every foot of coastline around the world), and with plastic production expected to double by 2050, the problem is set to get a lot worse.[8]

If our relationship with our planet was a romantic one, it would be labeled "toxic." Earth's best friends would probably be telling her she could do better. And we must do better. We need to build a more balanced, sustainable relationship with our planet.

Yet the emerging climate disaster is probably the biggest challenge we've ever faced. So how do we overcome something of this magnitude? In his book *How to Avoid a Climate Disaster*, Bill Gates says that we're adding 51 billion tons of greenhouse gases to the atmosphere every year. To stop global warming and avoid the worst impacts of climate change, Gates says we need to get that number down to zero by 2050. Let me say that again: zero.

The problem, of course, is that most zero-carbon energy solutions cost more than their fossil fuel counterparts. (Gates refers to the price difference as "Green Premiums.") He says that using Green Premiums as a decision-making tool can help us decide which zero-carbon solutions should be deployed now, which nongreen goods should be priced higher, and where we need to invest in new innovations because the current zero-carbon alternatives aren't cheap enough. (Some of the innovations Gates promotes include nuclear fusion, sea-based carbon removal, and direct air capture of carbon.)

Gates's book is a fascinating read and I urge everyone to read it. But while he has brilliant and practical ideas, we can't ignore the fact that solving the climate crisis is a global responsibility, requiring countries to work together and take collective action. The fact that global economic and political power structures are also undergoing huge changes will only make the job harder. This leads us to the next topic.

Trend 2: Shifts in Economic and Political Power

The economic and political world order is changing and, by 2050, the list of the most economically and politically powerful countries in the world will look very different to today.

Take China as an example. Due to the impact of the coronavirus crisis, China's economy is now predicted to overtake the United States by 2028, five years earlier than previously thought.[9] China is one of the so-called E7 emerging countries – alongside India, Brazil, Mexico, Russia, Indonesia, and Turkey – countries whose economies are expected to exceed those of the G7 advanced economies.

Let's look at a few stats that highlight the startling shifts in power that are coming our way:[10]

- By 2050, the EU27's share of global GDP will be just 9 percent, while China's is expected to be 20 percent.

- BY 2050, India will rank second in the global GDP rankings, putting it behind China and ahead of the US. Indonesia will rank fourth. The UK could be down to 10th place.

- E7 economies could grow around twice as fast as the G7. In fact, the combined economic power of the E7 economies could be double that of the G7 by 2040 – that's from being the same size as the G7 in 2015 and half the size in 1995.

And then there are the "next 11" emerging economies, including Bangladesh, Egypt, Nigeria, Pakistan, and Vietnam. These economies are projected to overtake the EU27 in global power as early as 2030.[11]

Bottom line, the West has been on the rise for centuries, but that is about to change. The E7 and next 11 economies will increasingly hold more sway in the global economy and, in turn, in world politics. Earlier in this chapter, I mentioned that China is building close links with African nations for access to land and rare resources, and this is just one example of China extending its global influence.

This power shift will no doubt bring new tensions, particularly as the world's most precious resources become scarcer. We may also see a new Cold War emerge around technology. China has said it wants to be a world leader in artificial intelligence by 2030, and has introduced measures to control the export of AI technologies by Chinese companies.[12] President Trump's ban on Huawei's products and telecoms equipment gives us another glimpse of how countries may seek to restrict the technological capabilities of other countries. In other words, rather than bringing the world closer together, technology may be yet another thing that exacerbates global tensions and contributes to growing divergence.

Trend 3: Growing Divergence and Polarization

After decades of globalization has brought countries closer together, there are signs that countries (and the alliances and systems they participate in) are beginning to decouple. There have been some notable examples of political fragmentation and growing divergence in recent years. We've seen it in the US, when President Trump withdrew from the Paris Agreement on climate mitigation, announced plans to withdraw America from the World Health Organization, and even spoke about withdrawing from NATO. And we've seen it in the UK, with the country leaving the European Union. In the UK, Brexit really emphasized the way large sections of society have shifted toward extreme sides of arguments, with little or no ability to see the other side's perspective. People fell out with friends, neighbors, and family members because of their political opinions, and American voters experienced the same thing during the 2020 election. Groups are becoming more divided along ideological lines, and that goes for groups of voters, and groups within society (think of the often vitriolic debates around feminism or trans rights). A 2019 survey by the Pew Research Center found that partisan division and animosity have deepened since 2016; 63 percent of Republicans said Democrats were "more unpatriotic" than other Americans, and 55 percent said they were more immoral. Meanwhile, 75 percent of Democrats said Republicans were more close-minded than other Americans, and 47 percent said they were more immoral.[13]

In short, the world feels more polarized than ever. I find this both crazy and disturbing. When did society become so polarized that you're either a staunch Democrat or Republican (or a Brexiter or Remainer, or any other position, political or otherwise), with nothing in between? And when did the other side become immoral and less patriotic? Losing all concept of the other side's perspective is, to me, a danger to our democracy and society. Yet that's exactly what's happening.

When information and analytics company IHS Markit set out its prediction of how the world would look in 2025, it said the "fragmented world" scenario is the most likely. In this scenario, the US, China, the EU, and other key players retreat from globalization and turn their focus inwards to concentrate on domestic challenges.[14] It's only a prediction, of course, but the COVID-19 crisis and the resulting economic fallout is likely to exacerbate the desire to turn inwards and focus on domestic problems.

There are a number of reasons why divergence and polarization have grown. There's no global enemy or external threat keeping disparate countries united. And, of course, we can't ignore the impact of social media ghettoes that show people only what they want to see. Thanks to social media algorithms, we simply don't all see the same news. Instead, we're served a stream of content that's personalized to our habits, interests, and beliefs. This is known as the "filter bubble." Trapped in our bubbles – because this is something we're all susceptible to – we may begin to believe the world is *exactly* as we see it. Fake news spreads quickly in this environment, because the people in your filter bubble share the same views as you, and it's much easier to believe a fake news story when people you follow are sharing and talking about it. Meanwhile, real problems and issues – and the need to work together to solve society's problems – get lost in the noise.

Technology, then, may play a key role in this growing divergence and polarization. I've already raised the prospect of a technology "Cold War," and we see hints of this with China restricting companies from exporting technology services, and preventing citizens from accessing certain websites. China is the best-known example of a country with its own isolated internet, and this is something we may see more of in the future. This splintering of the internet even has a name: the "splinternet." Indeed, Russia has already confirmed that it has created a system that would allow the country to completely decouple from the rest of the world's internet and operate its own independent internet.[15]

Another factor that may be fueling polarization and divergence is racial and ethnic diversity. While diversity is a long-term benefit for society, in the short term it can trigger social and political conflict and a breakdown in trust. Which brings us to the next subject.

Trend 4: Shifting Demographics

The global population in 2050, or even 2030, will look very different from today. Depending on where you are in the world, the population is growing and aging. We're seeing greater urbanization and more megacities. And, as I've previously mentioned, climate change may mean hundreds of millions of people are displaced and forced to migrate to other areas.

Let's get a quick overview of how the population is changing:

- According to a UN forecast, the world's population was expected to increase by 2 billion in the next 30 years, from 7.7 billion in 2020 to 9.7 billion in 2050.[16]

- However, recent estimates suggest the population may peak sooner than that, at 9.7 billion in 2064, and then decline to 8.8 billion by the end of the century.[17] In other words, it looks as though population growth is slowing, not least because more and more women can now choose to have fewer children.

- While the total global population is still growing, some countries are witnessing population decline due to factors such as migration and low birthrates. For example, Russia's population is expected to shrink by 18 million between 2006 and 2030, and Japan's population is projected to decrease by 11 million.[18]

- What's more, the world's population is growing older. As an example, in 1950, life expectancy in China was 40 years. By 2050, it will be 80 years.[19] This pattern is replicated across the world. In 2006, there were almost 500 million people in the world aged 65 and older. By 2030, that is projected to increase to 1 billion people, or 1 in 8 of the world's inhabitants.[20] This is good news because it shows that we have improved healthcare and living standards to allow people to live longer, but it does create societal and economic pressures.

- People are on the move, too. The number of people living in urban areas is rising rapidly. The world's urban population grew from 751 million in 1950 to 4.2 billion in 2018. Currently, 55 percent of the global population lives in urban areas, and this will increase to 68 percent by 2050. Asia is home to 54 percent of the world's urban population.[21]

- The number of megacities (classified by the UN as cities with 10 million or more inhabitants) is also on the rise. By 2030, there will be 43 megacities, up from 33 in 2018.[22]

- The cities that we live in will increasingly become "smart" and connected. There will be more than 25 global smart cities in 2025 (more than 50 percent of which will be in Europe and North America).[23]

- Meanwhile, the shift to more urban living will drive huge economic growth in developing economies. The emerging megacities in developing economies are expected to outperform developed megacities in terms of share of the world's GDP by 2025.[24] This, in turn, will lead to a growth in the consuming classes. By 2030, 66 percent of the world's middle classes will be living in Asia.[25]

Each of these factors creates opportunities and challenges. Longer lives, for example, must be planned for. Age-related chronic diseases will rise. The costs of healthcare and social insurance will rise. Patterns of work and retirement will shift. And societal aging as a whole may affect economic growth as the ratio of workers to retirees shifts. (Europe currently has four people of working age for every older person, but that will shrink to two workers per older person by 2050.)[26]

In another example, the opportunities around the growing urban populations and middle classes are huge. But we must also ensure cities develop in a sustainable way and that we address global inequality. Currently, the world's richest 1 percent own 44 percent of the world's wealth, which hardly seems fair.[27] According to the UN, inequality affects more than

70 percent of the global population and is on the rise across the world, including in fast-growing economies like China.[28] This is just another example of global trends moving in opposite directions – more people are being lifted out of poverty and the middle class is growing, yet the gap between the very rich and the poor is also growing.

This rising inequality must be tackled at national and international levels. We may even need to rethink our economic and democratic systems and reshape systems that are no longer fit for purpose. If we don't tackle inequality, the problems of division, divergence, and polarization will be exacerbated, and economic and social development will be restricted.

Finally, let's turn our attention to the social and cultural shifts that are taking place.

Trend 5: Social, Cultural, and Workplace Shifts

I find it fascinating that, while the world seems more polarized than ever, we're also seeing greater convergence between cultures. Think of Hollywood films influencing other cultures, or the global appeal of South Korean boyband BTS, or the way a Chinese teenager's video on TikTok can go viral in the US. Globally, 65 percent of people agree that we have more things in common than things that make us different.[29] Yet this is also an age of diversity and individuality; research suggests that individualism is a global phenomenon, not just a Western trend.[30] Once again, we see how global trends can contrast with each other.

Let's take a brief look at how society, culture, and the workplace are changing:

- Marriage is on the decline, and single-person households are the fastest-growing household profile in the period to 2030.[31]

- The gender gap remains a frustratingly stubborn problem. Women still remain less likely to participate in the labor market than men, are more likely to be unemployed than men, are overrepresented in vulnerable employment, are constrained from achieving the highest leadership positions, and are paid less than men.[32] On top of that, it looks as though the socioeconomic impacts of the COVID-19 crisis have disproportionately affected women.[33]

- Closing the gender gap is important, not just for women but for the benefit of society as a whole. There is a strong positive correlation between countries that are successfully closing the gender gap and their economic performance, and narrowing the gender gap means the global income per person will increase by at least 20 percent by 2030.[34]

- The number of Gen Z (those born after 1997) and millennials (Gen Y, born between 1981 and 1996) in the workplace is on the rise and baby boomers are retiring. As the workforce demographic changes, so too do the needs and expectations of workers. To baby boomers, putting in long hours was often seen as essential for success, but those entering the workplace now prioritize flexibility and work–life balance. In this age of personalization and individualism, Gen Z are also looking for an employee experience that is tailored to them. They expect training and mentoring, as well as challenging, meaningful work.[35] They increasingly expect to identify with their employer's brand identity; as an example, 65 percent of people want to work for an organization "with a powerful social conscience."[36]

- How we work is changing, too. One in five global employees now work remotely at least some of the time,[37] and the coronavirus pandemic will accelerate this "work from anywhere" culture. (Indeed, major companies like Twitter said early in the pandemic that workers wouldn't have to return to working in the office if they didn't want to.) The pandemic proved that remote working is feasible and beneficial across many industries, and as such we'll see the global job market accelerate – meaning tech workers no longer have to move to Palo Alto and so on.

- This work-from-anywhere culture will likely fuel more "free agents" entering the workforce and the continued rise of the gig economy. The hierarchical organizational structures of the past may dwindle in favor of flatter, team- and project-based structures, where people can move between and within organizations depending on where their skills are needed at any one time.

- Diversity is also becoming more important as the global job market accelerates, and as more Gen Z-ers (who are more racially and ethnically diverse than previous generations)[38] enter the workplace. In a survey by Deloitte, two-thirds of business leaders said diversity was important or very important to their business.[39] This includes diversity of thinking, as well as demographic diversity; in fact, diversity of thinking may increase innovation by 20 percent and reduce business risks by 30 percent.[40] The high-performing teams of the future, then, will be both demographically and cognitively diverse. Furthermore, organizations with inclusive cultures – where people feel valued, respected, and that they belong – are eight times more likely to achieve better business outcomes and twice as likely to meet or exceed financial targets.[41]

- There's also an increasing emphasis and less stigma around mental health and well-being – another trend that has been accelerated by the pandemic. Going forward, there will be increasing pressure on employers to make sure their people have the right work–life balance and that employees have access to mental health support through third-party providers.

Now that we've got a broader view of what's happening in the world, let's dig into some specific technology trends that are also impacting our world and how we live in it.

PRACTICAL LESSONS

All of these global shifts indicate where the biggest opportunities and risks lie for future success. So how should businesses be embracing or planning for these shifts? Here are a few key takeaways:

- The climate crisis. According to Ipsos, globally 73 percent of people agree we're on course for a climate disaster.[42] With a global majority agreeing that the world is facing a huge crisis, customers will increasingly gravitate toward more sustainable options. Businesses will have to do everything they can to maximize their green credentials and communicate that to customers.

- Economic shifts. As the E7 and next 11 economies grow, it will no doubt become more expensive for businesses to outsource their production and services to these countries. On the flip side, these economies will become much more attractive markets for products and services.

- Growing divergence. If the trend toward divergence and delinking continues, companies may potentially find themselves restricted from certain markets. A reliance on any one market is a risky strategy.

- Demographic shifts. For businesses, the growing consuming classes and greater urbanization around the world present huge possibilities, but participating in these new markets will mean adapting to different cultural and political environments.

- Social, cultural, and workplace shifts. Businesses must assess whether they are offering Gen Z, women, and global workers an attractive work environment, one in which people have flexibility and work–life balance, where they can be individuals and connect meaningfully with the brand.

Notes

1. Impacts of 1.5°C global warming on natural and human systems; IPCC; https://www.ipcc.ch/sr15/chapter/chapter-3/

2. Effects of global warming; National Geographic; https://www.nationalgeographic.com/environment/article/global-warming-effects

3. Climate change and resource scarcity; PwC; https://www.pwc.co.uk/issues/megatrends/climate-change-and-resource-scarcity.html

4. Emissions by sector; Our World in Data; https://ourworldindata.org/emissions-by-sector

5. Beyond the Noise: The Megatrends of Tomorrow's World; Deloitte; https://www2.deloitte.com/content/dam/Deloitte/nl/Documents/public-sector/deloitte-nl-ps-megatrends-2ndedition.pdf

6. Why Rare Earths May Leave Europe and U.S. Vulnerable; Bloomberg; https://www.bloomberg.com/news/articles/2021-02-16/why-rare-earths-are-achilles-heal-for-europe-u-s-quicktake

7. Double food production by 2050? Not so fast; Futurity; https://www.futurity.org/food-production-2050-1368582-2/

8. The world's plastic pollution crisis explained; National Geographic; https://www.nationalgeographic.com/environment/article/plastic-pollution?cmpid=int_org=ngp::int_mc=website::int_src=ngp::int_cmp=amp::int_add=amp_readtherest

9. Chinese economy to overtake US "by 2028" due to Covid; BBC News; https://www.bbc.com/news/world-asia-china-55454146

10. The world in 2050; PwC; https://www.pwc.com/gx/en/research-insights/economy/the-world-in-2050.html

11. Economic power shifts; European Commission; https://knowledge4policy.ec.europa.eu/foresight/topic/expanding-influence-east-south/power-shifts_en#:~:text=The%20%E2%80%9CNext%20Eleven%E2%80%9D%20(Bangladesh,in%20global%20power%20by%202030.

12. Why is China Introducing New Export Controls?; China Briefing; https://www.china-briefing.com/news/chinas-new-export-control-law-restrictions-imposed-23-items-technology/

13. Partisan Antipathy: More Intense, More personal; Pew Research Center; https://www.pewresearch.org/politics/2019/10/10/partisan-antipathy-more-intense-more-personal/?utm_source=link_newsv9&utm_campaign=item_268982&utm_medium=copy

14. Geopolitics in a post-pandemic world: A fragmented world; IHS Markit; https://ihsmarkit.com/research-analysis/geopolitics-in-a-postpandemic-world-a-fragmented-world.html

15. Russia "successfully tests" its unplugged internet; BBC News; https://www
.bbc.com/news/technology-50902496

16. Growing at a slower pace, world population is expected to reach 9.7 billion in
2050 and could peak at nearly 11 billion around 2100; United Nations; https://
www.un.org/development/desa/en/news/population/world-population-
prospects-2019.html#:~:text=The%20world's%20population%20is%20
expected,United%20Nations%20report%20launched%20today

17. World population in 2100 could be 2 billion below UN forecasts, study
suggests; Guardian; https://www.theguardian.com/world/2020/jul/15/
world-population-in-2100-could-be-2-billion-below-un-forecasts-
study-suggests

18. Why Population Aging Matters; National Institute on Aging; https://www
.nia.nih.gov/sites/default/files/2017-06/WPAM.pdf

19. 10 Mega Trends that are (re)shaping our world; Ipsos; https://www
.ipsos.com/sites/default/files/10-Mega-Trends-That-are-Reshaping-
The-World.pdf

20. Why Population Aging Matters; National Institute on Aging; https://www
.nia.nih.gov/sites/default/files/2017-06/WPAM.pdf

21. 2018 Revision of World Urbanization Prospects; United Nations; https://
www.un.org/development/desa/publications/2018-revision-of-world-
urbanization-prospects.html

22. Ibid.

23. World's Top Global Mega Trends to 2025 and Implications to Business,
Society and Cultures; Frost & Sullivan; https://www.thegeniusworks.com/
wp-content/uploads/2016/01/Megatrends-2025-Frost-and-Sullivan.pdf

24. Emerging megacities to outperform developed megacities by 2025; GlobalData;
https://www.globaldata.com/emerging-megacities-to-outperform-
developed-megacities-by-2025-says-globaldata/

25. 10 Mega Trends that are (re)shaping our world; Ipsos; https://www
.ipsos.com/sites/default/files/10-Mega-Trends-That-are-Reshaping-
The-World.pdf

26. Why Population Aging Matters; National Institute on Aging; https://www
.nia.nih.gov/sites/default/files/2017-06/WPAM.pdf

27. Global Wealth Report; Credit Suisse; https://www.credit-suisse.com/about-us/en/reports-research/global-wealth-report.html

28. Rising inequality affecting more than two-thirds of the globe, but it's not inevitable; UN News; https://news.un.org/en/story/2020/01/1055681

29. 10 Mega Trends that are (re)shaping our world; Ipsos; https://www.ipsos.com/sites/default/files/10-Mega-Trends-That-are-Reshaping-The-World.pdf

30. Individualistic Practices and Values Increasing Around the World; Association for Psychological Science; https://www.psychologicalscience.org/news/releases/individualistic-practices-and-values-increasing-around-the-world.html

31. 10 Mega Trends that are (re)shaping our world; Ipsos; https://www.ipsos.com/sites/default/files/10-Mega-Trends-That-are-Reshaping-The-World.pdf

32. Facts and Figures: Economic Empowerment; UN Women; https://www.unwomen.org/en/what-we-do/economic-empowerment/facts-and-figures

33. Closing the Gender Gap Accelerators; World Economic Forum; https://www.weforum.org/projects/closing-the-gender-gap-accelerators

34. Beyond the Noise: The Megatrends of Tomorrow's World; Deloitte; https://www2.deloitte.com/content/dam/Deloitte/nl/Documents/public-sector/deloitte-nl-ps-megatrends-2ndedition.pdf

35. Gen Z Rising; Accenture; https://www.accenture.com/_acnmedia/pdf-50/accenture-strategy-workforce-gen-z-rising-pov.pdf

36. 10 Mega Trends that are (re)shaping our world; Ipsos; https://www.ipsos.com/sites/default/files/10-Mega-Trends-That-are-Reshaping-The-World.pdf

37. Ibid.

38. Early Benchmarks Show Post-Millennials on Track to Be Most Diverse, Best Educated Generation Yet; Pew Research Center; https://www.pewresearch.org/social-trends/2018/11/15/early-benchmarks-show-post-millennials-on-track-to-be-most-diverse-best-educated-generation-yet/

39. The diversity and inclusion revolution; Deloitte; https://www2.deloitte.com/content/dam/insights/us/articles/4209_Diversity-and-inclusion-revolution/DI_Diversity-and-inclusion-revolution.pdf

40. Ibid.

41. Ibid.

42. 10 Mega Trends that are (re)shaping our world; Ipsos; https://www
    .ipsos.com/sites/default/files/10-Mega-Trends-That-are-Reshaping-
    The-World.pdf

CHAPTER 2
THE TEN TECH MEGA-TRENDS EVERY BUSINESS LEADER SHOULD KNOW ABOUT

We are now entering the fourth industrial revolution. As with each industrial revolution before it – steam and waterpower, electricity, and computerization – this revolution represents a huge transformational shift that will forever alter how we do business, and even how we go about our everyday lives. Driven by data, artificial intelligence and the Internet of Things (IoT, the plethora of everyday devices that are now connected to the internet), the fourth industrial revolution is essentially turning the world around us into one huge information system, which is why I often refer to it as "the intelligence revolution."

No Ordinary Industrial Revolution

What makes this fourth industrial revolution different from the previous three is the sheer range of new technologies involved. Where each of the previous industrial revolutions were driven by one major technological advancement, the fourth industrial revolution is driven by numerous tech trends, including the increasing datafication of our world, huge leaps in artificial intelligence, the rise of cyber-physical systems (computer systems that control physical processes), and the vast spread of the Internet of Things, to name just a few examples. Each of these advancements on their own would be transformative; together, they can take us beyond anything we could imagine.

What's interesting about the fourth industrial revolution is that the unprecedented digital transformation that we've seen in recent years is being accelerated by the *interaction* between all these different technologies. The enormous leaps in AI, for example, have been made possible by the explosion of data, which in turn is being accelerated by the plethora of smart devices constantly generating data. These trends are influencing each other, and will continue to do so. This means, rather than the big step changes of previous industrial revolutions, this latest revolution may usher in a period of exponential growth that just carries on and on. In other words, there may not be a fifth industrial revolution; we may instead experience a continual acceleration of the fourth industrial revolution.

"Exponential growth" is a phrase you probably hear a lot, but let's take a moment to consider what it means in real terms. When I talk about the amount of data in our world growing exponentially, and the exponential growth in computing power, I'm talking about it doubling every few years – two years in the case of computing power (as per Moore's Law, which I'll talk about later), and roughly every four years for the amount of data being stored.[1]

Imagine if the speed of cars developed at such a pace. Initially, the progress would seem fairly sensible, starting with 50mph then doubling two years later to 100mph. But after eight years our cars would be traveling faster than the speed of sound (767 mph). Within 50 years, we'd be driving faster than the speed of light (670 million mph). That's fast enough to take a round-trip from Earth to the Moon and back in about 2.5 seconds. Clearly, such pace of change isn't happening in the automotive industry, or other industries for that matter. And that's what makes the pace of digital change so startling. It's something we've never seen before, and it's almost impossible to imagine this pace continuing. But that's precisely what may happen. There's no limit to what these technologies can achieve.

Crucially, these tech trends, which are all mingling and mixing together, will disrupt every industry, every organization (big and small), and even many aspects of society. This is why business leaders need to understand these trends and plan for their potential impact. In this chapter, I outline 10 technology mega-trends that will separate the successful businesses of the future from those that get left behind. Each of these trends deserves a book in its own right (indeed, I've written entire books on many of these trends). So consider this a whistle-stop tour – something to get you thinking about the future of your organization, and specifically how your business might use these trends to drive success.

Trend 1: Ubiquitous Computing

Digital technology is more readily available and more powerful than ever before. Let's take a quick look how we got here, to the point where computers are all around us, and see what's in store for the future of computing.

Advances in computing power

As processing power has increased and the size of computer microchips has shrunk, most of us have become used to computers and devices getting smaller, lighter, cheaper, and more powerful. Indeed, the average smartphone today is more powerful than the supercomputers of 10 years ago.

Moore's Law states that the number of transistors on a microchip doubles every two years, thus doubling the speed and capability of computers every two years. This law has been in place for an astonishing 55 years. Now, however, we're reaching the limits of Moore's Law. After all, there's only so far you can take the shrinking of transistors and computer chips. But this doesn't mean the end of advances in computing power. It's just that, instead of relying on microchips getting smaller, it's likely future advances will come from innovations in software and algorithms (especially when the coding is done by AI), quantum computing, and even new forms of digital storage, such as DNA storage. In other words, even as Moore's Law falters, new advances on the horizon will continue to push the boundaries of computing power. These gains may be a bit more irregular and uneven than we've grown used to with Moore's Law, but they will come.

Quantum computing

Traditional computers may have grown exponentially more powerful over the last half-century, but they're basically still very fast versions of the humble electronic calculator. They're only capable of processing one "bit" of information at a time, in the form of a binary 1 or 0.

A quantum computer, on the other hand, uses "quantumbits" or "qubits" to process data, and these qubits seem to be capable of existing in two states simultaneously, meaning they have some likelihood of being a 1 and some likelihood of being a 0 *at the same time*. Using these quantum methods, it's possible to build machines capable of operating far more quickly than the fastest computers available today – potentially hundreds of millions of times faster. While quantum computers won't replace traditional computers (using a quantum computer to write your memoir, for example, would be like using a rocket launcher to crack a walnut), they could be used to complete new, previously impossible tasks that traditional computers aren't capable of. In other words, they're ideally suited to solving problems that humanity (and computers) hasn't yet been able to solve, such as the climate crisis. Some quantum computers exist today, but their use is mostly confined to academia and highly theoretical work. However, companies such as IBM, Google, and Microsoft are investing heavily in developing large-scale quantum computers that could see quantum computing deliver more widespread practical applications.

Storing and processing data

Computers have had to get faster and more powerful, in part to keep up with the vast amounts of data we're generating and processing. I talk more about the increasing datafication of our world later in the chapter, but it's clear that we're creating a vast amount of data on a daily basis. And the technology to store all that data is now significantly cheaper, more powerful, and easier to access. As a simple example, in the mid-1960s a terabyte of storage would have cost $3.5 billion; today I can buy a 1TB hard drive for less than $50.

Cloud computing (where data and applications are stored and processed on other people's computers) has played a critical role in the digital transformation we've seen in recent years, bringing huge advantages in terms of storing data cheaply, keeping data secure, and being able to process data more easily (most cloud providers offer AI and analytics services that can help you interrogate data at the click of a button).

So it's no surprise that as much as 80 percent of all enterprise and mission-critical workloads are predicted to move to the cloud by 2025.[2] The cloud has become the backbone of the data-driven, app-based tech ecosystem that modern businesses operate in, and it continues to evolve. One trend that we can expect to see more of in cloud computing is multi-cloud approaches, or a breaking down of the barriers between different cloud service providers like Amazon, Microsoft, and Google. There are growing calls for the big providers to adopt a more collaborative approach and create bridges between their platforms, allowing, for example, an Amazon Web Services client to share data and access with a partner in their supply chain who works with Microsoft Azure.

Outside of the cloud, as devices have become more powerful, they've also been able to take on more of the processing grunt work. Known as *edge computing*, this means instead of pushing every bit of data to the cloud for analysis, some of it can be processed at the source, where the data was collected (i.e., in the device itself). This will become more important, and more useful, as 5G rolls out. Bringing with it superfast broadband and faster response times, 5G will make "the edge" much more powerful than it is today, effectively allowing us to turn everything around us into computers.

There are other data storage innovations to watch out for, the most exciting of which is DNA storage. Yes, you read that correctly. I'm talking about the ability to store data on DNA. Data centers are energy-hungry resources, and we can't ignore the impact all this data we're creating has on the planet. DNA-based storage could provide a solution to this problem, and a number of companies, including Microsoft, are working on DNA-storage technology. It's not as crazy as it sounds; DNA is already routinely sequenced (read), copied, and synthesized (written to), and storing DNA doesn't take much energy. What's more, DNA can store huge amounts of information – far more than any electronic devices. A block of DNA measuring just one cubic meter could meet the world's current data storage needs for a year.[3] Which is just as well, because the rise of smart, connected devices – devices that are constantly gathering and generating data – shows no sign of slowing down.

Trend 2: Connected and Smart Everything

You'll no doubt be familiar with the Internet of Things (IoT) from devices like smart TVs, smart watches, and smart thermostats. The IoT refers to the increasing number of intelligent devices and objects that are connected to the internet and are capable of gathering and transmitting data. The IoT is now growing at such a rate that we have intelligent, well, everything. It's hard to pinpoint the exact number of connected devices on the planet, but some estimates suggest that by 2030 as many as 50 billion IoT devices will be installed worldwide.[4] That's more than 6 times the number of people on the planet.

And by intelligent everything, I mean *everything*. Yoga mats, light-bulbs, cars, robots, drones, ships — these and many more are becoming "smart," meaning they're capable of connecting to the internet, gathering data on what's going on around them, communicating that data with other devices or platforms, and often making decisions or taking action based on the data. Looking ahead, it's clear that anything that can be connected, will be. One cool example comes from the US Navy's *Sea Hunter* autonomous unmanned surface vehicle prototype (basically, an autonomous drone ship). *Sea Hunter* has already sailed autonomously from California to Hawaii and back without the need for a crew, and is being integrated into a naval carrier strike group,[5] meaning sailors will have to get used to operating alongside unmanned ships.

And this notion of smart everything doesn't just relate to devices and products (although that is obviously a key consideration for businesses); it also relates to intelligent spaces. From smart, connected factories and offices to entire smart cities, the spaces around us are increasingly being equipped with the ability to monitor what's going on and act accordingly. For example, public transportation routes can be adjusted in real time according to demand, or traffic flows can be monitored and analyzed to improve congestion. Alibaba's City Brain system uses AI to optimize a city's infrastructure, and in the Chinese city of Hangzhou, it has helped reduce traffic jams by 15 percent.[6]

Of course, this pervasive connectivity brings with it increased security risks. Connecting anything to the internet makes it vulnerable to cyberattack, which makes securing connected devices and spaces all the more important.

This ability to connect things and places to the internet (and to each other) has the potential to transform many industries, including manufacturing, education, healthcare, and defense. Perhaps most importantly for many businesses, this notion of connected everything provides a unique insight into how customers (and employees for that matter) really behave, versus how they *say* they behave. Manufacturers of connected cars, for instance, can understand when, where, and how their customers drive. This sort of knowledge is profoundly useful to businesses in terms of understanding how customers use products, designing future products, increasing customer satisfaction, and more. This is why data can be considered one of the most important assets modern businesses have at their disposal. And that brings us to the next topic.

Trend 3: The Datafication of Our World

Ubiquitous computing and the IoT are both huge contributors to the sheer volume of data that's being generated on a daily basis. But alongside machine-generated data, we humans are also generating masses of data through our daily activities. Everything we do leaves a digital trace. From liking a video on TikTok to buying gas with your credit card, so many of our everyday activities generate streams of data. As such, we've seen huge advances in the way data is stored. It's not just about data warehouses anymore; now we have *data lakes*, where data is stored in a less-structured way, with *data rivers* continuously flowing into those lakes. And, as I've already mentioned, we have futuristic advances such as DNA data storage to look forward to.

For businesses, the obvious advantage of all this data is that it can be harnessed to design better products and services, improve business processes, enhance decision-making, and even create new revenue sources (take a company like John Deere as an example, which has been able to package up the data collected from its farming machinery and sell it back to farmers).

Two of the biggest concerns around data are privacy and security. When everything we do leaves a digital trace, this can have massive implications for our individual privacy, so it's vital that businesses take steps to protect people's privacy. For me, this means only collecting data that you really need (and not collecting everything for the sake of it), making people aware of exactly what data you're collecting (and why), and offering them the chance to opt out where possible. Looking ahead, we can expect to see a significant tightening of regulations designed to protect people's privacy. Security-wise, while the number of breaches has declined since 2019, the severity of breaches has increased – to the extent that 37 billion sensitive records were compromised in 2020, an increase of 141 percent on the previous year.[7] And in February 2021, the largest breach of all time was leaked online. COMB, or Compilation of Many Breaches, as it's being called, contained 3.2 billion emails and passwords – roughly 40 percent of the entire population of the planet.[8] Data is a valuable asset, but it also brings with it considerable business risk.

Another risk, of course, is that companies simply drown in all this data. Thus it's essential that companies develop smarter approaches to turning data into insights – and, in turn, ensure that those data-driven insights can be translated into action. Businesses must work to raise *data literacy* across the organization, and this means all decision makers in the organization must have access to the data they need, understand the value of that data, and have a basic ability to use that data. As such, we can expect to see more and more organizations implementing data literacy programs.

Artificial intelligence will help to raise data literacy and accessibility. Indeed, many off-the-shelf cloud data storage solutions offer some form of AI capability to help businesses make sense of their data. Going forward, *augmented analytics* will play an increasingly key role. Driven by AI, augmented analytics essentially means systems can automatically detect patterns in data by themselves, without being programmed according to a specific set of rules, and then push insights out to users without having to be asked specific questions. In other words, data will become more *democratized*, meaning people right across the organization will be able to exploit data, without the need for data science skills. This data democratization is an exciting trend to watch, and is just one of many advantages that have sprung from the rise of AI, which brings us to another trend.

Trend 4: Artificial Intelligence

The fact that our world is increasingly driven by data has brought about incredible leaps in artificial intelligence (AI). Data is a core enabler for AI, in the sense that the more data intelligent machines have to learn from, the better they become at spotting patterns, extracting insights, and even predicting what may happen next.

AI is developing at such an incredible pace that today's intelligent machines are now capable of carrying out a wide range of tasks previously reserved for humans. We have *machine vision*, where intelligent machines can "see" and interpret images or the world around them; *natural language processing*, where machines can learn to understand human language; *natural language generation*, where machines can generate human-like responses; and *robotic process automation*, where business processes are automated by software robots. To put it in everyday terms, AI is behind self-driving cars, facial recognition technology, recommendation engines, fraud detection, the content that shows up on your social media feed, and more. In 2020 alone, smart speakers answered 100 billion voice commands – 75 percent more than in 2019 – all thanks to AI.[9] This "conversational AI," where machines can use language with human-like accuracy, has made huge breakthroughs in recent years.

One of the most exciting recent advances in this vein is the GPT-3 AI. Created by OpenAI, a research company founded by Elon Musk, GPT-3 is better at creating any content that has a language structure – whether a human language or machine language – than any AI that has come before it. GPT-3 can answer questions, write essays, translate languages, summarize long pieces of text, take memos, and even create computer code. In one demo, GPT-3 created an app similar to Instagram – demonstrating how AI could play a huge role in software and app development in future.

Crucially, AI gives intelligent machines the ability to learn from data and make decisions, sometimes without human intervention. This is where the terms *machine learning* and *deep learning* come from. If we think of AI as the umbrella term, machine learning and deep learning are cutting-edge disciplines of AI that both involve getting machines to learn in the same way as humans do (i.e., by interpreting the world around us, sorting through information and learning from our successes and failures). Deep learning is the more advanced of the two because you can simply feed a deep learning system data and let it work out for itself how to find patterns.

One thing that hasn't yet been achieved is the idea of *general AI*, or the hypothetical ability of machines to understand the world as well as humans and learn any task. This is the AI of sci-fi movies and books. For now, AIs tend to carry out specific, narrow tasks. But just because general AI hasn't been achieved yet doesn't mean it's impossible. General AI is certainly the goal of several AI companies, and I suspect that if we put all the existing AIs together, they would be able not only to match what humans can do, but even exceed it.

That's why I believe AI is one of the most powerful developments we've seen as humans – matched only by gene hacking (more on this coming up). The takeaway for businesses is that, as our interactions with machines become increasingly intelligent, customers will expect all manner of products and services to feature some sort of AI capability. Then there is the potential for AI to enhance your internal business processes, whether it's through automation or helping human workers carry out their work and make decisions more effectively. In other words, every business is going to have to get smarter.

Trend 5: Extended Reality

As you can probably guess, advances in AI have fueled new developments in other technologies, including extended reality (XR). XR is an umbrella term representing the spectrum of immersive technologies we have today – virtual reality, augmented reality, and mixed reality – as well as those immersive technologies that are yet to be created. Currently, *virtual reality* (VR) offers the most immersive experience, by effectively blocking out the real world around the user and immersing them in a computer-simulated environment (usually with the aid of a VR headset). *Augmented reality* (AR), on the other hand, blends the digital and real worlds by overlaying digital objects or information onto the real world (often via a smartphone app or filter). Meanwhile, *mixed reality* (MR) sits somewhere between the two, creating an experience where the digital and real worlds can interact with each other – for example, letting a user manipulate virtual elements as if they were real.

XR is primarily known for immersive gaming, but it is finding very real, very practical uses across a wide range of industries – often being used to create more immersive, personalized experiences for customers. House buyers, for example, can go on immersive virtual house tours. Customers can try out products virtually (for example, by overlaying a new style of glasses over their face or digitally placing a new sofa in their living room). And sports fans can immerse themselves in the stadium experience from the comfort of their home. The list of exciting new XR applications goes on. But as well as giving organizations new ways to engage with customers and users, XR also brings exciting new opportunities to improve business processes, including training, education, and hiring. For example, trainees can learn in more immersive environments, with information being visualized in much more exciting ways.

The key takeaway here is that XR can help your business turn *information* into *experiences*. If you think about it, this has the potential to change pretty much everything, from the way we consume information to the way we interact with others. In the future, then, XR could extend to all aspects of life as we know it – to the point where we could potentially transform the world around us into something personalized, using special glasses, headsets, or even (looking further afield) contact lenses and implants. I believe our experience of the world will increasingly take place in this blurred space between the real world and the digital one. If you think of the time people spend on social media, crafting their online persona, it's clear the line between the digital world and the real one has already become pretty porous. I'm certain XR is going to accelerate this.

And that means we need to find innovative new ways to boost trust in the digital world.

Trend 6: Digital Trust

Digital trust can be defined as the confidence users place in organizations to build a secure digital world, where transactions and interactions can take place safely, securely, and easily. Many believe blockchain and distributed ledger technology will play a central role in raising digital trust and making transactions more secure. (When serving as CEO of IBM, Ginni Rometty said, "What the Internet did for communications, I think blockchain will do for trusted transactions.")[10] This technology already exists, but it has some way to go before it's truly accessible for all organizations. That said, advances in more ubiquitous computing, 5G, edge computing, and cloud computing may combine to make blockchain technology more accessible (for example, by harnessing distributed computing power around the world, instead of having entire server farms dedicated to running just one blockchain).

But let's back up a bit. What exactly is blockchain technology? In very simple terms, it's a super-secure way of storing data. Blockchain promises a practical solution to the problem of storing, authenticating, and protecting data, thereby providing a new way to authenticate information, identities, transactions, and more. This makes blockchain an increasingly attractive tool for industries like banking and insurance, but in fact blockchain can be used to provide a super-secure real-time record of pretty much anything: contracts, supply chain information, even physical assets.

To get a little more technical, a blockchain is a form of open, distributed ledger (i.e., a database), where the data is distributed (i.e., duplicated) across many computers and is typically decentralized. This means there's no one central point of attack for hackers to target – hence why blockchain is so secure.

How does it work? Records in a blockchain are called "blocks" and each block has a time and date stamp, noting when the record was created or updated. Each block is linked to the previous block, thus forming the "chain." The chain itself can be public (Bitcoin is a prime example of a public blockchain) or private (like a banking blockchain).

What about the difference between *blockchain* and *distributed ledger technology*? Although I use "blockchain" as a catchall term here, strictly speaking, the two terms aren't quite interchangeable. A good way to sum up the difference is this: a blockchain is typically open and permissionless, while a distributed ledger tends to be permissioned. Blockchains are generally public, creating a truly decentralized, democratic system where no one body or person is "in charge" (Bitcoin being the perfect example). A distributed ledger, on the other hand, could be private, meaning access is restricted by one centralized body (say, an organization). So a distributed ledger isn't necessarily decentralized and democratic, but it is still distributed and generally far more secure than traditional databases.

Blockchain and distributed ledger technology brings many advantages for businesses: securing data, removing intermediaries, increasing transparency, and supporting super-secure, frictionless, real-time transactions. But there are challenges to overcome – chief of which is how to implement this technology within the constraints of an organization built on legacy technology. The answer may lie in partnering with the many new innovators and entrepreneurs who are making real headway in the blockchain space. According to Deloitte, 45 percent of emerging disrupters have already brought blockchain to production, compared to less than 25 percent of enterprise businesses.[11] In other words, fully harnessing blockchain technology may require a complete rethink of operations, rather than trying to bolt this revolutionary technology onto existing systems.

And while we're on the subject of rethinking business processes, we can't ignore the potential for 3D printing to overhaul manufacturing.

Trend 7: 3D Printing

3D printing allows us to rethink how we produce things. It gives manufacturers the ability to make things that simply can't be produced with traditional methods, to streamline the manufacturing process, and easily create highly personalized products (even completely unique one-offs), all while eliminating waste and reducing costs.

Also known as additive manufacturing, 3D printing means creating a 3D object from a digital file, by building it layer upon layer. Traditional manufacturing tends to be a subtractive process, meaning an object is typically cut or hollowed out of its source material, using something like a cutting tool, which is hardly the most efficient way of manufacturing things. 3D printing, on the other hand, is an *additive* process, meaning you create the object by adding layers upon layers of material, building up until you have the finished object. (If you were to slice a 3D printed object open, you'd be able to see each of the thin layers, a bit like rings in a tree trunk.) So, with 3D printing, you start from nothing and build the object up bit by bit, as opposed to starting with a block of material and cutting or shaping it down into something.

The main benefit of 3D printing is that even complex shapes can be created much more easily, and using less material than traditional manufacturing methods (good for the environment and the bottom line). Transport needs are reduced, since parts and products can be printed onsite; a factory, for example, could 3D print replacement machinery parts rather than having to order and wait for components to be shipped halfway around the world. And one-off items can be made quickly and easily, without worrying about economies of scale, which could be a game-changer for rapid prototyping, custom manufacturing, and creating highly personalized products. What's more, the materials used for 3D printing can be pretty much anything: plastic, metal, powder, concrete, liquid, even chocolate. Even entire houses can be 3D printed. In 2021, a 3D printed house was listed for sale in the US for the first time. Priced at $299,999, and featuring over 1,400 square feet of living space (plus a 750-square-foot garage), the home was 50 percent cheaper than comparable newly constructed homes in the same area.[12]

As you can imagine, 3D printing has the potential to transform manufacturing, particularly when it comes to the mass personalization of products. As consumers increasingly expect products and services to be uniquely tailored to their needs (see Chapter 12), 3D printing allows manufacturers to customize products and designs to suit one-off requests and orders. So while 3D printing may not seem as exciting as something like AI or storing data on cubes of DNA, I believe it's still a transformative tech trend that companies should be preparing for.

But let's return to the more futuristic and sci-fi end of the tech trend spectrum.

Trend 8: Gene Editing and Synthetic Biology

As Steve Jobs once said, "The biggest innovations in the 21st century will be at the intersection of biology and technology." It looks like his prediction may be coming true.

We only understand around 2 percent of our genes at present, but even with this small amount, scientists have been able to achieve incredible things – not least the ability to alter the DNA encoded within a cell (known as gene editing). As we unlock more of the mysteries of our genes, we'll find new ways to understand and control them. Understandably, gene editing raises ethical issues for some, but it could deliver some drastic leaps forward in the fight against disease. Gene editing can have particular advantages when "bad" genes are detected – genes that could endanger the health of the organism or its descendants. These harmful characteristics can, in theory, be altered.

Given that the human body contains around 37 trillion cells, the microscopic scale involved in gene editing is truly amazing. The cell's nucleus, where most DNA resides, makes up around 10 percent of a typical cell, so the level of accuracy needed to cut something that tiny is almost inconceivable. At present, the CRISPR (pronounced "crisper") method of gene editing shows the most promise; it's the simplest way of making precise changes to DNA, such as adding some traits and/or removing others, not unlike the "find and replace" function in Microsoft Word. The CRISPR method was controversially used by Chinese scientist He Jiankui to alter the DNA in the embryos of twin girls to prevent them catching HIV.[13] Gene editing like this is banned in most countries and the experiment was widely condemned.

But we're not just talking about editing human DNA here. Plant health can be improved with gene editing. By editing plant genomes, their resistance to pests and diseases can be increased, leading to higher yields and less dependence on harmful chemicals. For example, researchers at Penn State University are working on creating genetically enhanced cacao trees that will be resistant to the disease and fungus that destroys up to 30 percent of the worldwide cacao crop before their pods can be harvested.[14] Creating disease-resistant crops like this will play a vital role in feeding our planet in future.

As well as editing genes, it is also possible to synthesize an organism's entire genome. As early as 2002, scientists were able to create the polio virus from scratch by synthesizing its genome. This brings us on to the topic of synthetic biology – or the field of science that's devoted to redesigning organisms. Synthetic biology is similar to gene editing (the ability to read and edit genes lies at the heart of synthetic biology), but while gene editing tools can be used to make *small* changes to DNA, synthetic biology can involve stitching together long strands of DNA and inserting them into an organism. As a result, the organism may behave differently, have new abilities, or be able to produce a specific substance (such as a fuel).

Harnessing microorganisms is an exciting area of synthetic biology. Life depends on tiny organisms that we can't see, and the idea is that harnessing these microorganisms could help us solve our biggest challenges. Newlight Technologies, for example, has been able to harness microbes to produce a carbon-negative, ocean-degradable thermoplastic that could replace traditional plastic.[15] Elsewhere, researchers in Israel have created a bacteria that can live on carbon dioxide directly from the air.[16] Some fragrances are already made using synthetic biology, as are cruelty-free leatherlike products and cultured meat, to name just a few examples.

But what does all this mean for businesses? Synthetic biology and gene editing may transform the way we produce products, feed the planet, treat illness, and solve some of the biggest crises facing humanity. Editing tools like CRISPR will help fuel advances in gene editing and synthetic biology, but so too will technologies like AI, which is ideally suited to crunching through vast quantities of data and identifying the right DNA configurations. (This is partly why the human genome can now be sequenced in a week, at a cost of $600, compared to the 13 years and $3 billion it originally took.)[17] As such, synthetic biology and gene editing may disrupt some of the world's largest industries, including agriculture, chemicals, and healthcare.

Trend 9: Nanotechnology and Materials Science

Judging by the advances scientists are making with microorganisms, it's clear powerful things can come in very small packages. Let's shrink that down even further and take a quick look at nanotechnology and materials science.

In simple terms, nanotechnology means controlling matter on a tiny scale, at the atomic and molecular level, so that we can manipulate and move those atoms around to create new things. In this way, nanotechnology is a bit like construction, but on a tiny scale. And I do mean *tiny*. The nanoscale is 1,000 times smaller than the microscopic level and a billion times smaller than the typical world of meters that we're used to measuring things in. A human hair, for instance, measures approximately 100,000 nanometers wide. A strand of human DNA is just 2.5 nanometers wide.

Nanotechnology is important because, when we look at objects and materials at a nanoscopic level, we can understand more about how they work. (Some substances also behave differently and have completely different properties at an atomic level.) As an example, silk may feel incredibly soft and delicate to the touch, but at a nano level, it's made up of molecules aligned in cross-links, which is what makes it so strong. We can use knowledge like this to manipulate other materials at a nano level, to create super-strong, state-of-the-art materials like Kevlar, or products that are lighter, or any other conceivable improvement to products and components. This is where the *technology* bit of nanotechnology comes in – using our knowledge of materials at a nano level to create new solutions. In this way, the study of materials at a nano level could be considered almost a subfield of *materials science*, the discipline that focuses on studying and manipulating materials.

Those tiny computer chips and transistors that are behind the ubiquitous computing trend? They're built using nanotechnology and materials science. Same goes for lots of products and materials, from smartphone displays and lithium-ion batteries, to tennis balls and stain-resistant fabrics. And there are many more exciting new developments to come. In time, we can expect advances in nanotechnology and materials science to feed into many other technology trends already mentioned, including smart devices, smart cities, autonomous vehicles, and 3D printing. One example comes from the Jenax J. Flex foldable battery, which could pave the way for the bendable gadgets of the future.[18]

I'm particularly excited about the potential for nanotechnology and materials science to help mitigate the climate crisis. As an example, scientists at Toyota have been testing materials for a battery that can fully charge or discharge in just seven minutes, making it ideal for electric cars.[19] Or consider perovskite solar cells, based on the properties of a light-sensitive crystal. Perovskite could improve the conversion efficiency of solar panels – how much captured sunlight can be turned into energy – from 16 percent to 66 percent.[20] Advances like this could make solar energy affordable and achievable for everyone, and it's just one of the many materials science breakthroughs that could make our world a better place. Which brings us neatly on to the next topic.

Trend 10: New Energy Solutions

Technology and energy are inextricably linked, so we can't discuss tech mega-trends without referring to new energy solutions. Renewable energy solutions, specifically wind and solar, have certainly grown in efficiency, affordability, and availability in recent years. But let's look at a couple of new energy sources that may be on the horizon: nuclear fusion and green hydrogen. (Head to Chapter 3 to see how the wider energy sector is undergoing a transformation.)

Nuclear fusion is often touted as the clean and potentially inexhaustible energy solution for the future, but realizing this dream has proven frustratingly elusive – the main sticking point being that maintaining a fusion reaction takes more energy than it produces! This understandably makes nuclear fusion not terribly viable on any large scale. But now scientists have taken a big step closer to making nuclear fusion viable. The International Thermonuclear Experimental Reactor (ITER) project – which is a collaboration between the European Union, India, Japan, China, Russia, South Korea, and the United States – is currently building a prototype fusion reactor (called a tokamak), which could be ready to conduct its first tests in 2025 and be generating full-power fusion as early as 2035.[21] There are more than a dozen similar research initiatives under way around the world.

Fusion is not to be confused with *fission*, the energy source in current nuclear power stations, which is created by splitting an atom's nucleus. *Fusion*, which is what powers the Sun, is created when two light atoms fuse into one under extreme temperature and pressure conditions – and because the mass of the newly created single atom is less than the original two atoms, the "spare" mass is given off as energy. Maintaining the extreme temperatures and intense pressure needed has proven difficult, but this is where recent progress has been made, largely thanks to advances in magnet technology. And this means we may see a nuclear fusion reactor deliver a net power output by 2035.

Green hydrogen is the other zero-carbon energy source that has tempted scientists for decades. When hydrogen burns, the only by-product is water, which is what makes hydrogen such a tempting energy source. Unfortunately, the traditional process for producing hydrogen involves exposing fossil fuels to steam, which obviously isn't very green at all. That is why this traditional process is known as "gray hydrogen."

In contrast, *green hydrogen* splits water into hydrogen and oxygen, creating no other by-products. This is done via a process of electrolysis, which, historically, has taken so much electricity that it has made green hydrogen unfeasible. That may change thanks to renewable electricity sources. As excess renewable electricity is becoming available on the grid, that excess energy could, in theory, be used to drive the electrolysis of water. What's more, electrolysis machines are becoming more efficient. As such, some companies are already working to develop electrolyzers that can produce green hydrogen as cheaply as gray hydrogen within the next decade.[22] For sectors that rely on gas and coal, where wind and solar power isn't feasible, green hydrogen could be a vital part of the solution.

Now that we've taken a broad look at the global and technology trends shaping our world, let's drill down to some specifics. In the next part, we'll explore some specific sectors and see how they transform themselves.

PRACTICAL LESSONS

This chapter has thrown a lots of information and technical jargon at you, so let's sum up with a few practical lessons and takeaways for business leaders:

- One of the key takeaways from this chapter is the convergence and interaction between all these different tech trends, and the sheer pace of change. This is what makes the fourth industrial revolution so different from the previous three. As such, simply bolting one new technology (such as machine learning) onto existing systems and processes isn't enough. Rather, organizations may need to rethink their entire operations and constantly redefine their business. Gone are the days of incremental tech upgrades; we're entering an era of continual and rapid evolution.

- With this in mind, businesses that are "digital natives" or "born digital" are better prepared for the constant influx of new technologies. Traditional organizations, with their (often) expensive legacy systems, face a tougher road. Not only will they need to invest in new skills, capabilities, and technology (sometimes by partnering with more agile start-ups), but they may need to enact a cultural shift as well, toward a culture of continual learning and agility.

- It's vital all organizations approach these new technologies strategically. Adopting technology for technology's sake is never a good idea; rather, organizations must look to prioritize and deploy new technologies in a way that delivers maximum returns for their business. This will be different for each company.

Notes

1. IDC's Global StorageSphere Forecast Shows Continued Strong Growth in the World's Installed Base of Storage Capacity; IDC; https://www.idc.com/getdoc.jsp?containerId=prUS46303920

2. Prediction: 80% Of Enterprise IT Will Move to the Cloud By 2025; Forbes; https://www.forbes.com/sites/oracle/2019/02/07/prediction-80-of-enterprise-it-will-move-to-the-cloud-by-2025/

3. DNA Data Storage Is Closer Than You Think; Scientific American; https://www.scientificamerican.com/article/dna-data-storage-is-closer-than-you-think/

4. Number of internet of things (IoT) connected devices worldwide in 2018, 2025 and 2030; Statistica; https://www.statista.com/statistics/802690/worldwide-connected-devices-by-access-technology/

5. Sea Hunter Will Operate with Carrier Strike Group, as SURFDEVRON Plans Heavy Test Schedule; USNI News; https://news.usni.org/2020/01/21/sea-hunter-usv-will-operate-with-carrier-strike-group-as-surfdevron-plans-hefty-testing-schedule

6. In China, Alibaba's data-hungry AI is controlling (and watching) cities; Wired; https://www.wired.co.uk/article/alibaba-city-brain-artificial-intelligence-china-kuala-lumpur

7. 2020 sees huge increase in records exposed in data breaches; TechRepublic; https://www.techrepublic.com/article/2020-sees-huge-increase-in-records-exposed-in-data-breaches/

8. COMB: largest breach of all time leaked online with 3.2 billion records; Cybernews; https://cybernews.com/news/largest-compilation-of-emails-and-passwords-leaked-free/

9. Big Ideas 2021; Ark Invest; https://research.ark-invest.com/hubfs/1_Download_Files_ARK-Invest/White_Papers/ARK%E2%80%93Invest_BigIdeas_2021.pdf

10. @IBM; Twitter; https://twitter.com/ibm/status/877599373768630273?lang=en

11. The future of blockchain and market disruptors; Deloitte; https://www2.deloitte.com/us/en/insights/topics/understanding-blockchain-potential/global-blockchain-survey.html

12. First permitted 3D-printed house hits the market for $300k; Builder; https://www.builderonline.com/building/building-enclosure/first-permitted-3d-printed-house-hits-the-market-for-300k_o

13. He Jiankui: Baby gene experiment "foolish and dangerous"; BBC News; https://www.bbc.com/news/health-48496652

14. Cocoa CRISPR: Gene editing shows promise for improving the "chocolate tree"; Penn State University; https://news.psu.edu/story/521154/2018/05/09/research/cocoa-crispr-gene-editing-shows-promise-improving-chocolate-tree

15. Newlight Technologies; https://www.newlight.com/

16. In possible climate breakthrough, Israel scientists engineer bacteria to eat CO_2; Times of Israel; https://www.timesofisrael.com/in-possible-climate-breakthrough-israel-scientists-engineer-bacteria-to-eat-co%E2%82%82/#:~:text=Sue%20Surkes%20is%20The%20Times%20

of%20Israel's%20environment%20reporter.&text=In%20a%20remark-able%20breakthrough%20that,carbon%20dioxide%20rather%20than%20 sugar

17. We are witnessing a revolution in genomics – and it's only just begun; World Economic Forum; https://www.weforum.org/agenda/2019/06/ today-you-can-have-your-genome-sequenced-at-the-supermarket/

18. Jenax J. Flex battery; https://jenaxinc.com/

19. Future batteries, coming soon: Charge in seconds, last months and charge over the air; Pocket-lint; https://www.pocket-lint.com/gadgets/ news/130380-future-batteries-coming-soon-charge-in-seconds-last-months-and-power-over-the-air

20. 3 Major Materials Science Breakthroughs – and Why They Matter for the Future; Singularity hub; https://singularityhub.com/2020/05/21/3-major-materials-science-breakthroughs-and-why-they-matter-for-the-future/

21. Scientists just got closer to making nuclear fusion work; World Economic Forum; https://www.weforum.org/agenda/2019/05/nuclear-fusion-could-solve-the-world-s-energy-problems-and-scientists-just-got-closer-to-making-it-work/

22. Top 10 Emerging Technologies of 2020; World Economic Forum; http://www3.weforum.org/docs/WEF_Top_10_Emerging_Technolo-gies_2020.pdf

PART II
RETHINKING KEY SECTORS

Building upon the global shifts and tech mega-trends outlined in Part I, in Part II we'll look at the implications for some key sectors, including opportunities, challenges, and some brief examples of exciting projects and initiatives. (You'll find many more real-world examples across Parts III and IV.)

I could write a whole book on the changes taking place in these sectors, so each chapter provides an overview and highlights some of the dramatic shifts taking place. And, of course, I wasn't able to include every possible sector or industry facing change. I wanted to highlight those sectors that touch all of our lives to ensure everyone can relate to them. Some sectors are deliberately not included here, because they're referred to so frequently across Parts III and IV. Retail is a prime example.

Bottom line, if your sector isn't explicitly mentioned in this Part, don't worry; many of the same challenges, trends, and transformations will be applicable to your organization, and there are many lessons to be learned from the changes taking place in these industries.

CHAPTER 3
HOW WE GENERATE ENERGY

The Three Trends Transforming
the Energy Sector

Our traditional ways of generating energy are exploitative, unsustainable, and designed for the world of the past (making the name "fossil fuels" particularly apt). Then there's the problem that energy producers who are reliant on fossil fuels aren't held accountable for the true external costs, particularly the cost to the environment and people's health. Coal, for example, is only considered cheap because coal-fueled power stations don't have to pay for the environmental and social costs associated with burning coal. In some parts of the world, this will no doubt have contributed to the reliance on fossil fuels continuing far longer than it should have.

Now that we understand the impact of fossil fuels, it's time to start approaching energy production differently. And it couldn't be more urgent because some of the emerging alternatives being mooted have a long lead time, meaning we need to start investing in these technologies now if we're to reap the benefits by, say, 2050.

It's no exaggeration to say that I consider transforming the energy sector to be one of the most important challenges we face in the world. But there are exciting and encouraging signs of change. In particular, three key trends are promising to overhaul how we produce energy:

- Decarbonization refers to the transition toward a clean, carbon-free world, largely by increasing the use of renewables. Increasing premiums on the use of fossil fuels would also fall under this.

- Decentralization refers to distributed energy production, instead of the highly centralized grids that we're currently used to.

- Digitization refers to the use of digital machines, devices, and technology to optimize energy production, infrastructure, and use. Think of it as "intelligent energy."

Let's explore each trend in turn.

Trend 1: The Decarbonization of Energy

Electrification is often touted as a key way to decarbonize energy, with the move toward electric cars being a great example. The electrification of our world is such a key trend that, over time, electricity demand could increase by four times in Europe, while the price of electricity falls due to increasing use of renewables.[1] Unfortunately, at present, fossil fuels still make up a huge percentage of electricity generation in many parts of the world (in the US, for example, fossil fuels are responsible for 60.3 percent of electricity generation).[2] For electricity to become emissions-free, we must move further toward renewable energy solutions such as wind, solar, biofuels, and tidal power.

The case for renewables

Switching to wind, solar, and water power worldwide could eliminate as many as 7 million deaths a year from air pollution, and slow (then, ultimately, reverse) the effects of global warming.[3] Roughly one-fifth of the world's primary energy supply already comes from renewable sources, and this is expected to continue growing by 2.6 percent each year until 2040.[4] Solar appears to be winning the market so far, making up 60 percent of the renewable energy capacity installed in 2019 and prompting technology giants like Apple and Google to invest in solar technology.[5]

Looking beyond the well-known option of solar panels on roofs, some of the most exciting solar projects to make headlines in recent years include:[6]

- A floating solar farm in the Maldives, which aims to provide clean energy to 360 million people who live in remote coastal areas
- A solar bike path in the Netherlands
- A solar-powered train tunnel in Belgium
- A solar-powered airport in India

Overcoming the challenges with renewable energy

The challenge with renewable solutions is that we need energy 24 hours a day, yet sometimes there's simply no wind or sun, a problem known as "intermittency." What's more, peak demand times may not coincide with peak energy production times. This means we need to find ways to store the energy produced, so that energy captured can be transmitted and used later. Currently, there's no effective way to store the electricity produced by renewable technologies for any real length of time. But this is one area where exciting changes are happening, such as the Advanced Clean Energy Storage scheme in Utah, a hydrogen-based renewable energy storage complex.[7] Or there's Swiss startup Energy Vault, which is developing energy storage technology for intermittent renewable energy sources, inspired by pumped-storage plants that rely on the movement of water to generate power. Power-to-X – an umbrella term for processes that turn electricity into heat, hydrogen, or renewable synthetic fuels – may also play a role in solving the energy storage problem, and, in turn, accelerate the shift to renewables.[8] So, too might distributed power generation (more on that later in the chapter).

There's also the uncomfortable fact that electric vehicles, solar panels, and wind turbines are using rare earth materials mined from the earth. China has a monopoly on these materials (see Chapter 1), meaning geopolitical challenges could play an increasing role in the energy sector.[9]

Investing in other energy alternatives

As well as investing in energy storage projects, we also need other clean energy alternatives – solutions that are able to generate a consistent, reliable supply of clean electricity when supply from renewable sources dips. For now, that means nuclear. I understand people's nervousness around nuclear power, but the technology is one of the safest and cleanest ways of producing energy. In the 60-year history of civil nuclear power, there have been three major accidents at power plants, with Fukushima Dai-ichi being the most recent in 2011 (imagine if the aviation industry had such a record), and, overall, nuclear energy results in 99.7 percent fewer deaths than coal and 97.5 percent fewer than gas (the safety record for wind and solar is even more impressive).[10] Modern nuclear reactors are much safer than the ones we build decades ago. Looking ahead, we also have nuclear fusion edging closer (see Chapter 2), with the world's largest nuclear fusion project beginning assembly in France.[11]

We may also see advances in other alternative energy sources that could help to support wind and solar. These include:[12]

- Tidal power, captured from wave energy. Portugal established the world's first commercial-scale wave farm in 2008.

- Space-based solar power, which has already been proven viable by the Japan Aerospace Exploration Agency.

- Human power, where we generate power through our own bodies. For example, UK researchers have developed a knee brace that can produce electricity as the wearer walks.

- Embeddable solar power, where potentially any window or sheet of glass can be turned into a photovoltaic solar cell. Researchers at Michigan State University are already working on scaling this technology.

Trend 2: The Decentralization of Energy

Decentralization is another trend driving the energy transformation. In simple terms, decentralization means shifting away from the traditional energy model in which monopolistic utilities providers with large power plants distribute energy to the end user. Instead, the energy networks of the future will be *distributed*, meaning more energy will be generated away from the main grid (thanks to a combination of renewable energy and localized "microgrids" – any localized energy grid that functions independently or as part of a larger, standard energy grid). With this model, consumers generate energy for their own needs. Many of us are already familiar with this idea through the use of rooftop solar panels, but decentralized schemes can serve anything from a single building to an entire city. This ultimately means organizations, local authorities, and consumers can take charge of their own energy portfolio.

The case for decentralized networks

Decentralized networks can help to cut energy prices, reduce carbon emissions, empower communities, and improve energy security by offering energy independence and protection during emergencies. To put it another way, it's a smart way to meet growing demand, while improving sustainability.[13]

Already decentralized networks are taking shape in the UK. Aberdeen City Council, for example, turned to district heating – the supply of heat from one source to a district or group of buildings – to solve the problem of fuel poverty in some of the city's housing stock, reducing typical fuel costs for tenants by 50 percent and cutting carbon emissions by 45 percent in the process. The council has plans to extend the network beyond the 1,500 flats and handful of municipal buildings initially connected in the scheme, and the team is also helping other local authorities realize the same benefits.[14]

Elsewhere in the UK, Bristol City Council has been working with the Carbon Trust to develop four district energy schemes across the city with a goal of reducing carbon emissions, cutting costs, and supporting future development in the city.[15] Meanwhile, in the US, startups like Urban Energy are enabling distributed energy by turning rooftops in New York into community solar gardens.

In other words, public bodies and consumers are already beginning to realize that they can do it better than established energy providers and are taking control of their own energy destiny.

Overcoming the challenges

But it's not all rosy. One of the main challenges with decentralized energy is the lack of institutional knowledge and experience on how to develop and implement such projects, although organizations like the Carbon Trust and Urban Energy are helping to solve this.

Another challenge is how to cope with fluctuating demand patterns within these smaller grids (unlike, say, huge energy providers that can easily produce enough power at peak demand times). This is where technologies like AI can help (more on the digitization of energy coming up later). Using data from smart sensors, and smart energy storage solutions, decentralized systems can better manage local energy requirements and ensure power is supplied where and when needed. An example of this comes from Cornwall's Local Energy Market, which announced in 2019 that it had reached a "flexibility breakthrough" after installing a combination of solar, battery systems, and monitoring equipment into 100 homes and 125 businesses across Cornwall, England.[16]

Related to this is the term "Internet of Energy" (IoE). Like the Internet of Things (see Chapter 2), the IoE relies on smart devices to increase efficiencies and improve control. As an example, US-based startup Lumidyne Consulting's SPIDER system applies data modeling to distributed energy resources, to predict impact on energy demand and aid the planning of energy distribution. Or there's British startup Distributed Energy, which provides demand management solutions to manage small and mid-sized companies' power requirements, enabling greater adoption of renewable energy. Tools like this will help to manage risk and uncertainty in decentralized networks and make moving away from standard grids a viable option for more energy users.

Trend 3: The Digitization of Energy

This final trend goes hand in hand with the first two. The future of the energy sector will involve smart, decentralized grids that can understand which houses and buildings need energy at which time. With the energy being produced by an increasing variety of zero-carbon sources, technology will play an essential role in managing these complex energy networks of the future.

What do we mean by digital transformation?

To realize this vision of smarter, more diverse energy grids, we need intelligent devices and technology that: a) help us communicate with the grid so demand can be monitored and managed, and b) help us all reduce our energy consumption. I briefly alluded to some examples in the previous section, but let's see what else is involved in the digitization of energy (many of which are key tech mega-trends covered in the previous chapter). Together, these digital solutions have given rise to the term *Energy 4.0*, a play on Industry 4.0 or the fourth industrial revolution that I referred to at the start of Chapter 2.

- AI and predictive analytics : These are used to analyze and predict demand, adjust where power is drawn from on distributed grids, and predict equipment failures. GE, for example, uses AI to predict failures ahead of time at wind and solar plants.[17]

- The Internet of Things: In particular, the use of smart home thermostats and home energy management systems such as Google Nest is helping consumers cut their energy usage and heat their homes more efficiently.

- Blockchain: From secure, smart contracts to facilitating distributed networks, blockchain could be a transformative technology for the energy sector. In one example, Turkish startup Blok-Z's blockchain technology enables anyone to access economical, transparent and traceable green electricity.

- Quantum computing: The sheer power of quantum computers is ideally suited to solving the unique and vast challenges facing the energy sector. As an example, US-based startup QC Ware provides quantum computing solutions to help optimize energy use (including energy prediction and demand management).

- Digital twins: A digital twin is an advanced digital duplicate of a real-life object, system, or process. By using information gathered from IoT sensors in the real world, organizations can model changes and try them out in the digital twin without making expensive or high-risk alterations to the real-life counterpart. BP, for example, uses digital twins to model new oil field production.[18] In another example, MHPS-TOMONI's digital twin technology can create a virtual replica of a power plant or even an entire grid.[19]

As that last example suggests, these technologies don't just apply to innovative decentralized energy grids and renewable sources. Even with traditional, centralized operators, digital innovation can help energy providers cope with uncertainty, make better decisions, and improve efficiency in an increasingly competitive field. According to McKinsey, energy companies that have invested in digital innovation have seen up to 10 percent improvements in production and yield, and up to 30 percent improvements in costs.[20]

Overcoming the challenges

So far, these digital technologies haven't been fully exploited by the energy sector. Finding the value from digital can prove tricky, particularly for traditional energy companies who can be slow to change.

Largely this is because energy providers face some unique complications, such as health and safety risks, the large amount of capital invested in existing assets (such as power plants, pipelines, and offshore platforms), and the capabilities of frontline workers (who are often operating in remote or hard-to-reach locations). What's more, many oil and gas companies are entrenched in an engineering mindset – which tends to favor caution, in-depth planning, and a "right first time" approach – versus the flexible, agile, fast-moving mindset that digital transformation often requires.

Many sectors are coping with similar challenges, but the energy sector must contend with them all at the same time, which makes digital adoption not impossible, but certainly challenging.

Now let's turn to another long-established sector that is undergoing rapid change driven by technology: healthcare.

PRACTICAL LESSONS

In this chapter, we've learned:

- It is vital that energy companies, policymakers, regulators, public bodies, city planners, and local authorities work to advance these three trends in unison. This is essential for meeting our future economic and energy needs, while mitigating the climate crisis.

- Outside of the energy sector, all business leaders can learn from the opportunities and challenges faced by energy providers. Identifying emerging technologies to incorporate into your business, accelerating digital change, dealing with competition from emerging startups, and coping with market fragmentation are things that many businesses can identify with.

- In particular, the need to commit to digital transformation is common to all industries. In my experience, COVID-19 provides an unprecedented window to accelerate this, as companies and their employees were forced to accelerate digital adoption in a very short space of time. The trick is to not slide back into normalcy when the pandemic is over, but to use it as a springboard to continuous change and evolution.

- Finally, for business leaders looking to learn from these energy trends, perhaps the biggest takeaway is not to delay. Taking early action is a critical part of gaining a competitive advantage.

Notes

1. 5 technologies changing the future of renewable energy; Wartsila; https://www.wartsila.com/insights/article/5-technologies-changing-the-future-of-renewable-energy

2. What is U.S electricity generation by energy source?; U.S. Energy Information Administration; https://www.eia.gov/tools/faqs/faq.php?id=427&t=3

3. Renewable energy could power the world by 2050. Here's what that future might look like; World Economic Forum; https://www.weforum.org/agenda/2020/02/renewable-energy-future-carbon-emissions/

4. The biggest energy challenges facing humanity; BBC; https://www.bbc.com/future/article/20170313-the-biggest-energy-challenges-facing-humanity

5. 5 technologies changing the future of renewable energy; Wartsila; https://www.wartsila.com/insights/article/5-technologies-changing-the-future-of-renewable-energy

6. Most Innovative Solar Projects Around The World; Solar Metric; https://solarmetric.com/learn/most-innovative-solar-projects-around-the-world/amp/

7. In Utah, Hydrogen and a Massive Salt Dome Are Winning the West for Renewable Energy; Forbes; https://www.forbes.com/sites/mitsubishi-heavyindustries/2020/03/13/in-utah-hydrogen-and-a-massive-salt-dome-are-winning-the-west-for-renewable-energy/#4ee0db095c52

8. 5 technologies changing the future of renewable energy; Wartsila; https://www.wartsila.com/insights/article/5-technologies-changing-the-future-of-renewable-energy

9. These are the biggest hurdles on the path to clean energy; World Economic Forum; https://www.weforum.org/agenda/2021/02/heres-why-geopolitics-could-hamper-the-energy-transition/

10. What are the safest and cleanest sources of energy?; Our World in Data; https://ourworldindata.org/safest-sources-of-energy

11. World's largest nuclear fusion project begins assembly in France; The Guardian; https://www.theguardian.com/environment/2020/jul/28/worlds-largest-nuclear-fusion-project-under-assembly-in-france

12. The Alternative Energy Sources of the Future; Visual Capitalist; https://www.visualcapitalist.com/alternative-energy-sources-future/

13. Decentralised energy: powering a sustainable future; Carbon Trust; https://www.carbontrust.com/news-and-events/insights/decentralised-energy-powering-a-sustainable-future

14. Ibid.

15. Ibid.

16. Cornwall Local Energy Market reaches "flexibility breakthrough"; Energy Live news; https://www.energylivenews.com/2019/11/11/cornwall-local-energy-market-reaches-flexibility-breakthough/

17. GE Uses AI to Increase Responsiveness of Thermal Power; Bloomberg NEF; https://about.bnef.com/blog/ge-uses-ai-increase-responsiveness-thermal-power-qa/

18. Energy 4.0: Digital transformation in energy & utilities industry; Mobidev; https://mobidev.biz/blog/digital-transformation-energy-utilities-sector

19. TOMONI: Transforming power plants into big-data powerhouses; Mitsubishi Power; https://www.changeinpower.com/our-solutions/data-and-a-i/tomoni/

20. Digital transformation in energy: Achieving escape velocity; McKinsey & Company; https://www.mckinsey.com/industries/oil-and-gas/our-insights/digital-transformation-in-energy-achieving-escape-velocity

CHAPTER 4
HOW WE STAY HEALTHY
The Seven Trends Shaping Healthcare

Our struggling healthcare systems are approaching a tipping point, exacerbated by the COVID-19 pandemic, growing populations and longer lifespans (see Chapter 1), a shortage of healthcare professionals (the global shortage of healthcare professionals could reach 9.9 million by 2030),[1] and the rise of lifestyle-related chronic diseases (which have now replaced infectious diseases as the leading threat to health).[2] Huge parts of the world have no healthcare, or no free healthcare. And even in more developed countries, healthcare is often too expensive, still too exclusive, and far too reactive (as opposed to proactive).

These healthcare systems were built for a different time – a time when people didn't live as long as they do now, when there were fewer instances of chronic disease, and, crucially, when the intelligent technology needed to support effective healthcare didn't exist. The world, and technology, has moved on. And, as the seven key trends in this chapter show, the healthcare sector is beginning to catch up.

Trend 1: Preventative Medicine

Traditional medicine follows a reactive model. People feel ill or experience certain symptoms, then medical professionals work to diagnose and treat the problem, often through a process of trial and error.

There is little emphasis, if any, on prevention of conditions, either physical or mental.

But thanks to data and AI (I'll talk more about digitization later in the chapter), healthcare has the power to become more predictive and preventative. Technology can reduce the risk of preventative illness in many ways, and here are just a few examples:

- Automate reminders for patients who need to take medication on a regular basis.

- Deliver personalized medical advice and dosage recommendations based on each patient's body and environmental factors (more on personalization later in the chapter).

- Analyze data and harness predictive modeling to predict when people might be at a higher risk of developing diseases, mental health issues, and even addiction. In one example, researchers used machine learning to predict the likelihood of opioid dependency.[3]

- Identify which patients might be at risk of unplanned readmission to hospital within 30 days of receiving treatment and helping those patients better manage their health. In one study, for example, researchers found that certain events during a hospital stay and the length of stay significantly affected the chances of a 30-day readmission.[4] Another used predictive analytics to identify patients who were on track to develop sepsis 12 hours before onset of the condition.[5]

- Predict which patients are more likely to skip an appointment without warning. In one example, researchers were able to predict which individuals were most likely to be no-shows.[6] Such insights could be used to send extra reminders to patients, offer them help in getting to their appointment, or offer them an alternative timeslot.

- Prevent suicide by identifying individuals likely to attempt suicide. One study that combed through the data of patients who had previously self-harmed predicted the risk of suicide attempts with an 84 percent accuracy.[7] Early identification of those at risk of suicide ensures patients receive the mental health support they need.

In other words, thanks to technology, we will see healthcare become more proactive over time. This is important because, when healthcare providers can identify the risk of developing chronic conditions earlier, patients have a much better chance of avoiding long-term health problems. In turn, the cost of treating those conditions comes down.

Trend 2: Democratized Healthcare

One of the biggest problems with healthcare is that it isn't available to all, or simply isn't affordable. According to the WHO, half of the world lacks access to essential health services and 100 million people are pushed into extreme poverty because of health expenses.[8] And even in developed countries like America, millions of people still don't have health insurance (28.9 million people in 2019, or almost 11 percent of the population).[9]

Now, however, technology is helping to give people around the world greater access to healthcare services. Here are just a few examples of how technology is beginning to democratize healthcare:

- We have apps that can assist in the diagnostic process and provide people with remote access to health advice (more about telemedicine later in the chapter). WebMD's Pain Coach app is just one example. Allowing people to track and monitor their pain levels, the app is designed to help people spot potential pain triggers and better manage their pain.

- Chatbots can also play a role in providing remote assistance. As an example, the Wysa app, developed by Indian firm Touchkin, is an AI-powered stress, anxiety, and depression therapy chatbot that allows people to vent their feelings, track their mood, and boost their emotional wellness. And when additional support is needed, the chatbot connects users with a human coach.

- Everyday wearable technologies are increasingly able to detect signs of potential illness and help people monitor their vital signs. For example, Fitbit's Sense smartwatch can monitor your temperature and score your stress level. The Apple Watch's heart-tracking EKG feature has been cleared by the Food and Drug Administration, and the latest Apple Watch can even monitor blood oxygen levels.[10] Obviously, such wearable technology isn't available to everyone at present, but as the technology becomes less expensive, more people will be able to benefit from real-time insights about their health.

This democratization of healthcare will be accelerated by increasing digitization and automation within the healthcare sector (more on this later in the chapter). Apps, chatbots, and wearables are also contributing to greater personalization within healthcare, which brings us to the next topic.

Trend 3: Personalized, Precision Healthcare

As healthcare becomes more predictive and proactive, and as more people have access to healthcare solutions and insights through apps, chatbots, and wearable technology, it will also become easier to deliver more personalized, precision healthcare, where an individual's health indicators are monitored more easily, conditions are predicted in advance, and tailored advice and preventative care is delivered.

Let's look at a few examples of healthcare becoming more personalized:

- As you might imagine, AI plays a huge role in providing personalized healthcare. Using AI algorithms, the Your.MR app (also known as Healthily) allows patients to discuss their symptoms with a chatbot. The app then combs through medical literature on more than 1,000 conditions and provides personalized, accurate responses on the patient's potential condition, before connecting them with a suitable local doctor.

- In another example, the Cornerstone4Care app, developed by diabetes drug company Novo Nordisk and digital health company Glooko, is a personalized tool for monitoring diabetes. Patients can track their blood sugar and meals, and get personalized recommendations for diet, exercise, and diabetes management.

- Beyond apps and chatbots, we may also see hospitals and health-care facilities offering more personalized, concierge-style services to help with nonmedical needs. That's exactly what New Jersey's Riverview Medical Center has done. The clinic offers a concierge service that, among other things, delivers reading materials for patients and booking hotel rooms for visiting family members.[11]

Add in the power of gene technology and synthetic biology (see Chapter 2), and the future of healthcare could lie in intensely personalized diagnostics and treatment plans. In one example, biotech company 23andMe offers personalized DNA testing to highlight genetic predisposition to health risks, such as celiac disease or Parkinson's. Customers simply provide a saliva sample and receive a personalized report of their genetic makeup, detailing which conditions could be linked to their DNA.

Looking ahead, the ability to analyze a patient's genome will inform specific therapies, including drug choices and doses. This is already possible for certain types of epilepsy; for example, people with epilepsy caused by mutations in the gene ALDH7A1 can be effectively treated with a type of vitamin B6, yet this would not work so well with types of epilepsy caused by other gene mutations.[12] No wonder, then, that many geneticists believe the future of medicine lies in being able to read a person's genome and then to prescribe care and treatment based on that.

Trend 4: Digitized Healthcare

The idea of remote access to healthcare and more patient-centric healthcare is facilitated by the wider digitization of healthcare. Some of the key subtrends in technology-driven healthcare include:

- Telemedicine – the remote diagnosis and treatment of patients via communications platforms and tools – allows patients in remote areas to access medical aid, but even for those who have easy access to medical care, virtual appointments save people from spending hours in waiting rooms. COVID-19 has certainly accelerated this shift toward remote care; my local GP practice switched to offering telephone consultations wherever possible and I'm sure many readers experienced the same thing. In the US, in April 2020, 43.5 percent of Medicare primary care visits were conducted via telemedicine methods as opposed to in-person consultations, compared to 0.1 percent in February 2020.[13]

- Electronic health records (EHR) also play a critical role since they can integrate with telemedicine apps, allowing patients and providers to access information within the app. If this data were linked to data from wearables, it would give healthcare professionals a deeper insight into their patients' overall health, fitness, and activity. Already this is beginning to take shape with apps like Apple Health integrating with medical records from some institutions across the US, Canada, and the UK, allowing people to access their medical data via their devices.[14]

- As I've already mentioned, AI plays a critical role in the digitization of health, facilitating everything from predicting disease and analyzing scan results to detecting pandemics and aiding vaccine development. As an example, the BlueDot app is a pioneer in developing early warning systems for identifying pandemics and was the first to publish a paper predicting COVID-19's spread across the world.[15]

- Extended reality (see Chapter 2) is another important technology with huge potential to enhance many aspects of healthcare, from medical training to improving patient visits. For example, early analysis demonstrates that virtual reality is more effective for helping stroke victims overcome motor deficiencies and reducing the risk of falls than conventional physiotherapy.[16]

- Looking further ahead, we may even see virtual patients – specifically, the testing of drugs and treatments on virtual patients to see how real patients might respond. There are signs that this could speed up vaccine development and slash medical trial costs. These so-called "in silico" clinical trials are already under way – the FDA is using computer simulations in place of human trials for evaluating new mammography systems.[17]

As healthcare becomes increasingly digitized, there are of course challenges and pitfalls to overcome, particularly around protecting patients' precious health data (read more about the datafication of healthcare later in the chapter).

Trend 5: Improving the Human Body

There is now an entire industry centered around improving the human body, and hacking the body to prolong life as much as possible. Genomics and gene technology could arguably fall under this umbrella, too, where it is directed at removing bad genes.

One of the key subtrends here is biohacking, the use of strategic interventions aimed at improving mental and physical performance, and even halting aging – DIY biology, in other words. While some techniques, such as intermittent fasting and exposing the body to cold temperatures, have been around for a long time, more recent techniques are seeing people take a highly technical approach to engineering their own bodies. Take nutrigenomics as an example –numerous companies can provide a personalized diet plan based on your DNA (i.e., a spit sample).

A subset of biohackers goes way beyond supplements. In one extreme example, Dave Asprey, founder of the multimillion-dollar Bulletproof coffee brand, had a doctor harvest stem cells from his bone marrow and inject those cells into every joint in this body – all part of his highly publicized (and eye-wateringly expensive) quest to live to 180 years old.[18] Elsewhere, companies are offering "young-blood" infusions as a way to combat aging, despite warnings from the FDA.[19]

The question, of course, is where do we stop with biohacking? Where do we draw the line before we create a new class of hyper-modified superhumans? The worry is that this trend, while empowering people to take more charge of their own health and well-being, could increase the gap between the haves and the have-nots.

On a more positive note, there have also been exciting advances in prosthetics and lab-grown body parts, which can help improve the lives of amputees and other patients. In one example, MIT's Media Lab is involved in a research project that combines special amputation surgery with intuitive prosthetic development.[20] Special robot prosthetics are being designed for 10 volunteers, and the hope is the volunteers will be able to operate their prosthetics via the nervous system. In the future, intelligent prosthetics like this, which respond to the individual's commands more intuitively, may become the norm.

Trend 6: Robots and Nanobots

From robots working in healthcare settings to injecting tiny nanobots into the human body, robotics and nanotechnology are on course to play a much larger role in healthcare.

Here are some of my favorite examples:

- In China, medical robots are supporting frontline medical workers by helping to clean and disinfect hospital wards and communal spaces, as well as taking patients' temperatures and delivering food and medical supplies to patients. In other countries, medical robots have also been used to curb the spread of coronavirus by distributing hand sanitizer and ensuring face masks are being properly worn.[21]

- Exoskeletons – basically, wearable robotic technology – are another key advance in robotics. Researchers in France, for example, helped a patient move all four of his paralyzed limbs thanks to an exoskeleton.[22]

- There are also robotic labs in the cloud, which are designed to make big pharma capabilities accessible to anyone with a laptop. Here, automation, robotics, big data, AI, and chemical synthesis combine to create an automated, remote lab environment that could revolutionize drug discovery. Strateos is one such example of a robotic cloud lab, and the company claims it can accelerate drug discovery and synthetic biology research.[23]

- Nanotechnology is also finding increasing applications in healthcare, particularly in drug delivery, where nanoparticles are used to deliver medication to specific cells, thereby increasing efficiency and reducing harmful side effects. As a simple example, the cancer treatment drug Abraxane is a nanoparticle treatment. As nano technology develops, nanorobotic drug delivery could be done with even more accuracy, to the point where microdoses could be administered when and where needed.

- Not quite in the super-small realm of nanotechnology, but something extremely cool nevertheless, is a small capsule being introduced by the National Health Service in the UK. Designed as an alternative to a colonoscopy, patients swallow the pill – which contains two tiny cameras – then the capsule transmits images as it travels through the colon. The capsule then passes out of the bowel and can be flushed away.[24]

- In the future, nanobots could potentially be injected into the bloodstream and used to protect the body against disease. This could be a reality within the next decade; indeed, tiny DNA robots are already being tested in animals to find and destroy cancer cells.[25] If applied to humans, this could be used to revolutionize the treatment of cancer, reduce plaque in veins, and more. Nanobots flowing through the bloodstream could also turn the body into a connected, smart device, much like your smart TV or smart thermostat; one research paper outlines a proof of principle for nanobots gathering data from within the body and transmitting it to the cloud for monitoring by healthcare professionals.[26]

Trend 7: The Datafication of Medicine

As you might expect, the increasing adoption of medical technologies is being facilitated by data. For our final healthcare trend, let's take a quick look at some of the key breakthroughs in the datafication of medicine:

- Big data in medicine. More than 4 trillion gigabytes of medical data are generated annually, and this is set to double every two years.[27] Applying AI to this data is what enables the predictive, preventative medicine referred to earlier in the chapter.

- Digital twins. In Chapter 3 we saw how digital twin technology can help energy providers increase efficiencies and cut costs. In healthcare, digital twins can be used to digitally recreate hospital wards or healthcare models – for example, to decrease the downtime of hospital machinery. In the future, this could even extend to digital twins of patients, where doctors have access to a constantly updated, predictive simulation of each patient.[28]

- The Internet of Medical Things (IoMT). You've heard of the IoT (see Chapter 2). Well, thanks to the rise in wearable devices and medical apps, we now have the IoMT – a market set to be worth more than $85 billion by 2027.[29] The data transmitted by these IoMT devices is a key enabler in the move toward more preventative, proactive, and personalized medicine.

- Blockchain (see Chapter 2). This technology could help healthcare providers to distribute healthcare data and transaction records to patients in a more secure way, and even allow individuals to take control of their medical data. The general idea is to improve the transparency and accessibility of medical data (thus helping to democratize healthcare even further). For example, a general practitioner could easily and securely share information with a specialist, and the patient could also assign permission for others to view their medical data. (This could potentially even extend to life insurance companies in the future.)

These are all exciting developments, but there is one major issue to contend with: privacy and data protection. This is extremely important because medical data is highly personal and precious information – information that patients understandably don't want getting into the wrong hands. In the US alone, there were almost 600 medical data breaches in 2020, a 55 percent increase from 2019,[30] demonstrating the need to defend medical data against cyber breaches. Blockchain and homomorphic encryption (a super-secure method of analyzing data while the data remains encrypted) are promising technologies for increasing data security in future.[31]

Now let's turn our attention from healthcare to another sector that's central to creating a better, more prosperous society: education.

PRACTICAL LESSONS

In this chapter, we've learned a lot about the future of healthcare, but how might these lessons apply to other sectors?

- All businesses must move away from the reactive business processes of the past and become more proactive and predictive. In part, this means using data and predictive analytics to anticipate what customers want (more on smart products and services in Chapter 11).

- Personalization is a huge trend across many industries, with companies big and small pushing to delight their customers with highly personalized products and services (read more about this in Chapter 12).

- The datafication and digitization seen in healthcare is happening across all industries. To ensure your business isn't left behind, consider how automation, remote operations, AI, data, and even immersive VR and AR experiences could improve your business.

- The spike in healthcare data breaches provides yet another warning to other sectors that customers' personal data must be protected.

Notes

1. What are the top healthcare challenges to overcome in the near future according to industry leaders?; HealthcareTransformers; https://healthcaretransformers.com/healthcare-business/future-healthcare-challenges-solutions/

2. The Global Risks Report 2020; World Economic Forum; http://www3.weforum.org/docs/WEF_Global_Risk_Report_2020.pdf

3. How to prevent opioid addiction before it begins; USC News; https://news.usc.edu/140583/battle-opioid-addiction-begins-data/

4. Is Smart Data Better Than Bigger Data for Predictive Analytics?; Health IT Analytics; https://healthitanalytics.com/news/is-smart-data-better-than-bigger-data-for-predictive-analytics

5. UPenn Uses Machine Learning, EHRs to Target Severe Sepsis; Health IT Analytics; https://healthitanalytics.com/news/upenn-uses-machine-learning-ehrs-to-target-severe-sepsis

6. Predictive Analytics, EHR Data Identify Appointment No-Shows; Health IT Analytics; https://healthitanalytics.com/news/predictive-analytics-ehr-data-identify-appointment-no-shows

7. Predicting Risk of Suicide Attempts Over Time Through Machine Learning; Clinical Psychological Science; https://journals.sagepub.com/doi/abs/10.1177/2167702617691560

8. World Bank and WHO: Half the world lacks access to essential health services, 100 million still pushed into extreme poverty because of health expenses; WHO; https://www.who.int/news/item/13-12-2017-world-bank-and-who-half-the-world-lacks-access-to-essential-health-services-100-million-still-pushed-into-extreme-poverty-because-of-health-expenses

9. Key Facts About the Uninsured Population; KFF; https://www.kff.org/uninsured/issue-brief/key-facts-about-the-uninsured-population/

10. Why Apple needed the FDA to sign off on its EKG but not its blood oxygen monitor; Verge; https://www.theverge.com/2020/10/7/21504023/apple-watch-ekg-blood-oxygen-fda-clearance

11. 10 Examples of Personalization in Healthcare; Forbes; https://www.forbes.com/sites/blakemorgan/2018/10/22/10-examples-of-personalization-in-healthcare/

12. The future of genomic medicine: can it fulfil its promises?; Pharmaphorum; https://pharmaphorum.com/views-analysis-patients/the-future-of-genomic-medicine-can-it-fulfil-its-promises/

13. HHS Issues New Report Highlighting Dramatic Trends in Medicare Beneficiary Telehealth Utilization Amid COVID-19; Department of Health & Human Services; https://www.hhs.gov/about/news/2020/07/28/hhs-issues-new-report-highlighting-dramatic-trends-in-medicare-beneficiary-telehealth-utilization-amid-covid-19.html

14. Institutions that support health records on iPhone and iPod touch; Apple; https://support.apple.com/en-us/HT208647

15. How this Canadian start-up spotted coronavirus before everyone else knew about it; CNBC; https://www.cnbc.com/2020/03/03/bluedot-used-artificial-intelligence-to-predict-coronavirus-spread.html

16. Immersive Virtual Reality in Stroke Patients as a New Approach for Reducing Postural Disabilities and Falls Risk; Brain Sciences; https://www.ncbi.nlm.nih.gov/pmc/articles/PMC7287864/

17. Top 10 Emerging Technologies of 2020; World Economic Forum; http://www3.weforum.org/docs/WEF_Top_10_Emerging_Technologies_2020.pdf

18. The Bulletproof Coffee Founder Has Spent $1 Million in His Quest to Live to 180; Men's Health; https://www.menshealth.com/health/a25902826/bulletproof-dave-asprey-biohacking/

19. FDA Issues Warnings About Young-Blood Transfusions; Scientific American; https://www.scientificamerican.com/article/fda-issues-warning-about-young-blood-transfusions/

20. 13 Prosthetic Arms and Legs and More That Appear to Have Come from the Future; Interesting Engineering; https://interestingengineering.com/13-prosthetic-arms-and-legs-and-more-that-appear-to-have-come-from-the-future

21. Three trends defining the future of healthcare; Gulf Business; https://gulfbusiness.com/three-trends-defining-the-future-of-healthcare/

22. The Future of Healthcare; Industry Europe; https://industryeurope.com/sectors/healthcare/the-future-of-healthcare-five-trends-in-medical-technology/

23. Running Your Pharma Company Out of a Starbucks: Drug Discovery Moves to the Cloud; Forbes; https://www.forbes.com/sites/johncumbers/2020/03/13/running-your-pharma-company-out-of-a-starbucks-drug-discovery-moves-to-the-cloud/?sh=17a379f33190

24. Colon Capsule Endoscopy; NHS Inform; https://www.nhsinform.scot/tests-and-treatments/non-surgical-procedures/colon-capsule-endoscopy

25. Nanobots Will Be Flowing Through Your Body by 2030; Interesting Engineering; https://interestingengineering.com/nanobots-will-be-flowing-through-your-body-by-2030

26. A Logic-Gated Nanorobot for Targeted Transport of Molecular Payloads; Science; https://science.sciencemag.org/content/335/6070/831

27. Trends in Healthcare 2020; ncube; https://ncube.com/blog/trends-in-healthcare-2020-get-ready-for-digital-transformation

28. The Future of Healthcare; Industry Europe; https://industryeurope.com/sectors/healthcare/the-future-of-healthcare-five-trends-in-medical-technology/

29. Wearable Medical Devices Market Size to Cross $86.5 Billion by 2027; MarketWatch; https://www.marketwatch.com/press-release/wearable-medical-devices-market-size-to-cross-856-billion-by-2027-2021-03 03

30. Report: Healthcare data breaches spiked 55% in 2020; MedCityNews; https://medcitynews.com/2021/02/report-healthcare-data-breaches-spiked-55-in-2020/

31. Homomorphic Encryption: The "Golden Age" of Cryptography; DarkReading; https://www.darkreading.com/edge/theedge/homomorphic-encryption-the-golden-age-of-cryptography/b/d-id/1339748

CHAPTER 5
HOW WE LEARN
The Two Main Shifts in Education

Education is a trillion-dollar industry, with OECD countries devoting 11.3 percent of public spending to education (although UNESCO has set a target for member states to spend 15–20 percent of public spending by 2030).[1]

Yet, much like our healthcare system, our education system was developed for a very different world – a world before the fourth industrial revolution. The pace of change in our world and the move away from "jobs for life" mean that our traditional front-loaded education system (where learning is generally crammed into the first 18 or 21 years of life) is no longer fit for purpose. Education institutions must adapt to reflect this shift, and to reflect the fact that the essential, in-demand skills of the future will be very different from what has been taught in the past. In other words, what we teach has to change.

How we teach must also change. The digitization that is taking place across other industries is starting to impact education. We now have more online content than ever before – the move toward digital learning courses and tools was under way before COVID-19 and certainly accelerated by it – plus new, immersive ways for students to learn.

Bottom line: education needs to be transformed over the next few years to make it more relevant to the fourth industrial revolution and to prepare students for life and work in the 21st century. This requires a major rethink of both what we teach and how we teach it.

Shift 1: Rethinking *What* We Teach

I'm a governor at my children's school (I'm also married to a teacher), and while I accept that schools are constrained by the curriculum set at a national level, I also feel that curriculum is far too narrow. As someone who grew up in Germany, was educated in Germany, and then later moved to the UK, the curriculum here appears too UK-centric, with not enough being taught about different cultures – or nature, or our changing world, for that matter. As a simple example, why are so many secondary schools still offering the standard French or German language options, instead of the world's most spoken language, Mandarin? Given what we know about the global shifts taking place (see Chapter 1), wouldn't that give students a better start in life?

In other words, I think our primary and secondary schools could do better when it comes to creating the global citizens of the future – people who will reimagine the world and who are equipped with the skills employers desperately need in the fourth industrial revolution.

I also believe university education will evolve. I'm on an advisory board for Lancaster University Management School, and I'm well aware that so many university courses don't talk about technology. Too many medical degrees, for example, don't talk about robotics, despite the fact that the doctors of the future will be operating alongside robots (see Chapter 4). Increasingly, employers will be expecting graduates to come equipped with the skills needed to do a job, and this will absolutely involve technology and digital skills. Therefore, in the future, I predict employers will care less about traditional degrees and more about *skills*.

What skills will students need to learn?

Many of the jobs today's schoolchildren will work in don't even exist yet. LinkedIn predicts 150 million new technology jobs in the next five years, and almost all of the roles in LinkedIn's "Jobs on the Rise" report for 2021 can already be done remotely.[2] All this means digital skills will have an even greater advantage in future. Our education systems must adapt to reflect this, and to teach children the skills that are necessary to thrive in this age of socioeconomic change, job disruption, and automation.

In their "Schools of the Future" paper, the World Economic Forum outlined essential characteristics that will define high-quality learning in future.[3] These include:

- Global citizenship skills (including awareness of the wider world, and sustainability)

- Innovation and creativity skills (including problem-solving and analytical thinking)

- Technology skills (including data science and programming, which I believe should be a standard offering as a language option)

- Interpersonal skills (including emotional intelligence, empathy, cooperation, and social awareness)

You'll notice that "soft" skills are included on this list, and I couldn't agree more. As machines are able to automate more and more tasks, our inherently human social and emotional skills will become more valuable in the workplace. So, to the above list, I would add:

- Ethics: AI ethicist is a job title that's beginning to gain traction as more companies look to deploy AI in an ethical way. In the future, there will be many more jobs like this, as organizations seek to balance new technologies with ethics.

- Diversity (cultural diversity and diversity of thinking): The number of people being hired as workplace diversity experts increased 64 percent in 2020.[4]

In time, more education institutions will begin to incorporate these essential technology and human skills into their teaching. It's already happening at some schools. For example, the Green School in Bali, Indonesia, is committed to providing education that promotes sustainability and global citizenship. Serving more than 800 students from ages 3 to 18, the school teaches students in a natural environment, including wall-less classrooms. Students are transported to school in a "BioBus" fueled by cooking oil, and in their early years they spend a lot of time in the school's gardens and kitchen, learning about nature and where food comes from. Later, students can learn in the Innovation Hub, a maker's space with woodworking equipment and 3D printers.[5]

Encouraging lifelong learning

Education must also move away from a system in which learning decreases over the course of our lifespan to one where everyone is encouraged to adopt a continuous learning mindset.

Think about your own education. Chances are you progressed from school to university, then left full-time education and (barring the odd workplace course) never looked back. Education institutions are missing a trick to create lifelong learning partnerships. Universities, for example, could be offering students the chance to come back and take microcourses for the rest of their lives. My hope is that the shift to lifelong learning will be supported by education partners. If not, education institutions risk being left behind as new providers step in to bridge the gap.

And this shift toward lifelong learning is already under way outside of education, as employers expect workers to continuously reskill. The workplace is a constantly changing, unpredictable thing – a far cry from the workplaces of previous generations. So it's no wonder that a World Economic Forum report from 2017 found that one in four adults reported a disconnect between the skills they have and the skills needed for their current job.[6] In other words, we're working in 21st-century jobs, but our education and skills haven't caught up. By the end of a traditional three- or four-year degree, the skills learned may already be out of date.

This is why the World Economic Forum's "Schools of the Future" report highlights lifelong learning as a key capability, alongside the technical and human skills listed. One model for achieving this comes from the UK's Skills Builder Partnership, a global partnership that connects schools and employers to build essential skills and create a "lifelong mechanism" for students to track their own skills development.

Developed in collaboration with employers, this framework prioritizes building essential skills such as problem-solving, presenting, creativity, resilience, collaboration, and leadership. The partnership is also working with employers to implement the framework in their own organizations, so that the skills young people build in school follow right through to employment.[7]

In another example, a government initiative in Singapore offers lifelong learning accounts. These provide funding for a person's education over the course of their lifetime and can be drawn upon as and when they need to boost existing skills or gain new ones.[8]

Shift 2: Rethinking *How* We Teach

Formal education still bears the hallmarks of its origin – around the time of the first industrial revolution – and our general approach to education has changed little since then. In classrooms and lecture halls around the world, students still mostly sit facing the front, listening to the teacher deliver content that they're expected to memorize.

I occasionally teach at university and can honestly say that the traditional method of delivering lectures isn't the best use of anyone's time. I often feel that students could get just as much value from watching a recording of me delivering the content, then the in-classroom time could be spent discussing that content and relating it to real-world contexts.

This isn't to criticize teachers and lecturers. Far from it. I'm filled with respect for the work that educators do. But in order to teach the skills that are necessary to thrive in the 21st century, and create the leaders that our world needs, the way in which education is delivered must adapt. Crucially, I believe the teachers of the future will become facilitators, rather than content deliverers. Some of the key enablers of this change are:

- More digitized content
- More personalized, self-paced, and self-directed learning
- More collaborative, project-based learning

- More bite-sized learning
- More immersive learning

Let's explore each one in turn.

More digitized content

Technology solutions can overcome many common barriers to education and make education available to those even in remote areas. Digital textbooks, for example, are cheaper than their print counterparts. Online learning is a particularly important trend, one that was dramatically accelerated by the pandemic as millions of students and teachers around the world switched to online lessons. According to research by Pearson, 88 percent of students globally believe online learning will be a permanent feature of education in future.[9]

More digital content also creates more data, which means there's a greater opportunity for AI to play a role in education. In particular, AI will enable more personalized learning that adapts to the individual needs of students.

More personalized, self-paced, and self-directed learning

In the traditional education system, teachers are teaching large, diverse classes and learning is generally standardized at the same pace, with some levels of differentiation and streaming for ability. Aided by technology, the education systems of the future will move away from this approach to one where learning is much more flexible, and paced to suit the needs of each student.

If you've ever used the Duolingo language learning app, you've seen how it provides a tantalizing vision of how learning can be personalized to suit each learner. In the app, users interact with the content in different ways, depending on how they're progressing. For example, AI algorithms can predict the probability of a user being able to recall a word in a given context, and can then figure out what the user needs to keep practicing.[10] The user experience is continually being personalized to their needs and, crucially, learners can proceed at their own pace. As more content is delivered digitally, there's no reason why this can't extend to learning in schools, colleges, and universities. The technology already exists. Technology can also free up teachers from administrative tasks such as grading and testing, to allow more time for developing student relationships. In this way, teachers become content *facilitators*, there to supervise learning and support students' needs, rather than directly delivering content.

In turn, learning will become more self-directed and independent. Here's an example of what this means in practice. The Pratham Hybrid Learning Program in India is designed to help local communities support student-centered learning. Serving over 90,000 children aged 10–14 across 1,000 villages in India, the program enables entirely student-led activities, with students choosing what they'd like to collaboratively work on, and with volunteers acting as facilitators. Children in the program performed 12 percentage points better than control groups in school curricular subjects.[11] This indicates how education can benefit from moving to a more independent, project-based learning style, which brings us to the next concept.

More collaborative, project-based learning

To reflect the 21st-century workplace, learning must become more focused on project-based and problem-based work, where students work in groups to define and complete their own projects, just as in the Hybrid Learning Program in India.

The idea is that students "learn by doing." Instead of setting the agenda and delivering a set program of content, teachers act as hands-on supervisors and facilitators, guiding students as they investigate real-world problems, questions, or issues. As well as encouraging students to become more independent and collaborative, this method of learning will also foster more critical thinking, creativity, and communication – skills highly valued by employers.

More bite-sized learning

According to a study by Microsoft, humans now have an attention span of around eight seconds – less than a goldfish.[12] This has dropped in the last 20 years as people have gotten used to an increasingly digitized lifestyle with near-constant use of technology.

This means the education systems of the future must become better at delivering more bite-sized, snackable content – micro- and nano-learning, to use the technical terms:

- Micro-learning means short, snappy content, ideally around 5 minutes long but potentially up to 10 or 15 minutes, depending on the subject.

- Nano-learning takes this one step further to deliver content that takes around two minutes of a learner's time – teaching them only what they need to know at that exact moment in time.

Again, the digitization of education and greater adoption of AI will enable the delivery of bite-sized content that keeps pace with students' progress and natural attention spans.

More immersive learning

As well as AI, other technologies will play a critical role in the future of education. Extended reality (see Chapter 2) is one of them. In particular, virtual reality (VR) and augmented reality (AR) have enormous potential to bring education to life and immerse students in subjects.

This will take many forms, from fully immersive VR lessons and field trips to AR-infused lessons where students can visualize content and interact with it in new ways. In a lesson about ancient Egypt, for example, students can literally step into that period thanks to a VR headset or goggles (which can be very inexpensive, if you use something like Google Cardboard). Or in a biology lesson, students can use an AR app to project information about the human body right in front of their eyes.

More and more platforms and apps are being designed to enhance the education experience through immersive technologies. Take Labster as an example. Dedicated to enhancing science education, Labster lets students experiment with hyper-realistic, simulated lab equipment, allowing them to conduct experiments in a risk-free way.

One study on virtual learning shows that students who practice with VR headsets outperform students who learn only via a desktop.[13] A similar study of high school classrooms also found that virtual simulations significantly enhance students' scientific knowledge.[14] This points to the incredible value extended reality can bring to the classrooms of the future.

PRACTICAL LESSONS

Clearly there are huge challenges in implementing these changes. Most of the changes I've outlined in this chapter will require a fundamental rethink of what we teach and how we teach it. It won't be easy. Policy makers, politicians, educators, and even employers will need to collaborate to redesign our education systems for 21st-century needs. The challenges are significant, but so are the potential rewards. To put it in monetary terms, if we can close the education skills gap and better prepare learners for the needs of the future, as much as $11.5 trillion could be added to global GDP by 2028.[15] In more personal terms, today's schoolchildren will help to envision the future of our world. We must give them the tools needed to do this.

Employers must also take note. Just as educational institutions need to be preparing students for the future, so too must organizations prepare their employees. Some key lessons to highlight are:

- Employers must invest in their workers' education, and cultivate the technology and human skills that are essential for success in the fourth industrial revolution.

- Organizations also need to become seedbeds for life-long learning, where curiosity and continual improvement are highly valued and embedded in the very fabric of the company.

- Employers should also take note of the move toward more personalized, bite-sized and immersive learning. These can all be applied to workplace training and education to improve the learning experience.

Now let's turn to another area that's ripe for change: how we feed ourselves.

Notes

1. The future of education; The Possible; https://www.the-possible.com/future-of-education-digital-campus-learning-teaching/

2. Jobs on the Rise in 2021; LinkedIn; https://business.linkedin.com/talent-solutions/resources/talent-acquisition/jobs-on-the-rise-us

3. Schools of the Future; World Economic Forum; http://www3.weforum.org/docs/WEF_Schools_of_the_Future_Report_2019.pdf

4. Jobs on the Rise in 2021; LinkedIn; https://business.linkedin.com/talent-solutions/resources/talent-acquisition/jobs-on-the-rise-us

5. Schools of the Future; World Economic Forum; http://www3.weforum.org/docs/WEF_Schools_of_the_Future_Report_2019.pdf

6. Accelerating Workforce Reskilling for the Fourth Industrial Revolution; World Economic Forum; https://www.weforum.org/whitepapers/accelerating-workforce-reskilling-for-the-fourth-industrial-revolution

7. Schools of the Future; World Economic Forum; http://www3.weforum.org/docs/WEF_Schools_of_the_Future_Report_2019.pdf

8. The Future of Jobs in the Era of AI; Boston Consulting Group; https://media-exp1.licdn.com/dms/document/C4D1FAQFqOc4A9XWHKA/

feedshare-document-pdf-analyzed/0/1616058778744?e=1616148000&v=
beta&t=vt-wO6XVoLOfATzUO67cgOEI9Rgj6yFfAF9SocFEoag

9. The Global Learner Study; Pearson; https://www.pearson.com/content/dam/one-dot-com/one-dot-com/global/Files/news/gls/Pearson_Global-Learners-Survey_2020_FINAL.pdf

10. The Amazing Ways Duolingo Is Using Artificial Intelligence to Deliver Free Language Learning; Bernard Marr; https://www.bernardmarr.com/default.asp?contentID=2121

11. Schools of the Future; World Economic Forum; http://www3.weforum.org/docs/WEF_Schools_of_the_Future_Report_2019.pdf

12. You Now Have a Shorter Attention Span Than a Goldfish; Time; https://time.com/3858309/attention-spans-goldfish/

13. A Structural Equation Modeling Investigation of the Emotional Value of Immersive Virtual Reality in Education; ResearchGate; https://www.researchgate.net/publication/322887672_A_Structural_Equation_Modeling_Investigation_of_the_Emotional_Value_of_Immersive_Virtual_Reality_in_Education

14. Virtual Learning Simulations in High School; Frontiers in Psychology; https://www.ncbi.nlm.nih.gov/pmc/articles/PMC5447738/

15. Closing the Skills Gap Accelerators; World Economic Forum; https://www.weforum.org/projects/closing-the-skills-gap-accelerators

CHAPTER 6
HOW WE FEED OURSELVES

The Two Key Innovations Needed to Transform Agriculture

We know that demand for food is growing. The predicted rise in the global population will require food production to increase by up to 70 percent.[1] And with a growing middle class generally comes increasing demand for meat over wheat, grains, and legumes.[2] Meeting this demand for more food, and more meat, brings huge challenges when you consider the environmental impacts of agriculture:[3]

- The food system accounts for one quarter (26 percent) of total global greenhouse gas emissions. Agriculture, forestry, and land use make up 18.4 percent of this (the rest is things like food processing, packaging, refrigeration, and transport).

- 70 percent of global freshwater withdrawals are used for agriculture.

- Livestock already outnumber wild mammals by 15 to 1, and of the 28,000 species threatened with extinction, agriculture and aquaculture is listed as a threat for 24,000 of them.

Therefore, when we talk about tackling the climate crisis, we can't ignore food production. The obvious answer is for people around the world to adopt a plant-based diet. Research shows that excluding meat and dairy is the single most impactful way for people to reduce their environmental impact, because meat and dairy provide just 18 percent of calories (and only 37 percent of protein), yet they account for 83 percent of farmland and are responsible for 60 percent of agriculture's greenhouse gas emissions.[4] The same study also found that without meat and dairy consumption, global farmland could be reduced by 75 percent. In other words, we could free up land equivalent to the size of China, the US, the EU, and Australia combined, and still feed the planet.

But, if we're honest, we're a long way from getting billions of people to adopt a vegan diet. Which means we need urgent new innovations in agriculture and food production. I see this coming from two main areas:

- Reimagining current farming methods to make them more efficient and less harmful

- Finding new ways to create food (especially meat) in the future

Innovation 1: Reimagining Our Current Farming and Agriculture Methods

In order to increase productivity while reducing environmental impact, the agriculture industry must embrace new methods. Previous evolutions in farming have largely been driven by mechanical improvements (bigger, better machinery) or genetic advances (better seed, more effective fertilizers, etc.). Now, the next big transformation in farming is under way – and it is largely being driven by digital tools.

More automation in farming

As with most industries, automation is beginning to play a much larger role in agriculture. Here are just a few examples of how automation can improve farming methods:

- Robots are now able not only to identify crops that are ready for picking, but also to pick them – even delicate soft fruits. One raspberry-picking robot is capable of picking 25,000 berries a day, versus the 15,000 that a human picker can manage in an eight-hour shift,[5] thereby allowing farmers to overcome labor challenges and increase output. The world's first fleet of autonomous farm robots capable of scanning weeds, zapping weeds, and planting crops is expected to be ready for deployment in 2022.[6]

- Drones can be used to monitor crops, apply products, and transport supplies (read more about drones in transportation in Chapter 8). Over the next 10 years, the agricultural drone industry is predicted to generate 100,000 jobs in the US alone,[7] which is mind-blowing.

- We also have autonomous tractors and sprayers that can manage fieldwork without human drivers. Leading agricultural manufacturer John Deere is just one company investing in autonomous electric tractors and drone sprayers.

- With the rise of more complex farming equipment comes – you guessed it – more data. As in any business, this data is a precious resource and can be used to better manage farms and crops.

- Even in fish farming, technology is helping to deliver new efficiencies. One Norwegian salmon farming company, Cermaq, is using machine vision to automatically recognize and track individual fish by their unique markings – like facial recognition for humans. Using this, the company can monitor the health of fish in the pen, and customize care and feeding for each fish.[8]

As you can probably imagine, increasing use of technology in farming allows farmers to be more precise than ever.

Precision farming

The manufacturing of fertilizers for crop production is another significant contributor to greenhouse gases,[9] so cutting the amount of fertilizer used is another way to improve farming. The same goes for pesticides – and water use, for that matter.

This brings us to precision farming. Rather than the traditional method of uniformly applying the same rate of irrigation, fertilizers, and pesticides at set times and frequencies, precision farming involves applying these factors at variable rates, depending on the needs of crops. To do this, farmers need tools to collect data from their farms, analyze that data, make decisions on what action is needed where, and then carry out the required action.

Many tools are now on the market or in development to improve the precision of farming. A simple example comes from sensors placed in the soil, which allow farmers to understand and plan for variables such as soil acidity and temperature.[10] Or there are tools like the CI-600 In-Situ Root Imager, which can provide images of plant roots to see how they are responding to fertilizers.[11] Other tools can detect weeds and direct where pesticides are really needed, reducing pesticide use by 80 percent.[12]

This sort of precision farming is possible with animal agriculture, too. For example, chips and body sensors can be used to monitor the temperature, blood pressure, and pulse of livestock to detect early signs of illness or stress. Already ear-tag technology is able to monitor cows' body heat, overall health, and location.[13]

Blockchain in farming

Blockchain technology (see Chapter 2) may also play a significant role in agriculture:

- Blockchain can deliver major supply chain advantages, particularly when it comes to tracing the origin of foods – something that's essential for ensuring consumer trust. The entire supply chain can be recorded on a blockchain, reducing the time it takes to trace a food's origin down to seconds. In the wake of a 2018 outbreak of E.coli in lettuce, Walmart is deploying this technology to, among other things, track leafy greens all the way back to individual farms.[14]

- The technology can replace traditional contract systems (for example, insurance contracts) with smart contracts, thereby improving burdensome crop insurance processes. Blockchain startup Worldcovr, for example, uses blockchain and satellite technology to monitor rainfall and automatically trigger payouts for loss of crops.[15]

- Blockchain can cut out the middleman and facilitate peer-to-peer transactions, which may help to create a level playing field for smaller farmers and urban farmers (more on urban farming coming up next). AgUnity, for example, uses blockchain to allow growers to form small cooperatives.[16]

However, it's fair to say that not all of the transformations coming in farming will be driven by digital technologies. A move toward more local farming and GM crops will also play key roles. Let's explore these in more detail.

More localized, urban farming

Half of the world's habitable land is already used for agriculture,[17] which seems astonishing when you consider the planet's projected population growth, and the fact that we'll need to produce even more food than we do currently. Couple this with the food miles involved in shipping crops around the world and the case for more localized farming (i.e., producing food close to the people who need it) seems pretty compelling.

Urban farming or urban agriculture could solve some of the biggest challenges around how we feed ourselves, helping to increase food security, decrease waste, reduce food miles, and reduce the amount of habitable land given over to farming. In very basic terms, urban farming just means growing food in a city or town, but rather than community gardens or grow-your-own, urban farming means growing food as a commercial enterprise – just like a regular farm, but in an urban space.

But how can we do this in densely populated cities? The answer lies in *vertical farming* – the practice of growing crops in vertical layers. This can be done on a small scale, against a spare wall or in a shipping container; on a medium scale, in otherwise unused buildings; or even on a huge scale, with factory-size vertical farms. The world's largest vertical farm – an ambitious $30 million dollar enterprise in Newark, New Jersey – is capable of producing 2 million pounds of leafy greens a year, without soil, sunlight, or water. Plants are anchored vertically in a reusable cloth made of plastic bottles, and plants are fed with a nutrient-rich mist in a technique known as *aeroponics*. According to creators AeroFarms, the vertical farm uses 95 percent less water than traditional methods, can grow a plant within 14 days (versus up to 45 days on a traditional farm), and is 390 times more productive per square foot than a field farm.[18]

Hydroponics – growing plants by immersing them in nutrient-rich water – is another method that could enable more urban, local farming. And since the water is recycled and reused in the system, hydroponic systems use far less water – 70 liters of water to grow a kilo (2.2 pounds) of tomatoes versus the 400 liters used in the conventional farming method.[19]

Genetic engineering in farming

Back in Chapter 2, we saw that gene editing is already making a huge difference in agriculture, giving us more drought-resistant crops, more pest-resistant crops, and more productive crops. These are what's known as GMOs or GM crops. GM crops are already embedded in the supply chain – more than 10 percent of the world's arable land is used for GM crops, with the US, Brazil, and Argentina being the leading producers.[20] There are very real advantages to growing genetically altered crops. As an example, the creation of a high-yield strain of dwarf wheat by American biologist Norman Borlaug played a central role in the "Green Revolution," an agricultural revolution that increased food production around the world and helped to avoid a food crisis.[21] He was awarded the Nobel Peace Prize for his efforts.

But there are certainly opportunities to do more of this to produce more diverse crops and higher yields. Indeed, the crop biotechnology market (where seeds are produced using genetic manipulation) is currently valued at $28.2 billion and is forecast to reach $44.3 billion by 2031.[22] The advent of gene editing techniques like CRISPR (see Chapter 2) is making gene editing more viable, and will be a huge driver of growth in GMO crops. In particular, gene editing is expected to open up new opportunities to improve yield in ways that were previously inaccessible.

That said, there is some resistance to GM crops, particularly in Europe, where genetically modified foods are tightly regulated. Regulators and consumers will need to be brought on board if the agriculture industry is to further capitalize on genetic engineering. Things are starting to look up in this respect. In 2016, the US Department of Agriculture announced that a CRISPR-edited non-browning mushroom fell outside of GM regulation because the mushroom did not contain any foreign genetic material – just an edited version of its natural genome.[23] And gene editing of crops (and livestock) may soon be allowed in England, now that the UK has left the EU.[24]

You might have noticed the mention of livestock there. Yes, it's not just crops that can be genetically modified. For example, scientists have been working to identify the specific genetically inherited gut microbes that influence how much methane cows burp (because burps, not farts, are responsible for 90 percent of cows' methane emissions). Manipulating these microbes could cut methane emissions by half, according to the researchers involved.[25]

Innovation 2: Finding New Ways to Create Food (Especially Meat) in the Future

One-third of croplands are used to grow livestock feed.[26] Wouldn't it make more sense to devote that land to growing crops for humans and find innovative new ways to create meat? Advances in cultured and plant-based meat could represent a significant shift in how we produce meat. Then there's the potential for 3D printing (see Chapter 2) to play a role in food production. Let's explore both in more detail.

Cultured and plant-based meat

The market for plant-based milk alternatives is already well established (accounting for 13 percent of milk sales in the US alone),[27] and if the alternative meat market develops in a similar way, it could account for 10 percent of the global meat industry by 2029.[28] The market certainly seems receptive. Plant-based pioneers Beyond Meat became one of the most successful IPOs in history after going public at $1.5 billion and being valued at $13 billion less than three months later.[29] And chains

BUSINESS TRENDS IN PRACTICE

like Burger King and TGI Fridays are now routinely selling plant-based burgers. This means plant-based meat could go a long way to reducing the food sector's environmental impact; an Impossible plant-based burger, for example, has a carbon footprint that's 89 percent smaller than a regular beef burger.[30]

That said, I recognize that meat is ingrained in many cultures, and encouraging everyone to buy plant-based meats will be a challenge. This is where cultured meat comes in.

Cultured meat is genetically the same as real meat but is produced from animal cells. It's real meat, then, but made without factory farms and slaughterhouses. (Because the cells used to start the process can be taken from biopsies of live animals, cultured meat does not require animals to be slaughtered.)

Could cultured or cell-based meat (or "lab-grown meat," to use its less appetizing name) convince die-hard meat lovers to make the switch? It'll be a while before we know for sure, but there are early signs that the market – and regulators – are coming around to cultured meat as a realistic alternative to farmed meat. In 2020, Singapore became the first nation to approve cultured meat for sale. US company Eat Just's cultured "chicken bites" – which are grown from chicken cells in a bioreactor and combined with plant-based ingredients – were approved for sale by the Singapore Food Agency and will initially go on sale in a restaurant.[31]

The science behind cellular agriculture has come a long way since Professor Mark Post created the first lab-grown burger in 2013, but there is still a long way to go. For example, those Eat Just chicken bites are, at the time of writing, more expensive than actual chicken, which will prove a significant barrier for many consumers. But this will change as economies of scale improve. In 2020, one of the leading cultured meat startups, Memphis Meats, announced it was about to build a pilot production plant in the US for making cultured meat – all part of a move to scale up production and drive the cost down.[32]

And, of course, it's not just cultured meat that is coming our way – cultured seafood may also positively disrupt the food market.[33] What's more, a team of researchers is working to create cheese using cellular agriculture methods – real vegan cheese, in other words, but not from animals.[34]

3D-printed food

If the idea of lab-grown meat puts you off, how about 3D-printed food? Barcelona-based startup NovaMeat is leading the way in 3D printing plant-based food and has already successfully created the world's first 3D-printed piece of "meat" that apparently mimics the fibrous nature of real meat.[35] This potentially means 3D printing could, in future, play a role in how we produce food. Not only could this be better for our planet (because 3D printing in general is less wasteful than traditional production methods; see Chapter 2), but it could potentially be better for our health too, allowing consumers to individually customize their own 3D-printed food to suit their individual nutritional needs.[36] Thanks to 3D printing, economies of scale will no longer apply.

All this means the future of food might be very different than it is today, with meat and seafood being grown in labs and customizable food being 3D printed to order. It's an exciting thought, but I can only hope that these new methods aren't too far down the road. We need innovation now if we're to stop the climate crisis and feed our growing population.

Now let's move from the production of food to the production of consumer goods and the construction of buildings.

PRACTICAL LESSONS

Whether or not you're in the agriculture industry, there are key lessons we can learn from these food and farming trends:

- All businesses, regardless of sector, must find technology-driven ways to increase efficiencies, be more precise, and automate more processes.

- Similarly, all businesses must look to reduce their environmental impact and make their operations more sustainable (see Chapter 18).

- The need for innovative new products is also universal. Increasingly, consumers will expect products that are more sustainable, less wasteful, and more intelligent (see Chapters 7, 11, 15, and 17).

Notes

1. Agriculture's connected future: How technology can yield new growth; McKinsey; https://www.mckinsey.com/industries/agriculture/our-insights/agricultures-connected-future-how-technology-can-yield-new-growth

2. Trending 2050: The Future of Farming; Syngenta; https://www.syngenta-us.com/thrive/research/future-of-farming.html

3. Environmental impacts of food production: Our World in Data; https://ourworldindata.org/environmental-impacts-of-food

4. Avoiding meat and dairy is "single biggest way" to reduce your impact on Earth; Guardian; https://www.theguardian.com/environment/2018/may/31/avoiding-meat-and-dairy-is-single-biggest-way-to-reduce-your-impact-on-earth

5. Robocrop: world's first raspberry-picking robot set to work; Guardian; https://www.theguardian.com/technology/2019/may/26/world-first-fruit-picking-robot-set-to-work-artificial-intelligence-farming

6. World's first autonomous farm robot fleet ready for 2022; Farmers Weekly; https://www.fwi.co.uk/arable/crop-management/worlds-first-autonomous-farm-robot-fleet-ready-for-2022

7. Trending 2050: The Future of Farming; Syngenta; https://www.syngenta-us.com/thrive/research/future-of-farming.html

8. The Amazing Ways You Can Combine AI, 5G, and Machine Vision to Transform Fish Farming; Forbes; https://www.forbes.com/sites/bernardmarr/2021/02/08/the-amazing-ways-you-can-combine-ai-5g-and-machine-vision-to-transform-fish-farming/?sh=9bd8c925fe82

9. Greenhouse gas emissions from synthetic nitrogen manufacture and fertilization for main upland crops in China; Carbon Balance and Management; https://cbmjournal.biomedcentral.com/articles/10.1186/s13021-019-0133-9#:~:text=A%20significant%20source%20of%20greenhouse,O%20emissions%20from%20agricultural%20soils

10. Smart Farming in 2020; Business Insider; https://www.businessinsider.com/smart-farming-iot-agriculture?r=US&IR=T

11. Precision farming in 2021; Felix Instruments; https://felixinstruments.com/blog/precision-farming-what-it-is-why-its-changing-everything-in-agriculture/

12. Ibid.

13. Agriculture's connected future: How technology can yield new growth; McKinsey; https://www.mckinsey.com/industries/agriculture/our-insights/agricultures-connected-future-how-technology-can-yield-new-growth

14. In Wake of Romain E.coli Scare, Walmart Deploys Blockchain to Track Leafy Greens; Walmart; https://corporate.walmart.com/newsroom/2018/09/24/in-wake-of-romaine-e-coli-scare-walmart-deploys-blockchain-to-track-leafy-greens

15. 8 Blockchain Startups Disrupting the Agricultural Industry; StartUs Insights; https://www.startus-insights.com/innovators-guide/8-blockchain-startups-disrupting-the-agricultural-industry/

16. Ibid.

17. Environmental impacts of food production: Our World in Data; https://ourworldindata.org/environmental-impacts-of-food

18. The world's largest, indoor vertical farm; DWIH New York; https://www.dwih-newyork.org/en/2020/10/01/the-worlds-largest-indoor-vertical-farm/

19. Urban Farming Ultimate Guide and Examples; GroCycle; https://grocycle.com/urban-farming/

20. What GM crops are currently being grown and where; Royal Society; https://royalsociety.org/topics-policy/projects/gm-plants/what-gm-crops-are-currently-being-grown-and-where/

21. Normal Borlaug; Nobel Prize; https://www.nobelprize.org/prizes/peace/1970/borlaug/biographical/

22. Genetic Engineering in Agriculture; IDTechEx; https://www.idtechex .com/en/research-report/genetic-technologies-in-agriculture-2020-2030-forecasts-markets-technologies/750

23. Ibid.

24. Gene editing of crops and livestock may soon be permitted in England; Guardian; https://www.theguardian.com/science/2021/jan/07/gene-editing-of-crops-and-livestock-may-soon-be-permitted-in-england

25. Cows Genetically Modified to Burp and Fart Less Could Cut Methane Emissions by Half; Newsweek; https://www.newsweek.com/cow-fart-burp-methane-genetic-modification-1447589

26. Livestock and Landscapes; Food and Agriculture Organization; http:// www.fao.org/3/ar591e/ar591e.pdf

27. Supertrends. Pushing for change; CreditSuisse; https://www.credit-suisse .com/media/assets/microsite/docs/supertrends/supertrends-2020-en.pdf

28. Analysts: Cell-cultured and plant-based meat could be 10% of the market by 2029; FoodDive; https://www.fooddive.com/news/analysts-cell-cultured-and-plant-based-meat-could-be-10-of-the-market-by/555573/

29. Missed Out On Beyond Meat?; Forbes; https://www.forbes.com/sites/oliviergarret/2019/09/11/missed-out-on-beyond-meat-buy-these-2-ipos-this-week/

30. Analysts: Cell-cultured and plant-based meat could be 10% of the market by 2029; FoodDive; https://www.fooddive.com/news/analysts-cell-cultured-and-plant-based-meat-could-be-10-of-the-market-by/555573/

31. No-kill, lab-grown meat to go on sale for first time; Guardian; https://www .theguardian.com/environment/2020/dec/02/no-kill-lab-grown-meat-to-go-on-sale-for-first-time

32. A startup says it's building a US pilot plant for cell-based meat; Quartz; https://qz.com/1788892/memphis-meats-plans-to-build-the-first-us-cell-based-meat-plant/

33. Seafood Without the Sea: Will Lab-Grown Fish Hook Consumers; https:// text.npr.org/720041152

34. Real Cheese: Planet-Friendly, Animal-Free; Real Vegan Cheese; https:// www.realvegancheese.org/#:~:text=Real%20Vegan%20Cheese%20 (RVC)%20is,plant%2Dbased%20fats%20and%20sugars

35. Harvesting the Long-Term Power of Plant-Based Meat Alternatives; Plant Based News; https://plantbasednews.org/lifestyle/long-term-power-plant-based-meat-alternatives/

36. The Future of Food; Forbes; https://www.forbes.com/sites/bernard-marr/2019/06/28/the-future-of-food-amazing-lab-grown-and-3d-printed-meat-and-fish/

CHAPTER 7
HOW WE MAKE AND BUILD THINGS

Eleven Trends to Watch Across Manufacturing and Construction

Looking at greenhouse gas emissions by sector, manufacturing, construction (particularly cement and steel production), and building use are all significant contributors to climate change. Urgent action is required to make these sectors greener and more efficient, and new technologies and products are emerging to meet this need. In this chapter, I delve into some of the most exciting trends in manufacturing and construction, including energy-efficient buildings. Let's start with manufacturing.

Seven Major Trends in Manufacturing

Manufacturing – the process of making physical objects repeatedly and at scale – is often described as a key building block of society. From cars to mobile phones, solar panels to children's toys, almost all of the everyday things we use are produced by manufacturers. Manufacturing has evolved significantly over time, from human-centered methods to machine-reliant assembly lines to the highly automated, robot-heavy factories we're beginning to see more of. Several trends are combining to transform manufacturing and, together, these trends can be referred to as "Industry 4.0" – essentially, the fourth industrial revolution applied to a manufacturing context.

Let's explore some of the biggest trends contributing to Industry 4.0.

Trend 1: The Industrial Internet of Things (IIoT)

You've heard of the Internet of Things; now we have the *Industrial Internet of Things* (IIoT), where interconnected devices (particularly sensors) are used at an industrial level to collect valuable data that can improve the manufacturing process. For example, sensors can be used to gather data from machines on the factory floor, and this data can be used to understand how machines are performing, optimize the maintenance process, reduce machine downtime, and even predict faults before they occur (more on predictive maintenance coming up later). Or they can be used to optimize much of inventory management by understanding exactly where items are in the supply chain. Or sensors can provide insights into energy usage. In highly automated factories, machines can even act on sensor data without human intervention (more on automation coming up).

At Japanese auto component manufacturer Hirotec, IoT sensors were initially used on cutting devices at the company's tool-building operation in North America, in order to monitor machine performance. This gave the team valuable insights into the status and performance of each machine (for example, that certain machines sit idle at certain times every day). The company then used these insights to make machines more productive. The first phase of Hirotec's IIoT experiment was so successful, the company has since decided to connect a whole production line at one of its Japan plants, meaning the entire production of auto components at this plant will happen in a connected, IIoT way.[1]

Trend 2: Predictive Maintenance

Unexpected machine downtime can be hugely costly to manufacturers, but the IIoT is enabling another key trend that could cut machine downtime and machine failure dramatically. This brings us to *predictive maintenance* – or the use of sensor data and AI to detect failure patterns in machinery and components. By understanding when a machine or part is *likely* to fail, manufactures can take preventative action and maintain their equipment more effectively.

I briefly mentioned an example of this in Chapter 3, with GE using sensors and AI to predict failures ahead of time at its wind and solar plants.

Another example comes from Siemens AG, one of the world's largest industrial manufacturing companies. Siemens has used sensors even on older motors and transmissions to bring them into the 21st century – and by analyzing the data from these machines, Siemens says it can draw conclusions about the machines' condition, detect irregularities, and fix machines before they fail.[2] This shows how, thanks to the IoT and AI, predictive maintenance can be applied even to legacy machinery and systems. Manufacturers don't need to invest in entirely new systems to reap the benefits.

Trend 3: Digital Twins

I briefly mentioned digital twins back in Chapter 3 – specifically how companies like BP use digital replicas of systems to model new processes before making expensive and high-risk alterations to the digital twin's real-world counterpart. Let's see how this works in a manufacturing context.

Digital twins can simulate any physical process or object. So in a manufacturing setting, this might mean simulating a new product's dimensions, or representing the equipment on the factory floor (how the machinery operates, for instance). It can even be used to visualize and simulate an entire supply chain. Digital twins could be so transformative in manufacturing that by 2022 as many as 70 percent of manufacturers may be using the technology to conduct simulations and evaluations.[3]

As an example, Unilever has successfully integrated digital twins into eight of its factories around the world. In these factories, data from IoT systems is fed into a digital twin of the entire facility, then algorithms analyze that data to identify pain points and areas for improvement in the production line.[4]

Trend 4: Automation and Dark Factories

Automation is another key trend that will shape the future of manufacturing, as it will with many other industries. Thanks to AI, machines are now capable of carrying out more and more tasks that were previously reserved for humans (think of the raspberry-picking robot from Chapter 6). So it's no wonder we're seeing more manufacturing processes become automated. For example, at 50-year-old design and manufacturing company Flex, roughly 50 percent of manufacturing processes were fully automated by 2017.[5] But there is still room for more automation. By one estimate, of the 749 billion working hours spent on manufacturing activities worldwide, more than 478 billion of them are automatable.[6]

Automation can bring many advantages to manufacturers, including higher productivity (machines don't get tired), higher accuracy, and lower costs. And the range of activities that can now be automated is so vast, we may see more entirely automated factories, or so-called *dark factories*. At these fully automated sites, production happens without direct human intervention on site.

Of course, there are very legitimate concerns about automation displacing human jobs, but we must remember that automation is largely used to replace jobs that are dangerous, dull, and, if we're really honest, not ideally suited to humans. Plus, while automation will inevitably lead to job losses, it is also expected to create new jobs – by one estimate, close to 15 million new jobs by 2027, and that's just in the US.[7]

Automation may also spark more *reshoring*, where manufacturing that was previously outsourced to countries with lower wages is brought back home. Indeed, in 2018, almost 1,400 organizations announced they were bringing manufacturing back to the US.[8] As it becomes easier to automate more manufacturing processes, and as the costs of manufacturing overseas increase (as those countries become more affluent), we may see more organizations reshore their manufacturing operations.

Trend 5: Robots and Cobots

Robotics is a key enabler of automation, but not all robots are there to replace human workers. For example, we have robotic exoskeletons – wearable robots that can help human workers lift heavy objects more easily and reduce injuries – that are already being used by manufacturers such as Ford, BMW, and Hyundai.[9] And we have cobots – collaborative, intelligent robots – that are designed to work safely alongside human workers, as at the Ford Fiesta plant in Cologne, Germany.[10] The majority of factories in the future, then, may not be fully automated, but highly automated spaces where humans and intelligent machines work together seamlessly.

This combination of AI, IoT sensors, and robotics seems particularly exciting. This new breed of intelligent, connected robots – known as *advanced robotics* to distinguish them from traditional robots – is set to transform manufacturing by increasing operational efficiency and reducing costs. (Read more about robots and cobots in Chapter 19.)

Trend 6: 3D Printing and Additive Manufacturing

Thanks to 3D printing and additive manufacturing, manufacturers may no longer need to produce and hold huge inventories. As 3D printing becomes more cost-effective, efficient, and scalable, manufacturers will increasingly be able to make products to order – with less waste and fewer materials than the traditional manufacturing process (see Chapter 2). What's more, because 3D printed parts and products are made using a single machine, processes like welding and screwing multiple parts together will no longer be necessary.

There are some very exciting advances in 3D printing to watch, and you might be surprised at what today's 3D printers are capable of. For example, assembly technologies company AMBOTS has combined the best of 3D printing and robotics to create *swarm 3D printers* – a group of 16 3D printers that can work together to produce complex parts and products. They also have chunk-based 3D printers that can make huge parts and products by dividing them into smaller chunks to be individually printed.

Could entire factories be filled with robots and 3D printers instead of traditional machinery? That's certainly the vision of Brooklyn-based startup Voodoo Manufacturing, which is building a robotics 3D printing factory to rival the productivity and cost of traditional injection-molding methods.[11]

Trend 7: Smart and More Sustainable Products

The emergence of smart, connected devices isn't just changing *how* products are manufactured, but *what* types of products are manufactured. These days anything from yoga mats to babies' diapers can be equipped with sensors and made "smart," and I don't see this trend abating anytime soon. Therefore, product manufacturers will increasingly have to explore new ways of giving customers the intelligent products they expect. Some manufacturers may even move away from focusing solely on physical objects toward providing customers with digital-only or hybrid products (see Chapter 10). Think of how the trend for smart fitness trackers has evolved into a slew of apps and services designed to help users track their calorie intake, daily exercise, heart rate, and even sleep.

At the same time, customers will increasingly expect the products they buy to be sustainable, reusable, and recyclable. I believe the throwaway culture of the past is coming to an end and this too will inform what manufacturers make in future. Waste will increasingly be designed out of our societies and economies, in favor of a *circular economy* – where economic activity is separated from the consumption of precious, finite resources and instead provides environmental and social benefits for all.

Head to Parts 3 and 4 to read more about trends such as smart products and services, sustainability, personalization, and fast innovation.

Four Major Trends in Buildings and Construction

Like many industries, the COVID-19 pandemic hit construction hard, prompting a new era of reflection, innovation, and efficiency. Let's look at four of the biggest trends that are changing construction for the better.

Trend 1: The Desire for Greener, Smarter Buildings

As I mentioned in Chapter 2, buildings and even entire cities are now becoming smart and connected, offering up insights on building performance and use, and even regulating themselves to be more efficient. Increasingly, then, new buildings will be built with these connective technologies in mind. Together with energy-efficient and renewable technologies, this will combine to make buildings much more efficient (even carbon neutral) and to reduce the impact buildings have on the environment. And this can't come soon enough, because energy use in buildings accounts for around 17.5 percent of global greenhouse gas emissions.[12] The percentage in the US is much higher; indeed, buildings account for 29 percent of US greenhouse gas emissions[13] and around 40 percent of all US energy consumption.[14]

This is why the green building movement is so important. And a big part of this movement is the design and build of *net-zero* buildings – buildings where the total amount of energy used annually is equivalent to (or less than) the amount of renewable energy generated on-site – buildings with zero net energy consumption, in other words.

Net-zero buildings can be small, such as a net-zero, entirely electric home in Lexington, Massachusetts, which is 58 percent more energy efficient than a standard home.[15] And they can be huge. One of the world's largest net-zero buildings is the 135,000-square-foot Unisphere building in downtown Silver Spring, Maryland, home to the United Therapeutics brand. Thousands of connected sensors and devices form a sophisticated system that tracks energy use and coordinates heating and cooling. There's even a pool in the center of the building that absorbs excess heat.[16]

Trend 2: Modular and Off-Site Construction

The market for modular and prefabricated construction is on the up, and is expected to hit $109 billion by 2025, up from $82.3 in 2020.[17] In part, this trend is driven by labor shortages and rising costs in construction, but new technologies also play a key role. Take 3D printing as an example. In Chapter 2 we saw how entire houses can now be 3D printed at a cost that's significantly cheaper than traditional construction methods.

But it's not just small residential properties that can be 3D printed or constructed off-site. The 21-story CitizenM Bowery Hotel in downtown Manhattan is the tallest modular construction in the US. Modular and prefab construction allows construction firms to build in more controlled, safe environments, often in less time and using fewer materials. So it's no wonder many major builders plan to scale back their traditional on-site construction efforts to as little as 25 percent by 2025, in favor of modular, off-site construction.[18]

Trend 3: Replacing Traditional Concrete and Steel

The production of concrete and steel have a huge environmental footprint, yet we seem to be using more of these materials than ever – and this is likely to get worse as we build more megacities (see Chapter 1). The manufacturing of steel (and iron) accounts for 7.2 percent of global greenhouse gas emissions,[19] and steel production has seen a tenfold increase since 1950, to the extent that the world is producing 240 kilos of steel for every single person in the world, *every year*.[20] Meanwhile, cement production – a key ingredient of concrete – is alone responsible for 8 percent of the world's carbon dioxide emissions, meaning if the cement industry were a country, it would be the third largest CO_2 emitter in the world.[21] It sounds mind-boggling, but not when you consider that, after water, concrete is the most widely used substance on the planet.[22]

We therefore need new alternatives to traditional concrete and steel that can provide the same advantages of strength and durability, without the dreadful environment cost. And while these new materials are being developed, we urgently need ways to make concrete and steel production much, much greener.

This is beginning to happen already. For example, a Korean company has developed a way of making steel that produces 90 percent fewer toxic emissions than traditional steelmaking methods.[23] And when it comes to concrete, lower-carbon approaches to producing cement (again, the fundamental ingredient in concrete) could have a huge impact. For example, one startup in New Jersey has adopted a chemical process developed by Rutgers University that cuts the carbon dioxide released in cement making by 30 percent.[24] And Montreal-based company Carbi-Crete eschews the cement altogether, instead using a by-product of steel-making called steel slag to make concrete.[25]

Trend 4: Technology Adoption in Construction

The construction industry isn't well known for embracing new technologies, but as these examples show, technology is beginning to play a larger role in the building process. Here are some of the most important tech subtrends in construction:

- Drone use in construction is rising by almost 240 percent year on year,[26] with drones being used for aerial surveys, heat maps and thermal images, and even on-site security.

- VR and AR are beginning to be used in number of ways, including creating 3D visualizations of construction projects, making safety training more immersive and inspecting sites.

- Blockchain can be used to create a more secure, efficient construction workflow. For example, smart contracts stored on a blockchain can allow all stakeholders in a project to buy, track, and pay for services related to the project – like an all-in-one project tracking tool.

Over time, we can expect to see greater adoption of these and other new technologies in the building process. Circle back to Chapter 2 to revisit some of the biggest technology trends affecting all industries.

Now let's turn from the making process to another key section of the supply chain: transportation.

PRACTICAL LESSONS

In this chapter, we've learned that the construction and manufacturing industries are in for a period of rapid change, driven by new technologies, increasing automation, and a desire for greener products and services. Regardless of your industry, some of the key takeaways from this chapter include:

- The work that humans do will change, as machines take on more of the dangerous, dull, and easily repeatable tasks. Employees and employers must prepare for this change and invest in reskilling for the 21st century.

- Thanks to the IoT, data, and digital twins, businesses can extract new efficiencies from legacy systems and processes. In other words, you don't have to overhaul entire business processes and equipment to start reaping the benefits.

Notes

1. Hirotec: Transforming Manufacturing with Big Data and the Industrial Internet of Things (IIoT); Bernard Marr; https://www.bernardmarr.com/default.asp?contentID=1267

2. Artificial Intelligence: Optimizing Industrial Operations; Siemens; https://new.siemens.com/global/en/company/stories/research-technologies/artificial-intelligence/artificial-intelligence-optimizing-industrial-operations.html

3. Digital twins: Bridging the physical and digital; Deloitte; https://www2.deloitte.com/us/en/insights/focus/tech-trends/2020/digital-twin-applications-bridging-the-physical-and-digital.html

4. The transformation of digital twins in manufacturing; Manufacturing Global; https://www.manufacturingglobal.com/procurement-and-supply-chain/transformation-digital-twins-manufacturing

5. 5 trends for the future of manufacturing; World Economic Forum; https://www.weforum.org/agenda/2017/06/what-s-going-on-with-manufacturing-b013f435-1746-4bce-ac75-05c642652d42/

6. How automation is shaping the manufacturing industry; GlobalTrade; https://www.globaltrademag.com/how-automation-is-shaping-the-manufacturing-industry/

7. 5 trends for the future of manufacturing; World Economic Forum; https://www.weforum.org/agenda/2017/06/what-s-going-on-with-manufacturing-b013f435-1746-4bce-ac75-05c642652d42/

8. Reshoring Was at Record Levels in 2018. Is It Enough? IndustryWeek; https://www.industryweek.com/the-economy/article/22027880/reshoring-was-at-record-levels-in-2018-is-it-enough

9. Industrial exoskeletons: New systems, improved technologies, increasing adoption; The Robot Report; https://www.therobotreport.com/industrial-exoskeletons/

10. The Future of Work: Are You Ready for Smart Robots?; Forbes; https://www.forbes.com/sites/bernardmarr/2018/08/29/the-future-of-work-are-you-ready-for-smart-cobots/

11. How We're Building a Robotic 3D Printing Factory; Medium; https://medium.com/voodoo-manufacturing/announcing-project-skywalker-bf9efa99a677

12. Emissions by sector; Our World in Data; https://ourworldindata.org/emissions-by-sector

13. Decarbonizing US Buildings; Center for Climate and Energy Solutions; https://www.c2es.org/document/decarbonizing-u-s-buildings/#:~:text=Fossil%2Dfuel%20combustion%20attributed%20to,respectively%2C%20since%20a%202005%20peak.

14. Buildings; Alliance to Save Energy; https://www.ase.org/categories/buildings

15. 5 Net Zero Energy Building Examples Worth Emulating; GB&D; https://gbdmagazine.com/net-zero-energy-building-examples/

16. The innovative design of one of the world's largest net zero buildings; Quartz; https://qz.com/1771906/the-innovative-design-of-one-of-the-worlds-largest-net-zero-buildings/

17. Modular Construction Market worth $108.8 billion by 2025; Markets and Markets; https://www.marketsandmarkets.com/PressReleases/modular-construction.asp

18. Top 10 Construction Industry Trends to Watch for in 2021; BigRentz; https://www.bigrentz.com/blog/construction-trends#green-building

19. Emissions by sector; Our World in Data; https://ourworldindata.org/emissions-by-sector

20. 240 kilos of steel for every single person in the world – every year; The World Counts; https://www.theworldcounts.com/challenges/planet-earth/mining/environmental-impact-of-steel-production/story

21. Climate change: The massive CO2 emitter you may not know about; BBC News; https://www.bbc.com/news/science-environment-46455844

22. Concrete: The most destructive material on Earth; Guardian; https://www.theguardian.com/cities/2019/feb/25/concrete-the-most-destructive-material-on-earth

23. 240 kilos of steel for every single person in the world – every year; The World Counts; https://www.theworldcounts.com/challenges/planet-earth/mining/environmental-impact-of-steel-production/story

24. Top 10 Emerging Technologies of 2020; World Economic Forum; http://www3.weforum.org/docs/WEF_Top_10_Emerging_Technologies_2020.pdf

25. Ibid.

26. Ibid.

CHAPTER 8
HOW WE MOVE PEOPLE AND GOODS
The Three Trends Revolutionizing Transportation

Mobility is another sector undergoing enormous change. And I'm not just talking about moving people (via cars, planes, ships, etc.), but also goods. Therefore, the changes taking place in mobility will affect most businesses, regardless of sector – after all, so many supply chains rely on the movement of goods.

The transformation of mobility is being driven by three major trends:

- The electrification of vehicles
- Autonomous, connected vehicles
- The servitization of mobility

Let's explore each trend in turn.

Trend 1: Electrification

Transportation is a major cause of greenhouse gas emissions. Looking at the US alone, transportation generates around 28 percent of total greenhouse gas emissions, with these emissions largely coming from the burning of fossil fuels (particularly gasoline and diesel) to run cars, trucks, ships, planes, and trains.[1] We urgently need to transition to greener vehicles – and, in the case of cars, that means electric vehicles (EVs).

The electric car revolution

As of 2020, EVs accounted for just 6 percent of global automotive sales, but that is projected to grow to 13 percent by 2025 and 22 percent by 2030.[2] Over time, factors such as the tightening of national emissions targets, greater urban populations, improvements in charging infrastructure, and the declining cost of the lithium-ion batteries that power EVs (already down 80 percent since 2010)[3] will combine to encourage mass adoption of EVs.

And automakers are investing big in EVs. The year 2019 saw the largest-ever volume of investment going into developing new EV models, with Volkswagen alone investing $44 billion (the company has said it wants to be selling 40 percent EVs by 2030).[4] And obviously there's Tesla, the EV pioneer, which became the world's highest-valued automaker in July 2020 – quadruple the combined value of Ford and General Motors.[5]

I take this as a sign that we're reaching a crucial tipping point in EVs. Consumer opinion certainly seems to be catching up; 30 percent of vehicle buyers in the US now consider an EV purchase,[6] which means EVs represent a significant opportunity for automakers.

Greening up other modes of transport

It's not just cars that are becoming electrified. We now have electric scooters, which could make a huge difference to pollution levels in the megacities of the future. Indian ride-sharing company Ola has invested massively in e-scooters and is preparing to launch its model in late 2021. The company's e-scooter plant in India is gearing up to produce 10 million electric scooters a year (that's one scooter every two seconds when the plant is at full capacity).[7]

Advancements are also being made in electric trucks. While we don't have the battery technology to electrify long-distance haulage, all-electric trucks could revolutionize regional and last-mile journeys. Considering journeys of less than 250 miles make up 80 percent of freight in the US,[8] the adoption of electric trucks could have a significant impact on the industry's environmental impact. Although less than 1 percent of fleet trucks are currently electric,[9] companies like Daimler are investing in electric truck technology. Daimler's 18-wheeler, 250-mile range eCascadia truck is due to go into production.

What about planes? Without huge advances in battery technology, we're a long way from electric planes becoming truly viable, although companies like Airbus and MagniX are working on electric flight technology. For now, the few electric planes in existence are designed for private travel only, but Airbus hopes to have 100-passenger versions ready to take off by 2030.[10] Electric flight would go a long way to reduce the environmental footprint of air travel, which currently accounts for 2.5 percent of global carbon emissions.[11]

Alongside the electrification of air travel, the hydrogen-powered plane is another area of research that looks promising. In the UK, a consortium is exploring the potential for a 19-seat, 500-mile range aircraft that can run on hydrogen, and Airbus is targeting green hydrogen as a zero-emission fuel for commercial aircraft by 2035.[12]

More progress is being made in shipping, where a number of shipping and cruise giants are working toward net-zero carbon emissions. For example, Viking Cruises made headlines when it announced it was building the world's first liquid hydrogen–powered cruise ship.[13] Meanwhile, the country of Norway is taking steps to electrify its coastal vessels. Norway has been running electric car ferries since 2015 and the country now aims to run an all-electric fleet by 2023, although ferries that embark on longer routes will have to be equipped with hybrid technology.[14]

Creating entirely new modes of electric transport: Introducing Hyperloop

In the future, will we even need electric cars, trucks, and planes to transport cargo and people on longer-distance journeys? Not if Hyperloop travel becomes the norm.

Hyperloop is hyper-speed travel – essentially, super-fast vacuum tube trains. With hyperloop travel, capsules travel along a low-pressure tube via electric propulsion – while floating above the track using magnetic levitation, no less – then glide along at speeds of 760 mph. This means a journey from London to Edinburgh, which would usually take five hours, could potentially take just 30 minutes.

The name was coined by Elon Musk back in 2013. But Elon Musk isn't the only pioneer working on Hyperloop travel. Other Hyperloop projects are beginning to pop up around the world, and the technology is already being tested in the US and France. In fact, some experts predict Hyperloop could be part of society as early as 2030.[15]

In 2020, Virgin Hyperloop announced that it had conducted the first test with human passengers. The pod, which had two people on board, successfully accelerated along the tube to 100 mph, then slowed to a stop (Virgin Hyperloop's record speed for an unmanned test was 240 mph).[16] Virgin is also working with DP World on a Hyperloop cargo initiative called DP World Cargospeed, which aims to deliver freight "at the speed of flight and close to the cost of trucking."[17]

I'm very excited by this technology and believe Hyperloop has huge potential to replace traditional intercity and cross-continental travel (for both humans and cargo). But, as you might expect with such an innovative new technology, one of the main challenges to overcome is cost. The infrastructure for SpaceX's Hyperloop Alpha solution is reported to cost around $17 million per mile, which is pretty eye-watering, but Hyperloop developers insist the cost to customers will be less than that of high-speed rail and air travel.[18]

Trend 2: Autonomous Vehicles

Autonomous vehicles provide a unique opportunity to revolutionize the way people and goods are transported, improve road safety, and ease congestion on our increasingly busy roads. The autonomous vehicles of the future could even help to boost productivity because people traveling in the vehicle will be able to focus on other things, while the vehicle itself takes care of the driving. What's more, huge parking lots will be a thing of the past, as driverless vehicles and even passenger drones will be able to drop us at our destination and come back for us later. Let's see how autonomous vehicles will positively disrupt transportation.

Autonomous cars

Our cars are increasingly smart and connected. And with this connectivity comes greater autonomy, meaning that the more a car understands about its surroundings (thanks to cameras, sensors, etc.), the more it can carry out actions by itself. Most of us are familiar with cruise control and assisted parking features, but today's cars are able to do much, much more.

There are various levels of autonomy, from Level 0 (where humans have to do all the driving tasks) to Level 5 (where the vehicle can carry out *all* driver tasks in *any* situation). Self-driving leader Tesla says its autonomous technology will be capable of Level 5 autonomy soon.[19] Many other automakers are working toward achieving Level 4 autonomy (where the vehicle can drive itself under certain conditions only) over the next few years.

So will we have fully driverless cars on the streets soon? It's already happening. Waymo, Alphabet's autonomous taxi service, launched fully driverless rides for the general public in 2020.[20] And in China, AutoX launched its fully driverless taxis in early 2021.[21]

Meanwhile, in freight, several companies are working to develop autonomous trucks, including TuSimple, which is working with UPS to conduct test operations in Arizona and Texas. At the time of writing, TuSimple trucks still have a driver on board ready to take the wheel, but the company plans to conduct its first driverless trials this year and start selling autonomous trucks in 2024.[22]

Autonomous ships and drones

It's not just road vehicles that are becoming more autonomous. The world's first autonomous ferry, capable of operating without a crew, was announced back in 2018, although we're realistically decades away from the majority of ships becoming fully autonomous.[23]

Drones too, will become fully autonomous in the future, able to fly and make decisions without a human operator. Drones may even challenge traditional delivery methods. Several operators are investing in drone delivery, including Alphabet's Wing Aviation subsidiary, which in 2019 became the first drone delivery company to be awarded air carrier certification from the Federal Aviation Administration.[24]

We even have passenger drones coming our way – flying taxis, in other words. Several companies, including German aviation company Volocopter, are working to develop passenger drones. Volocopter's flagship 2X eVTOL aircraft – which has a range of 22 miles and a top speed of 68 mph – took its first manned urban test flight in 2019, and the company expects to begin commercial flights in 2022, transporting passengers from one VoloPort to another.[25] In the future, it's not unthinkable that such passenger drones could be fully autonomous as well. Indeed, Chinese company EHang announced in 2020 that it was partnering with the city of Linz in Austria on a pilot program for its EHang 216 autonomous air taxi – the first pilot of its kind in Europe.[26] Trial flights are planned for the near future.

Solutions to the "last mile" problem?

One of the major challenges with autonomous vehicles – particularly when it comes to deliveries – is the "last mile" problem. Autonomous trucks and vans are best suited to highway travel and delivering freight to local storage hubs. So how can we get packages from local storage hubs to the recipient's address, via congested city streets, right to their front door?

One solution comes in the form of autonomous delivery robots, such as Starship robots. I've used these little delivery robots for years now (they operate in my hometown of Milton Keynes, UK) and certainly increased my reliance on them during the pandemic. But big players like Ford are also working on the last mile problem. Ford has teamed up with Agility Robotics to develop Digit – a two-legged delivery robot that can unfold from the back of a self-driving vehicle and "walk" the package to the customer's front door.[27] Digit can even go up and down stairs. Solutions like these, combined with autonomous cars and trucks, and drone deliveries, could utterly transform the supply chain over the coming years.

Trend 3: The Servitization of Mobility

I talk more about subscription and servitization in Chapter 13 so I'll keep this fairly brief. But it's safe to say that few industries will be left untouched by the servitization trend, and that includes mobility. As more and more of us live in densely populated megacities, and as concern grows over the climate crisis, the days of everyone owning and running their own cars are numbered. Instead, we'll turn to mobility-as-a-service (MaaS) providers to meet our transportation needs.

This trend is already beginning to show in the overall decline of car sales. Notwithstanding the impact of the COVID-19 pandemic, people are buying fewer cars.[28] Plus, with the rise of ride-sharing services like Uber and Didi Chuxing, transportation is now much more complex and multilayered than the traditional private ownership model.

But what is MaaS? Essentially, it's mobility on demand. A company like Uber could technically fall under this bracket, but the MaaS operators of the future will offer customers multiple mobility options via a single payment channel and interface, rather than one single mode of transport. This may include bus, metro, ride-hailing, car-sharing, bicycle-sharing, e-scooter sharing, and so on. With an MaaS provider, you could borrow a car for a few hours one day, pick up an e-scooter in town later that day, and hop home on public transport – all via one platform. The key notion here is *access* to mobility, rather than ownership. In the future, the majority of city dwellers may never need to own a car at all.

Now, for a final look at a specific industry, let's turn our attention to the financial sector.

PRACTICAL LESSONS

Across each of these trends, there are exciting opportunities for those in the transportation sector. MaaS, for example, provides a huge opportunity for ride-sharing services to meet more of their customers' needs. Electrification provides an opportunity to make transport and supply chains more sustainable. And autonomous vehicles could make transportation much safer and more efficient.

For those outside of the transportation sector, key takeaways from this chapter include:

- Companies must start choosing more sustainable mobility options, including electric company cars and autonomous delivery robots. (Read more about sustainable operations in Chapter 18.)

- The automation that is happening in mobility is happening across almost all sectors. This means organizations must strike a tricky balance between the work that humans do and automation. (Read more about this in Chapter 19.)

- The as-a-service model will also affect every industry, so start thinking now about how you can provide customers with tailored subscription services or shared services. (Read more about servitization in Chapter 13 and the sharing economy in Chapter 15.)

Notes

1. Sources of Greenhouse Gas Emissions; United States Environmental Protection Agency; https://www.epa.gov/ghgemissions/sources-greenhouse-gas-emissions

2. A Deep Dive into the Future of Mobility; Toptal; https://www.toptal.com/finance/industry/future-of-mobility

3. Electrification; McKinsey & Company; https://www.mckinsey.com/features/mckinsey-center-for-future-mobility/overview/electrification

4. A Deep Dive into the Future of Mobility; Toptal; https://www.toptal.com/finance/industry/future-of-mobility

5. Teslanomics: How to justify being the most valuable car company on earth; Fortune; https://fortune.com/2020/08/10/tesla-most-valuable-car-company-in-the-world-electric-vehicles-evs/

6. Electrification; McKinsey & Company; https://www.mckinsey.com/features/mckinsey-center-for-future-mobility/overview/electrification

7. World's largest e-scooter plant; Business Today; https://www.businesstoday.in/sectors/auto/worlds-largest-e-scooter-plat-in-india-bhavish-aggarwal-tweets-video-visuals-of-ola-future-factory/story/433275.html

8. 8 electric truck and van companies to watch in 2020; GreenBiz; https://www.greenbiz.com/article/8-electric-truck-and-van-companies-watch-2020

9. Ibid.

10. Top 10 Emerging Technologies of 2020; World Economic Forum; http://www3.weforum.org/docs/WEF_Top_10_Emerging_Technologies_2020.pdf

11. Ibid.

12. Net zero: Aviation and shipping; Energy & Climate Intelligence Unit; https://eciu.net/analysis/briefings/net-zero/transport-aviation-and-shipping

13. Viking Cruises to Build World's 1st Hydrogen-Powered Cruise Ship?; Offshore Energy; https://www.offshore-energy.biz/viking-cruises-to-build-worlds-1st-hydrogen-powered-cruise-ship/

14. Europe Takes First Steps in Electrifying World's Shipping Fleets; Yale Environment 360; https://e360.yale.edu/features/europe-takes-first-steps-in-electrifying-worlds-shipping-fleets

15. Around the world in Hyperloop; DNV; https://www.dnv.com/to2030/technology/around-the-world-in-hyperloop.html

16. Virgin hyperloop hits an important milestone: The first human passenger test; Verge; https://www.theverge.com/2020/11/8/21553014/virgin-hyperloop-first-human-test-speed-pod-tube

17. Hyperloop for cargo aims to deliver at over 600 mph; CNN; https://edition.cnn.com/2018/05/04/tech/hyperloop-dp-world-cargospeed-announcement/index.html

18. Around the world in Hyperloop; DNV; https://www.dnv.com/to2030/technology/around-the-world-in-hyperloop.html

19. Elon Musk says Tesla's Full Self-Driving tech will have Level 5 autonomy by end of 2021; Cnet; https://www.cnet.com/roadshow/news/elon-musk-full-self-driving-tesla-earnings-call/

20. Waymo is opening its fully driverless service to the general public in Phoenix; Waymo; https://blog.waymo.com/2020/10/waymo-is-opening-its-fully-driverless.html

21. China Officially Launches Fully Driverless Autonomous Taxis; HypeBeast; https://hypebeast.com/2021/2/china-autox-fully-driverless-autonomous-taxi-launch

22. This Year Autonomous Trucks Will Take to the Road with No One on Board; IEEE Spectrum; https://spectrum.ieee.org/transportation/self-driving/this-year-autonomous-trucks-will-take-to-the-road-with-no-one-on-board

23. The incredible Autonomous Ships of the Future; Forbes; https://www.forbes.com/sites/bernardmarr/2019/06/05/the-incredible-autonomous-ships-of-the-future-run-by-artificial-intelligence-rather-than-a-crew/?sh=669238c16fbf

24. Drone delivery taking off from Alphabet's Wing Aviation; Robot Report; https://www.therobotreport.com/drone-delivery-taking-off-from-alphabets-wing-aviation/

25. Introducing the Mindboggling Flying Taxis of the Future; Bernard Marr; https://bernardmarr.com/default.asp?contentID=2068

26. Linz, Austria to Be Added to List of EHang's Pilot Cities; Transport Up; https://transportup.com/headlines-breaking-news/vehicles-manufactures/linz-austria-to-be-added-to-list-of-ehangs-pilot-cities/

27. A smart little robot that can help make deliveries; Ford; https://corporate.ford.com/articles/products/autonomous-vehicle-robot-delivery.html

28. A Deep Dive into the Future of Mobility; Toptal; https://www.toptal.com/finance/industry/future-of-mobility

CHAPTER 9
HOW WE LOOK AFTER OUR MONEY

The Four Shifts That Will Shape the Financial Sector

So far in this book, I've looked at key cultural and societal shifts and the changes occurring in major business sectors. I couldn't ignore the financial sector. Love it or loathe it, money is an important part of society. And our relationship with money – how we use it, whom we trust to look after it, and how we as financial customers expect to be treated – is changing. In this chapter, I explore four key trends that will shape the financial sector over the coming years, starting with a broad look at the future of money.

Shift 1: The Future of Money May Be Very Different Than Today

The digitization of money is revolutionizing our relationship with money. People can now pay for goods and services at the tap of a screen via mobile apps, or by scanning their phone, or even by flashing their smile (a "Smile to Pay" facial recognition payment service is already in operation in China).[1] Physical money often doesn't come into it.

This digitization of money means that our personal data is becoming increasingly intertwined with our money – a trend that will only continue. Imagine a future in which even more of your personal details (for example, whether you're a student or a homeowner) are embedded into your money and transactions. Payment systems could become almost invisible in this environment, with payment being taken automatically based on our identity and status (automatically applying any relevant discounts based on status or membership).

This may change how we feel about money in general. Will we value money less when money is no longer physical, when transactions become less visible? Will we no longer need the currencies that we have today? Perhaps. You might be surprised to learn that more than 600 currencies have disappeared in the last 30 years,[2] and it's not unthinkable that more will disappear or be replaced by digital currencies – even major currencies. Indeed, the European Central Bank is already exploring the introduction of a "digital euro."[3]

It's impossible to imagine all the consequences of gradually removing money – physical money, that is – from our everyday transactions. Perhaps the monetary system of the future will no longer be defined by different economies, currencies, central banks, and politicians, but by highly integrated digital platforms and financial communities. Maybe, in the future, money will be replaced altogether by social currencies, where individuals and businesses exchange goods and services using "points" instead of money. Maybe lending will be done entirely on a community basis (an extension of the peer-to-peer lending platforms that have already sprung up), and banks will be written out of the equation altogether. Indeed, new tech startups are already challenging established banks and financial services providers (more on this coming up).

If this vision of the future feels vaguely unnerving, good. Those in the financial sector must quickly wake up to our changing relationship with money and realign their products and services accordingly. The good news is these digital technologies bring huge potential to improve financial services, particularly when it comes to personalization – more on that coming up later in the chapter.

But this future will also bring huge challenges. We already see alarming data breaches every year (see Chapter 2), and these could become all the more damaging when our identities are inextricably tied up in our digital transactions. Will these new financial systems be more open to data breaches, fraud, and even terrorism? They would certainly be attractive targets. But before we dwell too much on the security implications, let's explore this notion of digitization in more detail.

Shift 2: The Increasing Digitization of Money and Financial Services

There's no doubt the COVID-19 pandemic has accelerated the digitization of money. Online payments and contactless payments surged as people either stayed home or were reluctant to handle physical money in shops.[4] The trust that people have long placed in banks and traditional forms of payment is increasingly being placed in digital money. Cash is no longer king.

But what do we mean by digital money? Essentially, digital money refers to any form of money or payment that only exists electronically – and this can be as simple as a payment or money transfer that takes place online (facilitated by a traditional bank or credit card company), or as complex as an entire cryptocurrency like Bitcoin (which generally sits outside of traditional money institutions). Digital money can therefore involve credit cards, smartphones, apps, online banking, money transfer platforms, and cryptocurrency platforms – but however the transaction occurs, the key factor is that no tangible money changes hands.

These days, most traditional banks and other financial service providers facilitate digital money transactions and don't require the physical exchange of money. But they will have to expand this to keep up with the rise of nontraditional operators entering the finance market, especially through payment apps and digital wallet services (more on these nontraditional competitors later in the chapter).

Cryptocurrency is a particularly interesting area to watch. Cryptocurrency exists on decentralized networks using blockchain technology (see Chapter 2), which means no central bank or government is responsible for issuing or regulating the currency. Today, cryptocurrencies like Bitcoin – and the blockchain technology that underpins them – are becoming more trusted and widely used. Tesla, for example, now accepts bitcoin for their cars. Bitcoin's price hit an all-time high in January 2021 as support for the currency continued to grow.[5] And, as of 2020, the US Office of the Comptroller of the Currency (OCC, part of the Treasury) now permits federally chartered banks to provide custody services for crypto-assets, and allows banks to streamline payment functions via public blockchain networks.[6] Also in 2020, DBS, Singapore's largest bank, announced it was planning to launch a cryptocurrency exchange.[7] In other words, cryptocurrency is going mainstream.

This is overall a good thing because blockchain-based transactions are, by their decentralized nature, super-secure. After all, digital money is extremely vulnerable to payment fraud and data theft. The wider adoption of blockchain-based technologies (which can be used to facilitate non-cryptocurrency transactions as well as cryptocurrency) will help with this. So too will AI, by analyzing transactions and identifying patterns that indicate a fraudulent transaction. Mastercard, for example, uses AI to detect and stop billions of dollars' worth of fraud, and cut the rate of "false declines" (where a transaction is incorrectly flagged as fraudulent).[8]

Beyond cybersecurity, another challenge for traditional providers is how to maintain a personal relationship with customers when they no longer routinely interact with tellers in a branch. Yet the digitization of money actually provides many opportunities to personalize customer interactions and improve customer satisfaction (see later in the chapter).

Then there is the environmental impact of all this digitization. Bitcoin alone requires enormous amounts of computing power and uses nearly as much electricity as the entire country of Argentina.[9] For the digitization of money to truly benefit society, it will need to go hand in hand with renewable energy production. In Iceland and Norway, for example, cryptocurrency miners take advantage of hydroelectric and geothermal energy to power their systems.[10] (Read more about moving to digital products in Chapter 10, and sustainable operations in Chapter 18.)

Shift 3: The Rise of Finance Apps and Nontraditional Providers

Facilitating this new wave of digital money are mobile payment apps and so-called "digital wallets" – typically app-based services that allow users to pay for things (for example, via contactless payments) and transfer money to others. Some digital wallets can also hold other items that you might store in an ordinary, physical wallet, such as e-tickets for upcoming events or gift cards.

Crucially, many of these apps are offered by tech giants and digital-native startups, not banks. Powered by data and AI capabilities, this new breed of fintech providers is threatening the long-established monopoly that traditional banks and financial service providers have over money and payments.

Take mobile payment apps like Venmo, Apple Pay, Google Pay, and Samsung Pay as an example. PayPal-owned Venmo processed $159 billion in payments in 2020, representing a 59 percent year-on-year increase, and is used by more than 50 million people in the US.[11] Just think how long it would take a traditional bank to achieve that kind of customer growth – decades perhaps. Yet mobile apps are able to grow quickly through viral peer-to-peer interactions and lower cost structures. So much so that, in China, the volume of mobile payments has increased more than 15-fold in just five years to $36 trillion (that's more than double China's GDP for 2020).[12]

The use and value of digital wallets will continue to explode. Today, digital wallets are typically valued between $250 and $1,900 per user, but this could potentially increase to $20,000 per user by 2025 – a $4.6 trillion opportunity in the US alone.[13] This has to give traditional banks pause for thought.

Apps are also beginning to enter the world of unsecured lending, with services like Klarna, a buy-now-pay-later digital payment system popular with millennials. This again will take market share from high street banks and other lenders. Then there are digital banking solutions designed to rival the services of traditional banks, in a solely digital ecosystem. Chinese bank WeBank, the world's leading digital bank, is a prime example, providing financial services (including digital wallets and unsecured loans) to underserved individuals and small to medium enterprises (SMEs).[14] Or there's Ant Group, Alibaba's fintech spinoff, which started as a mobile payment company and now manages over $560 billion in wealth management.[15] Or Lufax, another Chinese fintech giant, which offers retail credit, wealth management, and peer-to-peer lending.

One of the reasons these tech companies and startups are able to compete so well is because they're not hampered by expensive legacy IT systems. As a result, these new fintech providers can be much more nimble in how they develop products and services, and serve their customers. This is a major challenge for traditional banks and finance companies to overcome – especially when you consider that, as of mid-2019, 70 percent of financial institutions were still reviewing their legacy core banking platform and 43 percent were still using COBOL, a coding language that dates back to 1959.[16]

Taking all this into consideration, it's perhaps no wonder that a PwC survey of the financial industry found that a quarter of the industry's business could be at risk of being lost to fintech companies within five years.[17]

Clearly, the digitization of money represents a big threat to traditional banks and middleman services, such as companies that process credit card transactions. (Read more about how technology is cutting out the middlemen in Chapter 14.) For now, let's turn to one of the main advantages of digitization in finance: the potential for personalization.

Shift 4: Consumer Expectations for more Personalized, Intelligent Services

I talk more about personalization in Chapter 12 and intelligent services in Chapter 11, but let's explore what personalization and intelligent services mean in the financial sector.

According to a recent PwC survey on technology in finance, customer intelligence will be the most important predictor of revenue growth and profitability.[18] The digitization of finance is creating whole new streams of data on what customers do with their money – and this information can be used to offer customers helpful insights about their spending, or even to cross-sell other relevant financial products and services in future.

As an example, independent UK bank Metro Bank has an intelligent tool called Insights, which analyzes customer spending patterns and makes predictions about whether a customer is likely to exceed their credit limit before their next paycheck or whether an unexpected expense could push them into the red. This is the sort of personalized, tailor-made service that banking customers will increasingly expect in the 21st century.

This shift toward intelligence and personalization – more customer-centric operations, if you like – has been driven by AI. So much so that 85 percent of banking executives now say AI is among their top tech priorities, and that AI implementation could deliver up to 25 percent improvement in customer satisfaction and sales.[19]

That brings us to the end of Part II. I hope that the trends, challenges, opportunities, and practical lessons outlined for each sector have reinforced the need to take action in your own organization. For many businesses, this will prompt a rethink of the very products and services they offer. This leads us neatly to the next part of this book.

PRACTICAL LESSONS

In this chapter, we've learned that the financial sector is being seriously disrupted by a new wave of fintech offerings, both from established tech giants and specialized startups. Whether your business is operating in the banking space or not, there are several key lessons to take away from this:

- All businesses must update their payment experience in line with the digitization of money. Integrating seamlessly with digital wallets and payment platforms may offer your business a key competitive advantage.

- You may also need to invest in the skills and tools needed to gather data on customers' needs. This is essential for designing more personalized products and services.

- Finally, I believe every organization must weigh the risk coming from digital-native startups and tech giants. Consider whether your sector is at risk of these digital-first companies taking market share away from traditional operators.

Notes

1. The Amazing Ways Chinese Face Recognition Company Megvii (Face++) Uses AI and Machine Vision; Bernard Marr; https://bernardmarr.com/default.asp?contentID=1883

2. What is the future of money?; World Economic Forum; https://www.weforum.org/agenda/2015/11/what-is-the-future-of-money/

3. The future of money – innovating while retaining trust; European Central Bank; https://www.ecb.europa.eu/press/inter/date/2020/html/ecb.in201130~ce64cb35a3.en.html

4. Ibid.

5. Bitcoin's Price History; Investopedia; https://www.investopedia.com/articles/forex/121815/bitcoins-price-history.asp

6. Big Ideas 2021; Ark Invest; https://research.ark-invest.com/hubfs/1_Download_Files_ARK-Invest/White_Papers/ARK%E2%80%93Invest_BigIdeas_2021.pdf

7. Ibid.

8. The Amazing Ways How Mastercard Uses Artificial Intelligence to Stop Fraud and Reduce False Declines; Forbes; https://www.forbes.com/sites/bernardmarr/2018/11/30/the-amazing-ways-how-mastercard-uses-artificial-intelligence-to-stop-fraud-and-reduce-false-declines/

9. How bad is Bitcoin for the environment really?; Independent; https://www .independent.co.uk/climate-change/news/bitcoin-environment-mining-energy-cryptocurrency-b1819545.html

10. Ibid.

11. Venmo Revenue and Usage Statistics (2021); Business of Apps; https:// www.businessofapps.com/data/venmo-statistics/

12. Big Ideas 2021; Ark Invest; https://research.ark-invest.com/hubfs/1_ Download_Files_ARK-Invest/White_Papers/ARK%E2%80%93Invest_ BigIdeas_2021.pdf

13. Ibid.

14. WeBank: The World's Leading Digital Bank Decoded; Cision PR Newswire; https://www.prnewswire.com/news-releases/webank-the-worlds-leading-digital-bank-decoded-300949025.html

15. How Ant Group Became the Biggest Fintech Company in the World; Marker; https://marker.medium.com/how-ant-group-became-the-biggest-fintech-company-in-the-world-7afae29ec1d3

16. Forging New Pathways: The next evolution of innovation in financial services; World Economic Forum; http://www3.weforum.org/docs/WEF_ Forging_New_Pathways_2020.pdf

17. Financial services technology 2020 and beyond: Embracing disruption; PwC; https://www.pwc.com/gx/en/industries/financial-services/publications/ financial-services-technology-2020-and-beyond-embracing-disruption.html

18. Ibid.

19. As banks shift to Intelligent Banking, AI takes center stage; Capgemini; https://www.capgemini.com/2020/12/as-banks-shift-to-intelligent-banking-ai-takes-center-stage/

PART III
RETHINKING WHAT BUSINESSES OFFER

If businesses want to continue adding real value and solving customers' problems, they will have to rethink their products and services to take account of the huge shifts taking place. This is no easy feat. It takes courage to reimagine your business and potentially cannibalize your existing business model (think of how Apple's focus on iPhones and Apple Music essentially made iPods obsolete). And it requires humility, too – the humility to look at other industries and organizations and identify where they're doing better. I hope the real-world use cases in this part will help business leaders on this challenging journey.

Each chapter here represents a key business trend, such as the move toward digital channels or the desire for more sustainable goods and services. When I work with business leaders to help prepare their organizations for the future, these trends are the lenses through which we examine their business. In other words, these are the key topics I discuss with business leaders pretty much every day.

Naturally, there are some overlaps among these trends but, collectively, these chapters should give you a good feel for how consumer demands and customer value propositions are shifting. The most prosperous businesses of the future will focus on all eight of these trends to ensure relevance and business success.

CHAPTER 10
CHANNEL DIGITIZATION AND EXPANSION

The Move from Physical to Digital/ Hybrid Products and Channels

Of course, most businesses have already embraced digital routes to connect with customers. But in the past this digitization journey has generally treated digital channels – websites, social media – as add-ons. Now the gear has shifted completely and customers increasingly come to a business via a digital channel. Digital comes first, in other words, and can no longer be considered an add-on.

Coronavirus has accelerated this digital transformation. One McKinsey global survey of executives found that the pandemic sped up the digitization of customer and supply chain interactions by three to four years – in the space of just a few months.[1] Even more eye-opening, the share of digital (or digitally enabled) products accelerated by seven years. What's more, survey respondents said this digital-first approach is here to stay, as indicated by funding priorities. Digital initiatives were proving to be more of a priority than anything else.

This fast transition means businesses must focus their efforts on building better digital-first interactions with customers. For me, this means focusing on three specific areas:

- Apps

- A seamless omnichannel experience (where customers can move seamlessly between different channels and still get a cohesive customer experience)

- New, digital-only products

Let's look at each area in turn.

The App (and Super App) Revolution

There are now around 7 million apps available[2] (more, I'm sure, by the time you read this). Chances are you use apps on a daily basis, whether it's to chat with friends, order groceries, measure your calorie intake, check your bank account, or whatever.

All industries are being disrupted by apps – and this includes traditional customer-facing industries like banking, healthcare, hospitality, and retail. Apps are, in short, fast transitioning from an add-on feature to the central point of contact with customers. The app is the gateway to the customer, in other words. It is a precious tool for acquiring customers, interacting with them, learning more about them, and improving their experience.

Let's look at some examples.

Starbucks

I talk more about Starbucks later in the chapter, so I'll keep this brief. But I wanted to highlight Starbucks here because it epitomizes how traditional customer-facing businesses are harnessing apps. Using the Starbucks app, customers can find local stores, browse the menu, place orders, and collect extra rewards through "challenges." So it's no wonder Starbucks has one of the most popular apps among chain restaurants.[3]

Spin Mobility App

I love this example because it ties in with the mobility trends of autonomy, electrification, and servitization highlighted in Chapter 8 – demonstrating how so many of the trends in this book are intertwined.

Ford-owned "micromobility" company Spin has partnered with software company Tortoise to provide tele-operated (i.e., piloted by a remote operations team), three-wheeled electric scooters that can be scheduled or hailed in real time via an app. The hailing service is expected to come to cities across North America and Europe, including my hometown of Milton Keynes. The remote operations feature means these scooters can easily be repositioned to wherever they're needed – hopefully meaning no more deserted e-scooters littering sidewalks! The future vision is that scooters like this will be completely autonomous, so there won't be a need for anyone to operate them remotely.

Healthcare and wellness apps

I talked about the digitization of healthcare back in Chapter 4, but I want to briefly mention healthcare again because it's the perfect example of how apps are impacting industries that are not just customer-focused, but also highly physical. And the impact is significant. In fact, around 200 new health-related apps are built each day[4] – a number that has probably increased since the pandemic.

Some of my favorite examples include Generis, which provides DNA-based health advice on health, fitness, nutrition, and supplements. (DNA is retrieved from databases such as Ancestry.com and 23andMe.) Or there's BetterHelp, the pioneering online counseling app that allows patients to have easier, more affordable access to qualified mental health professionals. Or, when you need to connect with a doctor, there's Teladoc, which connects patients to board-certified doctors through round-the-clock video or phone consultations. Teladoc doctors can even prescribe medication to be collected at the patient's pharmacy of choice. Here in the UK, the National Health Service endorses multiple apps for patient use, including the EXi app, which creates a personalized 12-week exercise plan.

The rise of the "super app"

Increasingly, we're seeing the rise of apps that function as a complete ecosystem – where customers can do anything from chatting with friends, to managing their money, to ordering a taxi, all within one app. Gojek, Grab, and WeChat are great examples of these so-called *super apps*.

Indonesian app Gojek, for example, allows users across Southeast Asia to access dozens of services, including digital payments, food delivery, transit, package delivery, and even getting a massage. Launched in 2015, it is now the largest consumer transactional technology group in Southeast Asia, processing more than 7 million orders a day.[5]

Also in Southeast Asia, Grab, which started out as the GrabTaxi ride-hailing service, has since expanded into multiple consumer services, including hotel booking and ticket purchasing services, on-demand video, grocery shopping, and financial services (such as mobile payments and small business loans).

But the pioneer in the super app space has to be WeChat, owned by Chinese conglomerate Tencent. The app, which has more than a billion monthly users,[6] started out as a WhatsApp-style messaging service, but now allows users to do a whole lot more, including flight and hotel bookings, ride-hailing, digital payments, and even gaming. One cool feature is each WeChat user has a unique QR barcode, meaning users can add new contacts simply by scanning the QR code on their phone.

The app *is* the business

The time has come when apps are no longer an extension of the business, but the business itself. And that means companies must reorganize themselves around this digital-first, app-centered model. All aspects of your business, from customer services to business development and marketing, must be working *with* the app. This may require new skills or partnerships – whether that means investing in app development in-house, partnering with specialists to create a bespoke new app, or leveraging third-party apps (such as having a customer enquiry chatbot feature in Facebook Messenger or Snapchat).

The key to success is the customer experience – in particular, how well the app integrates with the overall customer experience. This brings us to the next topic.

Creating a Seamless Omnichannel Experience

As if creating an engaging app experience wasn't enough of a challenge, businesses must increasingly create a successful hybrid world where customers can interact with the brand and its products/services across multiple channels in a highly integrated way. From offline to online and back again, you must create a seamless hybrid experience where customers enjoy a smooth, effortless encounter. This is what's known as an *omnichannel experience* – not to be confused with *multichannel*. In a multichannel environment, customers can connect with your brand in multiple ways, but those channels aren't necessarily joined up and cohesive. But with an omnichannel approach, the customer or user can move seamlessly between different channels – mobile app, desktop website, in store, on the phone – and enjoy a truly cohesive experience. Research shows that brands with a strong omnichannel strategy retain, on average, 89 percent of customers, in comparison to 33 percent of companies with a weak omnichannel approach.[7]

Let's look at some brands that are nailing this omnichannel experience.

Starbucks (again)

I gave a quick glimpse of the Starbucks app experience in the previous section, so let's start there. Not only does the Starbucks rewards app help customers keep track of and top up their loyalty card, it also helps customers locate their nearest store and place an order. The app also remembers how you like your coffee, and suggests other menu items that might go with your order. And once you arrive at the store, you can skip the line and your coffee will be ready and waiting for you (as a Starbucks Rewards member, you can even get free refills on your coffee). In-store payments can also be made with the app. And, finally, if you like a song you hear while you're in store, the app integrates with Spotify, so you can identify the song and add it to a playlist.

Timberland

Another way apps can integrate with the in-store experience is by near-field communication (NFC) tags that allow customers to scan products and get more information. Timberland has used this to create a more connected customer experience in its stores. Shoppers are given a tablet that, when held next to products and signage throughout the store, gives more info on that product or offer. As customers look up more items, the system learns about their preferences and begins to suggest other suitable products, thereby creating a more personalized in-store experience.

Disney

Plan a vacation at one of Disney's parks and you're in for an omnichannel treat. Your trip may start by booking on Disney's impressive website. Then you can use the My Disney Experience app to plan your vacation in more detail, including securing dining reservations and your Fast Pass. And once you arrive at the park, the app will help you locate your must-see attractions and let you know how long the wait times are for each attraction. Disney improves the in-person experience even further through its Magic Band – a physical wristband that integrates with the app and Fast Pass program. The band also acts as a hotel room key, food ordering tool, and photo storage device.

Domino's

Food ordering and delivery are now routinely done via digital channels. But, like Starbucks, the most successful chains are making sure that customers receive the same effortless experience whatever channel they use.

For me, Domino's is a great example of this. As a 60-year-old pizza company, Domino's has seen a lot of changes in how customers order pizza. Today, the chain has more than 15 ways for customers to order pizzas, including calling the local restaurant, using the dedicated app, sending a pizza emoji over social media messaging, and even ordering via Alexa. Whatever channel I use, it's consistently hassle-free.

This hybrid offline and online experience is taking shape right across the food industry, from huge chains like Domino's and McDonalds right down to my local fish and chips shop. Yes, even my local fish and chips shop, Moore's Fish & Chips, has an app that lets me order our Friday night takeaway online and collect it from a dedicated entrance at the store. Or for even more convenience, I can request a Starship deliver robot to bring me the food. Which goes to show that even tiny businesses must be thinking about integrating their digital and physical channels to create one seamless customer experience.

Wild Turkey whiskey tasting

As well as in-store, apps, online, and e-commerce, there are also new channels to consider integrating into the customer experience – particularly voice-activated devices like Alexa. This is the route Wild Turkey decided to use when creating a guided virtual whiskey-tasting experience during the coronavirus pandemic. All customers have to do is ask Alexa to "open Wild Turkey tasting" and then they can listen to master distillers as they explain the different whiskeys, provide tasting notes, and deliver content based on questions.

This example shows how even traditional industries are embracing digital ways to connect with customers. But it's not just the customer experience and marketing/sales channels that are becoming digitized – products are, too.

Creating New Digital-Only Products

It should be clear by now that the boundary between the real world and the digital is becoming increasingly porous (if not meaningless). And this means many companies will want to start thinking about digital-only products. For many, this will mean smart, AI-driven products (which I talk more about in the next chapter).

So many sectors have already shifted from physical to digital goods. Music is a prime example, but there's also gaming, books, magazines, and even art. Let's look at some fascinating examples of new, digital-only products.

Rocket League

My two boys love this game, which is a bit like playing soccer in an arena but with cars. The makers have created a whole ecosystem where you can buy or trade fancier cars and accessories – and, with my kids at least, these are the products kids are talking about at school. So, rather than the latest must-have sneakers, kids increasingly want the latest must-have digital accessories.

Digital-only clothing

A similar thing is beginning to happen in the fashion industry, with companies offering digital-only clothing (designer clothing that's digitally applied to an image of you). It may sound weird, but with fast fashion contributing to the environmental crisis, I'm intrigued by zero-waste digital fashion. Take The Fabricant as an example. This "always digital, never physical" brand creates digital-only fashion that can be used and traded in virtual realities. Or there's DressX, which offers to outfit your digital image with a wide range of digital-only clothing and accessories so you can look amazing in new outfits that you can show off on your Instagram.

There's even an all-digital modeling agency now. Created by Cameron-James Wilson, the Diigitals modeling agency has a portfolio of virtual models – including Shudu, the digital supermodel who has been featured in *Vogue*.

Digital art

In March 2021, the world's "first robot citizen," Sophia the Robot, became the first robot to auction its own digital artwork – building on the growing popularity of the NFT (non-fungible token) digital art market, where art is stored on a blockchain. The 12-second video entitled "Sophia Instantiation" (created in collaboration with human artist Andrea Bonaceto) was purchased for $688,888. In fact, NFT sales are beginning to outperform the prices being achieved for physical artworks by some of the world's most famous painters; in March 2021, a jpeg file by artist Beeple sold for $70 million.[8]

Synthetic media

Thanks to AI, the *synthetic media* trend – where media (text, images, video, and voice) is generated by computers – has made huge leaps forward in recent years. We routinely interact with digital assistants like Alexa and Google Assistant, and these will only become more lifelike as time goes on.

You can even create realistic synthetic versions of yourself. There's a company called Synthesia, which allows you to create professional-looking synthetic videos, using a realistic digital avatar of yourself (including your own voice, if you like). And because the content is created by intelligent machines, videos can be created in minutes. As you can probably imagine, this could revolutionize how companies create digital content.

PRACTICAL LESSONS

This digitization of channels and products creates huge opportunities for organizations of all shapes and sizes. Let's recap the key practical takeaways from this chapter:

- All businesses, regardless of size and sector, must have a digital presence. We're now living in a digital-first world, and apps are playing a huge role in this transformation.

- The customer experience must be seamless, integrated, and effortless across multiple channels (online and offline). As organizations increasingly interact with customers across multiple touchpoints, a smooth omnichannel experience is essential.

- While apps and websites are obviously important, don't overlook the importance of new channels, such as voice interactions.

- Business leaders must also start to think about the impact digital-only products may have on their industry.

Of course, one of the major advantages of investing in digital channels and products is that you get to collect even more data on customer actions and preferences – and this can help you design smarter products and services (see Chapter 11) and personalize your products and services (Chapter 12). Let's move on to those trends now.

Notes

1. How COVID-19 has pushed companies over the technology tipping point – and transformed business forever; McKinsey & Company; https://www.mckinsey.com/business-functions/strategy-and-corporate-finance/our-insights/how-covid-19-has-pushed-companies-over-the-technology-tipping-point-and-transformed-business-forever

2. Era of Mobile Apps; Mobile App Daily; https://www.mobileappdaily.com/how-mobile-apps-are-changing-our-lives

3. Starbucks, Panera lead the way in digital, report finds; Restaurant Business; https://www.restaurantbusinessonline.com/technology/starbucks-panera-lead-way-digital-report-finds

4. 8 Best Healthcare Apps for Patients; Rootstrap; https://www.rootstrap.com/blog/healthcare-apps/

5. Gojek; https://www.gojek.io/

6. Everything you need to know about WeChat – China's billion-user messaging app; CNBC; https://www.cnbc.com/2019/02/04/what-is-wechat-china-biggest-messaging-app.html

7. Digital customer experience: Everything to know in 2021; Qualtrics; https://www.qualtrics.com/uk/experience-management/customer/digital-cx/

8. The Latest Artist Selling NFTs? It's a Robot; New York Times; https://www.nytimes.com/2021/03/25/arts/sophia-robot-nft.html

CHAPTER 11
COGNIFYING PRODUCTS AND SERVICES

Smarter Products, Smarter Services

As we saw in Chapter 2, there's no escaping AI and the IoT. It is inextricably part of our everyday lives. This is demonstrated by the increasing number of products that are called "smart," which means they can gather, send, and receive data. These days, the "cognifying" of products – a phrase coined by Kevin Kelly, founding executive editor of *Wired* magazine – is being applied to a wide range of everyday products and machines, from coffee makers and fridges to cars and huge industrial machines in factories (see IoT, Chapter 2). In fact, given the shrinking size and cost of sensors, pretty much anything can be made smart.

But it's not just products that are becoming more intelligent; as we'll see in this chapter, so too are services.

Smarter Products

It's the connectivity of smart products that's so important. By gathering and transmitting data, these smart products can learn to react to their surroundings and/or the user's preferences, thereby making the interactions between consumers and products more meaningful and, importantly, more useful. This means there's no point making a product smart for the sake of it – it must add value for the user.

Let's look at some of my favorite examples.

Smart home thermostats

While there are many smart thermostats to choose from these days, Google Nest is the company that pioneered the cognification of home thermostats. What I love about the Nest thermostat is it learns how you use your home and then regulates your heating automatically. So if you get home from work at 6 p.m. most days, it will learn your routine and start to heat or cool your home just before you get in. It also comes with activity sensors that can assess whether anyone is at home and adjust the temperature accordingly.

Smart cars

For me, Tesla is a great example of adding AI into a product in a meaningful way. AI (specifically, machine learning) is the technology that powers Tesla's autonomous driving features. Two AI chips make separate assessments of what's going on around the vehicle, and these assessments are then compared; if the assessments are the same, the car is guided accordingly. This enables better control and safety in autopilot mode. And because autopilot is, for now at least, intended to assist drivers, not replace them altogether, drivers are frequently reminded to keep their hands on the wheel; if they don't, the car gives a series of warnings and will eventually slow down and stop. Plus, there's sentry mode, which monitors the car's surroundings and takes video clips when the vehicle is unattended.

Smart robot vacuum

At CES 2021, Samsung unveiled the world's first AI-driven robotic vacuum, the JetBot 90 AI+. The vacuum uses sensors and AI to respond to its environment, recognize objects, and optimize its cleaning route.

It can lower itself under furniture, and recognize and maintain a safe distance from fragile or delicate objects.

AI-enabled coffee machines

JURA Australia, makers of premium coffee makers, have been making a smart coffee machine since 2019. The Z6 uses AI to learn and predict user's coffee choices, and update the display screen with a personalized menu of coffee options, based on what the user has selected before.

Smart fridges

Samsung has clearly gone all in on the smart home products. It even has a Family Hub smart refrigerator, which is equipped with AI-enabled cameras that can identify the food inside and let you know what items you're running low on. (You can also access the cameras from a smartphone, which is useful when you're out shopping and can't remember if you're out of cream.) There's also a meal planning feature where you can plan meals for the week ahead and create a smart shopping list for required ingredients.

Smart light bulbs

Philips makes a range of smart LED lights that can be controlled remotely and create a mix of colors and lighting effects. The Philips Hue smart bulbs are compatible with Alexa and Google Home devices, so you can control them with voice commands, and lights can turn off automatically when the system senses there is no one in the room. There's also a Philips app, Philips Hue Sync, where you can synchronize lighting to flash in time with music, video, and movies.

Smart, autonomous ships

The Mayflower Autonomous Ship – a collaboration between nonprofit ProMare, IBM, and other partners – is a 15-meter scientific research vessel that is completely crewless. According to the project's head of communications, Johnathan Batty, eliminating humans from research vessels reduces the requirements for the many facilities and conveniences we need to keep ourselves alive and comfortable, which means the ship can be more efficient.[1] The ship is packed with sensors, cameras, and processors that allow it to sail safely and carry out its research missions – all entirely autonomously (although it can also be monitored and remote-controlled from land).

Intelligent dog doors

MyQ Pet Portal is an intelligent pet door and winner of the CES 2021 Best of Innovation Award in the smart home category.[2] If your pup wants to go out for a tinkle when you're not home, the smart door uses cameras and AI – combined with a Bluetooth collar sensor – to recognize your pet and let her out and back in again. Or there's a "by request" function where the system alerts you when your pet comes up to the door, then, using an accompanying app, you can see and talk to her before releasing the door yourself. And the door itself is fitted with a noncontact sensor to ensure it never closes on your pooch's tail.

I find this example especially inspiring because MyQ is a division of Chamberlain Group, a corporation founded in 1954 that designs and manufactures garage door openers and gate entry systems. My point is that this isn't a digital-native company. And yet they're still creating award-winning smart products for the 21st century.

Robotic lawn mowers

Bored of mowing the lawn? Then you might be interested in Husqvarna's Automower, a robotic, GPS-equipped lawnmower that keeps your lawn in perfect shape. It automatically adjusts its operation to suit various factors, such as grass length, weather conditions, and tricky areas (like slopes and obstacles), and connects with your smartphone, so you can keep track of the mower's progress. It can also be voice controlled with Alexa and Google Assistant.

Smart flying security cameras for your home

In 2020, Amazon unveiled its Ring Always Home Cam, an autonomous, drone-like camera that flies around your home to monitor and record disturbances while you're out. It's connected to sensors placed within the home, and when a sensor detects a potential break-in, the camera will automatically fly on a preset path to the designated part of the home. You'll also receive an alert to your phone, allowing you to watch the footage from inside your house in real time. This means homeowners don't need to install multiple devices around the home – because the Ring will fly to wherever it's needed.

I hope these examples demonstrate how the cognification of products will impact almost every industry and almost every type of product. But it's not just products that will be affected by this trend. We're now entering an era of intelligent, AI-enhanced services as well.

Smarter Services

AI-enhanced services may mean a couple of different things. First, AI can be used to improve the existing service you provide to customers. Or there may be an opportunity to develop entirely new services and business models that are driven by AI. (There is also "AI-as-a-service," where AI providers offer access to AI tools on a subscription model, but I talk more about that in Chapter 13.)

Thanks to data and AI, businesses can now develop a much better understanding of their customers than ever before – their actions, their preferences, how they engage with services, and so on. Armed with this knowledge, organizations can design much more responsive, intelligent solutions and deliver more personalized services (more about personalization in Chapter 12). Amazon's personalized recommendation engine is a prime example of an intelligent service that adds real value for customers.

Whether your organization is already a service-based business or you're considering branching from products into services, AI is vital to delivering the kind of service customers want and need in the 21st century. If your customers don't already expect a smarter, more personalized service, I can guarantee they soon will. And that means if you don't offer more intelligent services, you risk being overtaken by other providers; think back to Chapter 9 and how traditional banks are losing market share to tech giants and startups.

Let's look at some examples of AI-enhanced services.

Google maps

Every day, Google Maps helps drivers navigate more than 1 billion kilometers, across 220 countries. Two of the key features of Google maps are traffic (i.e., whether there's a huge traffic jam on the way) and routing (the best way to get from A to B). Both are powered by AI.

What's really clever about Google's traffic feature is that it doesn't tell you current traffic conditions (which isn't that helpful when you're already stuck in a traffic jam) – it *predicts* what traffic will look like in the near future. To do this, it analyzes both historic traffic patterns and live traffic conditions and then uses AI to generate traffic predictions. That's why Google is able to predict the estimated time of arrival with 97 percent accuracy, and how it was able to cope with dramatic changes in driving patterns during the pandemic.[3]

Google's predictive traffic models also help determine the best route for your journey, along with other factors, such as road quality, the size/directness of roads, tolls, speed limits, and so on. Google also gathers incident reports from drivers to monitor when road conditions change unexpectedly.

AI-driven social media content from TikTok

All social media platforms use AI algorithms to serve up content to users, but video-sharing platform TikTok is a brilliant example. So that it can recommend relevant videos, the app closely monitors user reaction to and engagement with videos – including positive engagement such as likes, shares, watching a video all the way to the end, and negative reactions such as swiping away from the video. In a very short space of time, it absorbs enough intel to provide highly accurate predictions on what videos the user will be interested in. And this, in turn, means users spend more time in the app. It's perhaps no wonder that, in December 2020, TikTok overtook Facebook as the most downloaded app globally.[4]

Self-healing, autonomous database by oracle

Oracle says its Autonomous Database reduces operational costs by up to 90 percent and provides 417 percent ROI over five years.[5] How? By using AI to automate database tuning, security, backups, updates, and other routine tasks. In other words, it does things like patch your database for security vulnerabilities and protect against user errors – all without human intervention.

AI-powered meeting notes

Alongside autonomous databases, a range of other business tools are also becoming smart. Otter is one such example. With Otter, you can generate accurate notes from meetings, interviews, lectures, and other voice conversations. (It integrates with Zoom, or you can record conversations using your phone or web browser.) You get real-time streaming transcripts, then, within minutes of the conversation ending, rich, searchable notes are available to export and share.

AI chatbot for help with domestic abuse

Chatbots are another AI-powered way to deliver smarter services to users. These days there are customer service chatbots, helpdesk chatbots, wellness chatbots, and even chatbots that will help you plan and book the perfect holiday. One interesting example comes from the rAInbow – or "Bo" – chatbot. Hailing from South Africa, Bo is a friendly bot that's available to chat anytime about domestic abuse or relationships that don't feel right. Many people are reluctant to share concerns with friends and family, and sometime it isn't always obvious whether a relationship is becoming abusive, so Bo provides a safe space to voice concerns, ask questions, and get advice. The bot is designed to help users spot the signs of abuse, understand what's healthy behavior and what's not, and access helpful resources – rather like having a nonjudgmental friend on hand 24/7.

Merging Smart Products and Services

In this age of personalization and servitization (see Chapters 12 and 13), the line between products and services is becoming increasingly blurred. Take smart home assistants like Alexa and Google Assistant. These are AI-driven services, delivered via smart devices such as the Amazon Echo and Google Home speakers (read more about the "add-on" servitization model in Chapter 13).

For now, let's focus on a non-tech example, this time from the world of insurance. Technically, insurance is a transactional product that you buy (and, all being well, rarely use). Yet savvy insurers are beginning to develop a more meaningful, value-adding, service-based relationship with their customers – by creating a service that supports customers and makes their lives easier, healthier, and so on.

My favorite example of this comes from health and life insurance provider Vitality Health. Rather than paying for sickness, as traditional health insurance providers do, Vitality pays for wellness. The company uses data and AI to track and reward customers' healthy behavior, thereby creating a shared value system where customers benefit from lower insurance premiums (and, of course, healthier lives) and the insurer benefits from lower payouts.

Vitality starts by assessing a new member's baseline health and lifestyle information – such as smoking, drinking, height, blood pressure – and this information is used to determine the customer's Vitality Age. (Interestingly, 79% of people surveyed have a higher Vitality Age than their biological age.)[6] Then, Vitality creates what it calls a Personal Pathway for each member – designed to help customers improve their Vitality Age by making healthier choices. To track how customers are doing, Vitality gathers data from compatible wearable technologies, like the Apple Watch, and collects data from partners, including gyms. And when customers stick to their Personal Pathway, they're rewarded with points that can be redeemed against discounted services. The healthier the lifestyle, the bigger the rewards. Vitality also uses the data gathered to price policies more accurately and adjust premiums based on how engaged a member is with their individual program.

Personally, this is exactly the sort of intelligent service I want from my insurance providers. I want insurance companies to add value, be more proactive, solve problems before they occur, and help me save money. In the future, more service providers (not just insurance companies) will be providing intelligent services as standard.

As I've already mentioned, cognifying your products and services creates enormous opportunity to personalize your offering for individual customers. In the next chapter, we'll explore how brands are capitalizing on the huge trend that is personalization.

PRACTICAL LESSONS

Whether your organization is a product-based business, a service provider, or a mixture of the two, here are some key takeaways from this chapter:

- AI-driven products and services are no longer the sole domain of big tech firms.

- In the future, almost every product and every service will have some element of AI to it. Ultimately, everything is becoming smarter – and this trend isn't going to go away. Every company must therefore consider how this desire for smart anything and everything will impact their own product and service offerings.

- There are many advantages to making your products and services more intelligent. You can build a better understanding of your customers – how they use your product or service, their habits and preferences, and so on – and use this data to improve your offering, engage customers more deeply, create better products and services, and drive future success.

- Looking ahead, integration with voice control and smart assistants like Siri and Alexa will become even more important for smart products (and perhaps even for smart services).

Notes

1. The Mayflower Autonomous Ship: Pushing the Boundaries of Self-Driving Robot Ships on Our Oceans; Bernard Marr; https://www.linkedin.com/pulse/mayflower-autonomous-ship-pushing-boundaries-robot-ships-bernard-marr/

2. The Hottest Tech at CES 2021 Is for the Dogs; Wired; https://www.wired.com/sponsored/story/the-hottest-tech-at-ces-2021-is-for-the-dogs/

3. Google Maps 101: How AI helps predict traffic and determine routes; Google; https://blog.google/products/maps/google-maps-101-how-ai-helps-predict-traffic-and-determine-routes/

4. What Is TikTok and How Is AI Making It Tick?; Analytic Steps; https://www.analyticssteps.com/blogs/how-artificial-intelligence-ai-making-tiktok-tick

5. Oracle Autonomous Database; Oracle; https://www.oracle.com/uk/autonomous-database/

6. Vitality: A data-driven approach to better health; Digital Initiative; https://digital.hbs.edu/platform-digit/submission/vitality-a-data-driven-approach-to-better-health/

CHAPTER 12
RIGHT TIME, RIGHT PLACE, RIGHT FOR YOU

The Rise of Micro-Moments and Personalization

The mass marketing strategies of the past are dying. In this age of hyper individualization, people want to feel special. They expect brands to understand and respond to their individual needs. They want something that's unique to them. And they want it fast.

To put it another way, your customers are craving a more meaningful, immediate connection with your brand. Which brings us to perhaps one of the most important trends in this book: the rise of micro-moments and personalization.

The Speed of Now

As we saw in Chapter 5, humans' average attention span is now worse than that of a goldfish. We're time-poor and bombarded with content all the time. And this means we need quick solutions. In this fast-paced, digital-first age, the challenge (and opportunity) for businesses is to pinpoint those exact moments when customers are looking for a specific thing (a product, information, or whatever), and then quickly give it to them. And I do mean quickly. The opportunity to serve customers what they're looking for may be just a few seconds – if you don't deliver, they'll move on to the next option. This is what Google refers to as "micro-moments" (also dubbed the "catch me in seconds" trend).

Introducing micro-moments

These intent-rich moments are when a person picks up a device because they want to know, do, or buy something or go somewhere. They may be looking for information on a topic, attempting to complete a task, looking to purchase something, or trying to find a local business,. Whatever it is they want, they want it now – and they'll be drawn to brands that can deliver. According to Accenture (which refers to micro-moments as "momentary markets"), 85 percent of executives agree real-time (or near real-time) delivery is the next big wave of competitive advantage.[1]

In other words, business success is no longer just about capturing markets; it's about capturing *moments*. Google says this means businesses need to:[2]

- **Be there** when those intent-rich moments occur (which means being able to anticipate those micro-moments for your target audience). To achieve this, your business may need to improve forecasting techniques, and may even need more data. And, of course, to be there at the right moment, you need to be connecting with customers through digital channels (see Chapter 10).

- **Be useful**, by serving up a relevant digital experience and quickly connecting people with what they're looking for.

- **Be accountable**, by creating a seamless experience across all channels, and measuring impact.

But identifying and delivering in these moments of need is just one side of the coin. Businesses must also combine this with *personalization* –customers don't just want their needs met instantly, but they also want to feel they're unique. (Seventy-one percent of consumers express frustration when they feel a shopping experience is impersonal.)[3] This means brands must catch customers when they need something most, and instantly meet that need, while providing a personalized experience (which may be through personalized search results, recommendations, customized products, or whatever). Think of it this way: personalization now means personalizing your offering for individuals *and moments*. And all on a large scale.

From mass production to mass personalization

Customers increasingly expect to shape the products and services they consume. According to Deloitte, the majority of consumers are not only willing to pay a 20 percent premium for a customized product or service, but they would also like to be actively involved in the process (for example, deciding how it should be personalized to them).[4] A simple example is buying a new car and choosing the options and accessories that best suit you. And now we can customize pretty much anything, from sneakers and skincare products to music playlists.

The challenge, of course, is that personalization contradicts the dominant business model of mass distribution of products or services at high volume. The good news is that technology exists to make personalization possible on a large scale. We have recommendation engines that can point customers to the products and services they're most likely to want. We have more data than ever before and the intelligent analytic solutions to turn that data into insights on what customers really want. We have product configuration tools that allow customers to decide what they want in a product. And with advances in manufacturing technology (including 3D printing), delivering customized products is becoming easier and more cost-effective. Therefore, the next wave of personalization coming our way is *mass personalization*, where customers can be offered a unique product or service at scale, profitably.

(As an aside, marketing, too, is transitioning from mass marketing to hyper-individualized activities, with the potential side effect of the end of traditional customer segments and personas. We shall see.)

Another big challenge around personalizing products and services is data privacy. Personalization can come off as creepy (case in point: the oft-mentioned example of Target predicting that a teenage customer was pregnant and then sending her personalized offers, before she had informed her family). So organizations must strike a delicate balance. They need to create trust, so that the customer is happy to hand over some data without feeling like Big Brother is watching them. One of the best ways to do this is to be transparent about what data you're collecting, and why – and demonstrate value in return. As a customer, I'm happy for a company to use some of my data, if it means I get a better, more personalized service or product (that is genuinely useful) in return.

Let's explore some examples of organizations who are getting it right, and delivering a slick "right time, right place, right for you" experience.

Inspiring Examples of Personalized Services

Two potent examples of personalized services are Google's personalized search function and Netflix's personalized content recommendations. Both of these are driven by recommendation engines.

A quick look at recommendation engines

A recommendation engine is any system that suggests information, products, and services based on data about the user (age, gender, etc.), past activity (such as ratings, reviews and purchases), and the behavior of similar users ("people who bought X also bought Y"). Recommendation engines are an incredibly efficient way for businesses to provide customers with personalized products, services, and information – and generally provide a better, more meaningful user experience.

Based on the amount of data Google now has about most of us, it can go way beyond a traditional web search engine (which yields results based on web ranking factors) and instead functions more as a recommendation engine, by serving up results based on what it knows about you. That means that if you and I both searched the same keyword or phrase on Google, we would see quite different results come up, because

Google bases its results on factors like demographics, location, interests, and search history.

Netflix is another great example of this in action. When you log into Netflix, the system serves up a handy selection of content that you're likely to enjoy, based on things you've watched previously (and whether you watched it all the way through), and what similar viewers have enjoyed. Netflix even personalizes the thumbnail images that you see for each series or movie – in theory, showing an image most likely to grab your attention. Take the movie *Good Will Hunting* as an example. If you watch a lot of comedies, you might be presented with a thumbnail showing Robin Williams. But if you're more of a romance fan, your thumbnail might show a still of Matt Damon and Minnie Driver gazing lovingly at each other. (This has landed the streaming giant in hot water in the past for allegedly serving up thumbnails based on ethnicity – for example, showing a black viewer a thumbnail with a black character, who it turns out has only a minor role in the movie.)[5]

But there's no doubt the recommendation engine helps Netflix deliver an experience that's personalized to each user. And it works – 80 percent of Netflix content watched is discovered through the recommendation system.[6] According to estimates, this saves Netflix around a billion dollars a year in cancelled subscriptions because, well, fewer people want to cancel.[7]

Let's explore some other examples of companies successfully deploying personalized recommendations and services.

Personalized news and video feeds from ByteDance

ByteDance is the company behind TikTok – the video sharing app beloved by people much younger than me – and Toutiao – a cross between a search engine and a social media platform that delivers a continuous, personalized stream of content to hundreds of millions of users every day.

What's special about Toutiao in particular is you don't have to "like" anything for the system to learn your preferences; the AI simply learns what you like by tracking what you read (and how long you spend reading those items). It then provides more of the same sort of content, so your entire news feed is customized perfectly for you. Of course, there are problems with this approach – not least the danger of people getting more entrenched in their "bubbles" (see Chapter 1) – but it goes to show how anything, even news, can become personalized.

Facebook's highly targeted ads

Facebook is another one of those companies that knows a lot about you. And because the social network has so much personal data on users, it's able to target super-specific audiences with ads – a service that it sells to advertisers. The platform can tell, for example, whether you're feeling down that day, whether you're a newlywed, or even weird stuff like whether you're friends with expats. The company has also developed an algorithm that can predict when a consumer is likely to switch from one product brand to another – information that's pure gold for advertisers.[8]

This all makes sense because Facebook is able to gather masses of data on its users. But what if you're not a tech giant and you don't have access to such detailed personal information? As these next examples show, personalization is still possible.

Pull&Bear: How to pull off a personalized experience without data

Clothing retailer Pull&Bear takes an interesting navigational approach to personalized recommendations. In other words, it's not based on what the company already knows about customers (which is only possible when you have personal data) but is instead based on what the customer says and does at that moment. So, when a new visitor arrives at the company's website, they're first asked whether they want to browse women's or men's clothing, then the site continues to personalize the browsing experience from there. User choices can be remembered for future browsing, but it's not essential, and the experience becomes even more personalized if a user creates an account and buys products. I love how this example proves you don't need masses of user data in order to provide a personalized customer experience from the first touchpoint.

Vivino wine app: The Netflix for wine

"Digital sommelier" Vivino, the largest wine e-commerce platform in the world, has a mobile app that is more Netflix than wine shop. Users can simply take a photo of a bottle of wine via the app to see pricing, reviews, and tasting notes – and, crucially, get personalized Netflix-style recommendations on whether they're likely to enjoy the wine. This recommendation feature, called Match For You, is available once a user has rated five wines on the app (and gets more accurate the more you rate). Basically, judging by past purchases and preferences, you see a customized percentage match for each wine you view, instead of just the general Vivino rating for each wine. Vivino saw a 157 percent increase in wine sales during the pandemic,[9] and it's this additional data that has allowed the company to launch its Netflix-style recommendations.

Personalized insurance

These days, insurance arguably straddles both products and services, but let me cover it here, before we move on to personalized products. A whopping 90 percent of insurers agree the integration of customization is the next big wave of competitive advantage in insurance.[10] But how does personalized insurance work? A great example comes from Vitality Health, which provides customers with a personalized Vitality Age and recommendations on how to live a healthier life (circle back to Chapter 11 for more on this use case). Another way is by allowing people to easily purchase insurance "add-ons" as and when they need them – for example, adding maternity coverage to a health insurance policy for the duration of a pregnancy only. Health insurance provider Bind offers precisely this kind of personalized, on-demand health insurance plans.

As an aside, healthcare itself will also become more personalized, thanks to technology such as digital twins, the IoT, and AI. (Circle back to Chapter 4 for more on this.)

Personalization in Products

It's not just services that are becoming increasingly personalized. A wide range of products can also be customized to suit your needs. Let's look at some of my favorite examples.

Nike's customized sneakers

The Nike By You feature allows sneaker fans to customize certain Nike designs. The customer starts by choosing a shoe, then they can personalize it with unique colorways and even personalized text. As 3D printing scales up, it will be possible to offer even more customized products on demand, challenging the traditional mass-production approach.

Bespoke beauty and skincare products

From apps and web experiences to in-person consultations, beauty and skincare brands are now offering a variety of ways for customers to personalize their products, based on skin type, problem areas, and beauty goals. For example, Skin Inc's signature product My Daily Dose allows consumers to build a custom skin serum from three different "boosters" that can be mixed and matched according to what the skin needs most at that time of day or night. Similarly, Clinique iD offers three base formulas for type of moisturizer, then combines that with five different boosters that address different skincare concerns, such as fine lines or uneven skin tone.

Mackmyra reserve: Your own personal whiskey

Swedish whiskey maker Mackmyra offers whiskey lovers a unique opportunity to create their own personal 30-liter cask of whiskey and follow it through maturation to final bottling. Everything from the whiskey's final odor, color, and flavor to the type of cask and maturation period can be customized – and you can even be there when the cask is filled and visit your cask during the maturation period. The company already has around 10,000 cask owners and co-owners who are looking forward to supping their personalized single malt.[11]

Increasing personalization is also opening up new revenue streams for businesses – in particular, the opportunity to create ongoing revenue through subscription services. Let's see how companies of all shapes and sizes are applying the "Netflix approach" in their field.

PRACTICAL LESSONS

Let's finish with some final takeaways from this chapter:

- Across both products and services, the successful businesses of the future will be those that can identify consumers' momentary needs as they happen, and respond to those needs with personalized solutions.

- Achieving this will likely involve some investment in new technology and tools that can forecast demand. It may even potentially mean rethinking the manufacturing process to be more agile.

- Remember, personalization can come off as creepy, so it's vital you take a privacy-conscious approach. For me, this means being transparent about what data you're gathering, giving customers the chance to opt out where possible, and making sure you offer real value in return.

Notes

1. The Post-Digital Era Is Upon Us; Accenture; https://www.accenture.com/_acnmedia/PDF-94/Accenture-TechVision-2019-Tech-Trends-Report.pdf#zoom=50

2. The Basics of Micro-Moments; Think with Google; https://www.thinkwithgoogle.com/consumer-insights/consumer-journey/micro-moments-understand-new-consumer-behavior/

3. The Post-Digital Era Is Upon Us; Accenture; https://www.accenture.com/_acnmedia/PDF-94/Accenture-TechVision-2019-Tech-Trends-Report.pdf#zoom=50

4. Made to order: The rise of mass personalization; Deloitte; https://www2.deloitte.com/content/dam/Deloitte/ch/Documents/consumer-business/ch-en-consumer-business-made-to-order-consumer-review.pdf

5. Film fans see red over Netflix "targeted" posters for black viewers; Guardian; https://www.theguardian.com/media/2018/oct/20/netflix-film-black-viewers-personalised-marketing-target

6. This is how Netflix's top secret recommendation system works; Wired; https://www.wired.co.uk/article/how-do-netflixs-algorithms-work-machine-learning-helps-to-predict-what-viewers-will-like

7. A simple way to explain the Recommendation Engine in AI; Medium; https://medium.com/voice-tech-podcast/a-simple-way-to-explain-the-recommendation-engine-in-ai-d1a609f59d97

8. Facebook's Targeted Ads Are More Complex Than It Lets On; Wired; https://www.wired.com/story/facebooks-targeted-ads-are-more-complex-than-it-lets-on/

9. How digital sommelier Vivino is becoming a Netflix for wine; Fortune; https://fortune.com/2021/01/30/vivino-virtual-digital-sommelier-buying-wine-online/

10. MR Markets: Meeting needs at the speed of now; Accenture; https://insuranceblog.accenture.com/my-markets-meeting-needs-at-the-speed-of-now

11. Mackmyra reserve; https://mackmyra.com/whisky/mackmyra-reserve/

CHAPTER 13
SUBSCRIPTION AND SERVITIZATION
The As-a-Service Revolution

To me, this is one of the most important trends in this book. Driven by the increasing cognification of products and services, organizations of all kinds can now delight their customers with thoughtful subscription-based services and products. This trend is all about moving from a traditional business model where the customer buys a product or service as and when they need it, to one where they sign up to receive that product or service on a regular basis. The customer benefits from convenient auto-renewals, and builds a deeper connection with the brands they love (see Chapter 12). Meanwhile, the business generates predictable revenue – because, so long as you continue to provide value for the customer, they will continue to pay for it – and enjoys all the business benefits that come with boosting customer engagement.

A subscription or servitization business can be defined as any business that sells its products or services on a scheduled basis (such as monthly), thereby generating recurring revenue. Apple is a great example of a company that has transitioned from a straightforward product manufacturer to a subscription business – from iPhones and iPads and Apple Watches to services like Apple News, Apple TV, and Apple Music. This is something appearing across all markets now. Even something like mobility is now being offered as a service (Chapter 8).

In the future, we'll hardly own anything at all. Everything from cars, phones, clothes, music, and movies, to housing and even the roads that we drive on will all be offered "as a service." However you feel about that on a personal level, there's no denying it creates a great opportunity for businesses. In fact, research shows that subscription businesses achieve five times faster revenue growth than the S&P 500.[1]

In this chapter we'll look at four key subscription/servitization models:

- Streaming/content services

- Technology as a service

- Subscription boxes

- Products with added subscription services

Streaming/Content Services

For obvious reasons, this is also often referred to as the "Netflix model." Netflix may not have invented streaming or the subscription business model, but they certainly brought it to the masses. An astonishing 46 percent of customers already pay for an online streaming service, and in many cases, that means Netflix.[2]

With this subscription model, the organization provides content that subscribers can access anywhere, anytime via a channel or platform. But this doesn't just apply to movies and TV. Other examples might include online learning courses, online fitness or yoga classes, music streaming services, and e-book subscription services, like Kindle Unlimited. One thing that often keeps Netflix customers (and other content subscribers) coming back for more is personalized recommendations on what to watch/read/listen to next – meaning this trend is inextricably linked with the personalization trend (see Chapter 12) and cognification (see Chapter 11).

At the start of this chapter, I mentioned Apple as a company that has successfully repositioned itself as a subscription business. Let's explore that in a little more detail.

Where Apple leads, others will follow

For several years now, Apple has been gradually migrating much of its business toward subscription-based services. That's not to say Apple will stop selling devices like the iPhone – just that they have recognized the importance of recurring revenue.

Apple's services division – which includes things like Apple Music, Apple Fitness+, Apple Pay, Apple News, and Apple TV – has grown so much in recent years, it generated $15.76 billion in the first quarter of 2021, and is now second only to the revenue generated by iPhone sales.[3] In other words, Apple services already bring in more revenue than iPad sales.

And in 2020, Apple announced that it would be making subscriptions more accessible by allowing customers to bundle up to six services together into one monthly subscription, called Apple One. The company is also reportedly toying with the idea of hardware-and-service combos (more on this product plus add-on subscription model later in the chapter).[4]

The evolution of Amazon Prime

What started as a free shipping service for an annual fee has now blossomed into a service that includes Prime Video, Prime Music, Audible books, and more. And this recurring revenue is crucial for Amazon because its retail model wasn't hugely profitable. But with Prime customers paid up for a year at a time, the business benefits from predictable revenue and improved profit margins – because Prime customers spend more money on Amazon than non-Prime members (between double and quadruple more, in fact).[5] What's more, customer retention is high because, once they've had a taste, customers are loathe to give up their Prime benefits. Of customers who accept the free 30-day trial, 73 percent convert to paying Prime customers, and 91 percent go on to renew their Prime membership for the following year.[6] What business wouldn't be happy with retention stats like that?

Technology as a Service

With advances in cloud computing and AI have come a whole raft of providers offering technology solutions on a subscription basis.

Software and cloud computing as a service

"As a service" is now the go-to business model for software and computing providers. With this model, the vendor provides access to software (through a cloud interface) or computing infrastructure (such as cloud storage) for a monthly or annual fee. So instead of purchasing hardware and software outright, and then having to purchase new versions as and when needed, the customer pays for continued access to the tools they need. For customers, this delivers many advantages:

- It offers easy access to technology solutions, often without the need for in-house expertise.

- Scalable solutions flex as the company's needs change.

- It saves the hassle of buying, installing, maintaining, and upgrading software and hardware (because the vendor manages it all at their end).

- Applications are accessible anywhere in the world.

- Better security: with data in the cloud, there's no single point of failure.

Key examples of software and computing as a service offerings include Salesforce, Amazon Web Services, Microsoft Azure, Google Cloud, and Alibaba Cloud, to name just a few.

AI as a Service (AIaaS)

Those businesses I just mentioned also offer AIaaS, meaning that customers have easy access to AI tools like facial recognition, natural language processing, natural language generation, advanced analytics, and more. Often, these can simply be switched on and off, like an optional extra, giving businesses of all shapes, sizes, and expertise access to AI tools without the expensive price tag. IBM is a major player in the AIaaS game. The company's Watson platform offers a wide range of business-ready tools and, crucially, users can ask questions in natural language (no coding expertise required). As more organizations recognize that AI is critical to meeting customer needs (indeed, it underpins so many of the trends in this book), demand for AIaaS will skyrocket.

Robots on subscription?

Yes, now we even have robotics as a service (Raas), where companies can literally hire a robot to complete a task (either a real physical robot or, in the case of robotic process automation, software robots). The RaaS market is growing rapidly, with an estimated 1.3 million installations of RaaS by 2026 (making it a $34 billion market).[7] Companies like Amazon, Google, Microsoft, and even Honda are all getting in on the RaaS act.

But what does RaaS mean in practice? Obvious use cases come from the manufacturing sector, where the ability to have robots on subscription could revolutionize the production process. But let's look at a rather more unusual example.

Startup Trombia Technologies has developed an autonomous robotic street sweeper service called Trombia Free that local governments can subscribe to and have up and running the next day. Think of it as a bit like a Roomba home vacuum device, but for city streets! The company says its street sweeper – which is designed to operate autonomously in all weather conditions – will offer a more cost-efficient, easier, and faster alternative for sweeping paved areas. And best of all, it's more sustainable, using less than 15 percent of the power used by traditional heavy suction street sweeping technologies.[8] I love this example because it pulls together so many strands from this book, such as self-driving technology, servitization, and sustainability.

Meanwhile, in the case of robotic process automation, there may not be a physical robot involved at all – rather software "bots," typically accessed via a cloud solution, are used to automate processes that are rules-based, structured, and repetitive. In one example, a large consumer and commercial bank used 85 software bots to run 13 processes that handled 1.5 million requests in a year. This allowed the bank to add capacity that equaled 230 full-time employees at just about 30 percent of the cost of recruiting more staff.[9]

Subscription Boxes

So far we've talked mostly about service subscriptions. But what about products? With the subscription box business model, pretty much any product type – no matter how niche – can be offered as a subscription. Here, products are delivered direct to the customer's door (in a box, hence the name), on a regular basis. Often there is some sort of customization element involved, where the contents of the box can be personalized to the customer's preferences, habits, previously liked products, and so on. And customers may have the choice to preselect these items themselves or have them chosen for them (i.e., surprise or mystery boxes).

Let's look at some of my favorite examples of subscription boxes.

Hunt a Killer Mystery Box Subscription

This murder mystery game turns quiz nights into something a little bit more immersive and unusual. Every box contains beautifully designed clues and information to help at-home detectives solve the latest murder mystery.

Flex: Feminine Hygiene Subscription

Instead of picking up feminine hygiene products at the store, Flex customers receive a personalized monthly box of Flex feminine hygiene products delivered to their door every two months. Packages are customized according to the customer's cycle, flow, and lifestyle, and members get access to expert advice via phone, chat, and text.

Blacksocks: Sock Subscriptions for the Busy Businessman

Socks on subscription? It may sound a bit daft, but if you go through socks like I do, and find shopping for socks to be one of the most boring retail experiences going, it kind of makes sense. Step forward Blacksocks, which will deliver socks to your door once or three or four times a year, depending on your preference. Primarily aimed at businessmen, the service has now expanded to include underwear, T-shirts, and shirts. If this example doesn't show you that pretty much any product can be offered as a subscription, I don't know what will.

Stitch Fix: Intelligent fashion

Stitch Fix is a great example of how you can combine the subscription model with AI to create an intelligent subscription offering. Customers detail their size, style preferences, and lifestyle in a questionnaire (they can also link to their Pinterest account). Then, using AI, the system preselects clothes that will fit and suit the customer, and a (human) personal stylist chooses the best options from that preselected list. And voilà, the perfect clothes for you arrive every month. If you don't like or need an item, you simply return it, and the system learns more about what you do and don't want for the future.

YCloset: Clothing rentals in China

In the future, maybe we won't even need to own clothes. Not if companies like YCloset take off. Operating out of a massive warehouse in Nantong, China, the company offers women access to an endlessly rotating wardrobe of clothes for a flat monthly fee. Customers simply select clothes via the platform's app, then send them back after they're finished wearing them. The clothes are then cleaned, ready for the next customer to rent. With 20 million registered users, YCloset provides an interesting glimpse of the future of fashion.

Birchbox Beauty Boxes

For just $15 per month, Birchbox, a leading beauty box subscription service, will send you the latest beauty products. Customers answer questions online to get boxes that are tailored to their needs and beauty goals.

Craft Gin Club: "Mother's Ruin" Direct to Your Door Every Month

The UK's largest subscription club for gin lovers, Craft Gin Club selects the best small-batch gins for you every month (or two or three months, if preferred). Every box contains a full-size bottle of craft gin, plus selected mixers, snacks, and an accompanying magazine.

Dollar Shave Club: Cheaper Grooming Products on Subscription

Launched in 2011, Dollar Shave Club has expanded from razor blades to other grooming products, such as shave butter and antiperspirant – basically, anything men need for their personal grooming conveniently delivered to the home. Customers become a member of the club when they buy the first product from the company, and with free shipping and low prices, customers are incentivized to remain a member.

Products with an Add-on Subscripton

Increasingly, when you invest in a product, you can tap into additional services available as a subscription. A great example is the Amazon Ring home security camera that I mentioned in Chapter 11. With the Ring Protect paid-for plan, you can store footage from Ring cameras and access them 24/7, whereas without the paid-for plan, the system will not store any recorded footage – it will just notify you when motion is detected and let you view the footage in real time.

Let's explore a couple of quick examples of products with add-on subscriptions.

Google Nest Aware: One Subscription for All Your Nest Home Security Devices

If you're more of a Google person than an Amazon person, the Nest Aware paid-for subscription service will be up your street. While Google used to ask customers to pay for added services on a per-device basis (meaning per camera, speaker, or display), it has now simplified this to one subscription covering all devices. The subscription includes 30 or 60 days of storage for videos where the cameras have detected motion, and 24/7 video recording is available as an optional extra.

Peloton: Fitness Hardware and Subscriptions

You've probably seen the adverts. You buy a Peloton connected indoor cycle or treadmill, then, thanks to a monthly subscription service, have access to virtual group workout sessions, viewed on the bike's or treadmill's built-in touchscreen monitor. Peloton's products aren't cheap, yet the company has been able grow quarterly sales by 128% during 2021, giving it quarterly sales of over $1 billion[10] – largely because of the value added by the exclusive sports and fitness content, which at $49 a month for All Access Membership compares very favorably to gym membership prices. Other fitness brands are now getting in on the act, including ProForm, which sells similar bikes for less than half the price of Peloton.

In the future, I can see all kinds of products being delivered with an "as a service" option. One major construction company that I work with is even exploring the idea of "roads as a service." So, rather than a normal road-building contract where they get paid to build the road and that's it, the construction company would own or co-own the roads they build, and then maintain those roads on a subscription basis for the government or local authority. It's a pretty mind-blowing idea, but they clearly sense the magnitude of this trend and are rethinking their business accordingly.

PRACTICAL LESSONS

Whether you're a product or service business, the subscription trend is absolutely relevant to your business. Here are some key things to bear in mind about this trend:

- Literally any business can migrate to a subscription model, and with demand for smarter, more personalized products and services on the rise, customers will increasingly turn to subscriptions to meet their everyday needs.

- When thinking about applying this trend in your business, start by considering your goals. Do you, for example, want to grow revenue, reach more customers, improve customer retention? Your goals will inform pricing structure and what exactly you offer on subscription.

- If you want to acquire and keep customers, it's vital the customer experience is excellent. Ask yourself, how will you add real value for customers and ensure they can't bear to quit your subscription? Think of Amazon Prime's impressive customer retention.

- You'll absolutely need a reliable, seamless, and simple subscription billing system. If it's too complicated, customers will look elsewhere.

There's an interesting side effect of the subscription business model: middlemen can be completely taken out of the equation. Blacksocks, for example, is able to bypass retailers and wholesalers to build a direct relationship with consumers. This leads right into an exploration of another key business trend.

Notes

1. Subscription Business Model: 10 Amazing Industry Examples; Gary Fox; https://www.garyfox.co/subscription-business-model/

2. Thinking inside the subscription box; McKinsey & Company; https://www .mckinsey.com/industries/technology-media-and-telecommunications/ our-insights/thinking-inside-the-subscription-box-new-research-on- ecommerce-consumers

3. Apple's revenue from iTunes, software and services from 1st quarter 2013 to 1st quarter 2021; Statista; https://www.statista.com/statistics/250918/ apples-revenue-from-itunes-software-and-services/

4. What You Need to Know About Apple's New Subscription Packages; Forbes; https://www.forbes.com/sites/vidhichoudhary/2020/08/13/what-you- need-to-know-about-apples-new-subscription-packages/?sh= 2dd82a642916

5. What the Amazon Subscription Model Can Show Entrepreneurs; Minute Hack; https://minutehack.com/opinions/what-the-amazon-subscription- model-can-show-entrepreneurs

6. What the Amazon Subscription Model Can Show Entrepreneurs; Minute Hack; https://minutehack.com/opinions/what-the-amazon-subscription- model-can-show-entrepreneurs

7. Manufacturing: How Robotics as a Service extends to whole factories; Internet of Business; https://internetofbusiness.com/how-robotics-as-a- service-is-extending-to-whole-factories-analysis/

8. Trombia Free autonomous street sweeper launched by Trombia Technolo- gies; The Robot Report; https://www.therobotreport.com/trombia-free- autonomous-street-sweeper-launched/

9. 10 Amazing Examples of Robotic Process Automation in Practice; Bernard Marr; https://bernardmarr.com/default.asp?contentID=1909

10. Peloton Quarterly Sales; CNBC; https://www.cnbc.com/2021/02/04/ peloton-pton-reports-q2-2021-earnings.html

CHAPTER 14
CUTTING OUT
THE MIDDLEMEN

How Brands Are Going Direct
to the Consumer

This trend has been going on for a while now, with brands across all sectors finding new, direct routes to customers via online channels (see channel digitization in Chapter 10). I believe all businesses must consider how they can build new ways to connect directly with their customers. And for intermediary organizations, such as banks and retailers, this trend obviously represents a significant challenge. These intermediaries – who have been quite powerful in the past – are being pushed out of the equation, which means middlemen organizations of all kinds must begin to assess the potential impact of this trend on their business.

Delving into the Direct-to-Consumer Trend

Also known as *disintermediation*, the direct-to-consumer (DTC) trend essentially means bypassing traditional intermediaries in the supply chain – such as retailers, wholesalers, distributors, and advertisers – to connect directly with the end consumer. DTC channels are nothing new; think of farmers selling their wares at farmers' markets while also working with retailers. The difference now is that there's a whole new swathe of businesses skipping the middlemen altogether, with the Dollar Shave Club (see Chapter 13) being a great example. And as well as new businesses springing up to sell directly to customers, established brands such as L'Oréal and Disney are also embracing the DTC trend.

Why is this trend so potent? One word: online. These days, customers head online to purchase everything from groceries and household items, to clothes and medicine, to flights and vacations. This means it's easier than ever for middlemen retailers and other businesses who have traditionally facilitated this customer journey to be eliminated.

Naturally, DTC poses some challenges for organizations. For example:

- It can add to some business costs, such as marketing and distribution (while reducing other costs, it's fair to say).

- It requires a strong, authentic brand, often with some sort of sustainability vibe (see Chapters 17, 18, and 22). Communicating your brand's mission, values, and sustainability is critical for building lasting customer relationships.

- It requires a digital-first mindset and strong online presence, often including an app. What's more, the digital customer experience must be seamless (see Chapter 10).

- Plus, this strategy runs the risk of alienating sometimes long-standing relationships with middlemen channels. Businesses must strike a balance by investing in DTC routes while still keeping existing partnerships alive.

On the flip side, DTC brings a number of business advantages, including these:

- There's no need to negotiate with third parties. For startups this can be particularly appealing because getting a foot in the door with big retailers can be a significant barrier to entry.

- You have total control over your brand image and the customer experience (as opposed to brands selling through retailers, who may have little control over how their product is presented and sold).

- Costs are reduced in some areas, potentially allowing you to price more aggressively.

- You get more of the profit, since there are no middlemen taking a cut.

- You build a better understanding of customers because, when you sell direct, you can gather valuable customer data. This can be used to upsell more products and services, improve your offering, and create personalized solutions (see Chapter 12).

There are advantages for the customer as well. As we saw in Chapter 12, customers increasingly seek a more personal connection with brands, and buying directly from brands helps to foster that connection. Buying direct from brands also cuts out a lot of the baffling choices that consumers are faced with when they go to a middleman retailer (who may have hundreds or thousands of products to choose from), creating a smoother buying experience. So perhaps it's no surprise that 81 percent of consumers in the US said they planned to buy from a DTC brand by 2023.[1]

DTC Products in Action

Let's look at some of my favorite examples of brands building strong DTC channels.

Tesla: Buying a car "the Amazon Way"

In 2020, 45 percent of people under 35 said they were considering buying a car, and this younger demographic is clearly fueling a desire for digital car-buying experiences – 46 percent of consumers said they would rather search for and buy cars online than go to a dealership.[2] We're so used to buying everything we want online. Why shouldn't that extend to cars? For automakers, this poses a tantalizing opportunity to sell DTC.

In the US, many states restrict the ability of automakers to sell to consumers, but Tesla is one manufacturer that seems to have gotten around these rules successfully. Today, you can easily buy a Tesla directly online (you can even pay with Bitcoin). Watch as more manufacturers follow suit, in the US and around the world. Indeed, I work with a large car retailer group that sells cars through showrooms, and they are already considering how this trend will threaten their business.

Warby Parker and DTC eyewear

The traditional glasses-buying experience isn't great. You go to a physical store and spend ages trying on multiple different frames, while an assistant follows you around. Warby Parker eliminated this hassle by letting customers try on eyeglasses and sunglasses at home – by selecting multiple pairs to try, then returning the ones they didn't want. This in itself was revolutionary, but Warby Parker upped its DTC game even further by introducing a virtual try-on solution using the iPhone X. Warby Parker's augmented reality app, which uses Apple's Face ID function, scans your face to recommend frames that will best suit you, then digitally superimposes the frames onto the image of your face so you can see how they'll look in real life.

BarkBox: Pet treats on subscription

I love this example because it brings together the DTC trend and the servitization trend from Chapter 13. Aimed at urban dog owners, BarkBox provides dog toys, treats, and goodies as a subscription service – with prepacked, themed monthly boxes. Crucially, BarkBox has built a community of customers who advocate for the brand online; at the time of writing there were more than 700k Instagram posts under #dogsofBark, and the brand donates 10% of proceeds to animal shelters. Indeed, many DTC brands cultivate a strong ethical, charitable, and/or sustainable stance, which helps to attract and retain a loyal community of customers.

DTC mattresses

Mattress shops could be a thing of the past, as more mattress brands embrace DTC channels. In 2019, 45 percent of mattresses sold were purchased online, with 12 percent of those coming from DTC brands – and this will only increase.[3] One cool example comes from mattress brand Casper, which eradicates the overwhelming choice of mattresses (soft, firm, semi-firm, gel, foam, hybrid) to provide one mattress that's reportedly perfect for everyone. The brand worked with social media influencers like Kylie Jenner to promote the brand and boost sales.

Another DTC mattress brand is My Green Mattress, created by founder Tim Masters, who was struggling to buy an all-natural, eco mattress for his allergy-stricken daughter. Today, My Green Mattress handcrafts certified organic mattresses from organic cotton, wool, and latex – meaning they're free of the chemicals often found in mattresses – and manufactures these mattresses in an environmentally and socially responsible way. This ties in with yet another key business trend: conscious consumption (see Chapter 17).

Disney goes DTC

Disney is a great example of an established brand that's investing heavily in a DTC strategy. Instead of relying on streaming services and cinemas to distribute its content, Disney has built its own content distribution platform, Disney+. And in 2020, the company announced it was reorganizing its media and entertainment division around Disney+, essentially making DTC streaming Disney's primary entertainment focus.[4]

Gymshark and Nike: DTC sportswear

Fitness apparel and accessories brand Gymshark is one of the fastest-growing businesses in the UK, expanding from a one-man, one-sewing-machine business operating out of a garage to a £100 million business in less than a decade.[5] For Gymshark, selling DTC has allowed the brand to leapfrog traditional barriers to entry, lower the cost of failure, and innovate more quickly (avoiding the "analysis paralysis" that traditional brands often face). Which demonstrates how DTC can be a powerful route for new businesses to exploit.

But what about established brands? Nike shows it is possible for traditional brands to pivot to a DTC model. The footwear and fitness brand has been significantly upping its digital offerings over the last few years, with e-commerce initiatives, mobile experiences, and customized products (see Chapter 12). The pandemic only accelerated Nike's e-commerce drive, and led to DTC sales accounting for 33 percent of revenues in 2020, compared to 13 percent a decade ago.[6] In other words, DTC hasn't been an overnight success at Nike – rather a steady and ongoing push, but one that's clearly paying off. Interestingly, the brand has also been investing in its own smaller neighborhood retail premises called Nike Live, which serve as pickup hubs, and huge flagship retail spots called House of Innovation.

DTC beauty products with L'Oréal

L'Oréal's tech incubator lab has played a central role in building DTC links. Launched in 2012, the incubator is responsible for innovations such as an app that lets customers virtually test eye shadows, and Perso, a smart device that lets customers tailor their own skincare formulations, foundations, and lipsticks at home (and virtually try new formulas via an accompanying app). Crucially, innovations like this allow the company to build direct relationships with customers and gather valuable data across more than 1.3 billion data points.[7] To put it another way, L'Oréal is taking back control of customer data from store retailers – and building recurring revenue at the same time. The company expects 50 percent of sales to come from e-commerce channels by 2023.[8]

The Blockchain Threat to Middlemen Service Providers

It's important to note that we're not just talking about DTC products here. Middlemen service providers like banks will also be threatened by this trend. Consider a money transfer between two friends – if they each bank with a separate bank, then there are two middlemen involved in this simple transaction. But with a money transfer app (see Chapter 9), this customer journey is massively streamlined.

Blockchain is one technology in particular that could threaten many traditional middleman businesses – not just banks, but also lawyers, real estate agents, insurance brokers, and more. Because blockchain facilitates peer-to-peer transactions, it may even threaten some of the newly introduced middlemen platform businesses that have sprung up, such as Uber, Airbnb, and Spotify. (Read more about platform businesses in Chapter 15.)

I talked more about blockchain technology back in Chapter 2, so I won't go into the technical stuff here. But suffice to say that blockchain is gaining traction in many industries, and is slowly beginning to reshape supply chain structures, which means it ties in perfectly with this DTC trend.

A key feature of most blockchain technology is its decentralized nature, meaning no single entity owns the records on the blockchain (whether transaction records, smart contracts, or whatever) and all relevant parties can access the information they need whenever. This reduces the need for intermediaries to facilitate transactions and transfer information (or goods) between the relevant parties. In all kinds of transactions, this could reduce transaction costs and inefficiencies, and eliminate human error.

The blockchain threat is so real, many established middlemen industries are embracing blockchain as a way to improve their service and provide greater value for customers. Let's look at a few quick examples:

- Blockchain-based marine hull insurance platform Insurwave is the result of a collaboration between companies like ACORD, A.P. Moller-Maersk Group, and Microsoft. The platform was projected to facilitate 500,000 automated transactions in its first 12 months. But is also provides real-time info such as ship location and safety hazards to insurers and insurees; for example, if a vessel enters a high-risk area, the system detects this and factors it into insurance calculations.[9]

- Financial institutions like Western Union and Santander have partnered with blockchain provider Ripple to improve cross-border payments. Ripple's xCurrent blockchain product provides banks with a two-way communication protocol that allows real-time messaging and settlement.[10]

- Russia-based S7 Airlines uses blockchain-based smart contracts to issue and sell tickets. Not only does this improve security and convenience, but it has also reduced airline/agent settlement times from 14 days to 23 seconds![11]

Blockchain is so powerful because it effectively transforms material information and goods into digital tokens. And when you think of it like that, pretty much anything can be traded or facilitated using blockchain. Just look at the non-fungible token trend – used to trade anything from photos and memorabilia to hugely expensive artworks (see Sophia the Robot, Chapter 10). Among other things, this could forever alter the music industry, by removing existing intermediaries like Spotify and allowing artists to trade directly with fans. Take blockchain-based platform Opus as an example. Through smart contracts, artists can be paid directly upon the purchase or stream of their music (or receive a share of the ad revenue from freemium users), thereby increasing the amount of royalties that artists receive.[12]

The Contradiction That Is Reintermediation

If disintermediation (DTC) is one side of the coin, *reintermediation* – or the introduction of new intermediaries into the supply chain – is the flip side. (Remember I said in Chapter 1 how some of the trends in this book are contradictory? This is a perfect example.)

Alongside the growth in DTC channels, we're also seeing new intermediaries enter the market to facilitate transactions and interactions between suppliers and customers. Take Deliveroo or DoorDash as an example. These online food delivery companies partner with restaurants to take care of the whole takeaway process for them – customers order through the Deliveroo or DoorDash app, then a driver collects the food from the restaurant and drops it at their door. This is great because it allows more restaurants to offer a delivery service when they might not otherwise have the infrastructure or funds to do so. There's no need to hire drivers or invest in a delivery vehicle – the delivery company will take care of it all. In this case, it's more efficient and cost-effective to work with an intermediary than to try and go it alone.

Sometimes, though, this reintermediation can work in tandem with disintermediation. For example, news outlet the Guardian has been building its own DTC channel for years, through its app, subscription revenue, and donations. But it also works with news aggregator Apple News to distribute its content, showing how a blended approach can work well.

PRACTICAL LESSONS

Whether you're a product or service business, a supplier or the intermediary, you can be sure this trend will impact your business in one way or another. Here are some practical takeaways from this chapter:

- Intermediary companies must start to ask themselves, "What value are we offering for customers? Is this enough for them to stick with us? Will customers skip us altogether in future?"

- To build a successful DTC strategy, you need digital channels, a seamless customer experience, and a strong brand.

- Many successful DTC brands emphasize their eco, ethical, or charitable activities, and this can be a way to foster customer loyalty.

- Remember, DTC gives you valuable customer data, and this data can help you build a stronger business in future.

- And finally, the flip side of disintermediation (DTC) is reintermediation (the introduction of new middlemen platforms). The right way forward for your business may be a balanced approach that blends DTC channels with value-adding intermediary channels.

The dynamic between disintermediation and reintermediation is particularly interesting and leads us nicely on to the next chapter – the growth of platform businesses as a new kind of middleman.

Notes

1. 81 percent of consumers plan to shop direct-to-consumer brands; Retail Dive; https://www.retaildive.com/news/81-of-consumers-plan-to-shop-direct-to-consumer-brands/539087/

2. COVID-19 and the automotive consumer; Capgemini; https://www.capgemini.com/wp-content/uploads/2020/04/COVID-19-Automotive.pdf

3. DTC Mattress Brands Optimize Marketing Strategies with Eco-Friendly Options and Charitable Partnerships; DMS Insights; https://insights.digitalmediasolutions.com/articles/mattress-wars-2020

4. Disney says its "primary focus" for entertainment is streaming – announces a major reorg; CNBC; https://www.cnbc.com/2020/10/12/disney-reorganizes-to-focus-on-streaming-direct-to-consumer.html

5. Gymshark your business; WARC; https://www.warc.com/newsandopinion/news/gymshark-your-business/42699

6. Nike Plans Steady Digital Push in 2021 as Direct-to-Consumer Sales Grow; DMS Insights; https://insights.digitalmediasolutions.com/articles/nike-ecommerce-dtc-digital-sales

7. "Everything we do is about DTC": Inside L'Oréal's tech hub; Digiday; https://digiday.com/marketing/everything-dtc-inside-loreals-tech-hub/

8. L'Oréal eyes at-home tech market to accelerate its DTC plan; Digiday; https://digiday.com/media/loreal-eyes-at-home-tech-market/

9. Fascinating Examples of How Blockchain Is Used in Insurance, Banking and Travel; Forbes; https://www.forbes.com/sites/bernardmarr/2020/08/05/fascinating-examples-of-how-blockchain-is-used-in-insurance-banking-and-travel/

10. Banking Is Only the Beginning: 58 Big Industries Blockchain Could Transform; CB Insights; https://www.cbinsights.com/research/industries-disrupted-blockchain/

11. Ibid.

12. Blockchain to Disrupt Music Industry and Make It Change Tune; Coin-Telegraph; https://cointelegraph.com/news/blockchain-to-disrupt-music-industry-and-make-it-change-tune

CHAPTER 15
FROM B2C TO "ALL TO ALL"

The Rise of Platforms, the Sharing Economy, and Crowdsourcing

The customer-to-customer (C2C) economy – where customers connect with other customers to communicate or trade goods and services – has given rise to massive platform businesses, like Uber, Facebook, and Etsy. There is value in facilitating these interactions and transactions, after all, and those platforms that can create a safe, easy way for customers to connect have seen enormous growth. This is part of the reintermediation trend that I mentioned in the previous chapter, where new businesses have sprung up to facilitate connections between relevant parties. Crowdsourcing – the process of sourcing ideas, skills, and services from a large group of participants via the internet – is also part of this trend, because crowdsourcing is underpinned by platforms.

Even if your business isn't a platform business, it's worth paying attention to this trend. There may be an opportunity to pivot to a platform model, or introduce a new business built around a value-adding platform. Or you may want to take advantage of crowdsourcing to source ideas, tasks, or talent. Read on to learn how other organizations have capitalized on this fascinating trend.

The Platform Business Model

Look at a list of the world's most valuable companies, and I bet the majority of them will be platform businesses. (At the time of writing this chapter, for example, 6 of the 10 most valuable companies in the world were platform businesses: Apple, Alphabet, Amazon, Facebook, Tencent, and Alibaba.)

What is a platform business?

The platform business model revolves around facilitating exchanges between users (typically consumers and providers, although I will use the term "users" as a catch-all). The platform business doesn't typically create or own inventory, like a traditional business does. Rather, the asset is the platform itself (including proprietary software, user data, etc.).

The platform adds value by creating large networks of users that other users can tap into – whether it's a craftsperson looking to tap into a large pool of customers (Etsy), a freelancer looking for contract work (Fiverr), a driver looking to find people who need a ride (Uber), a business looking to target its adverts at specific customer groups (Google), or simply someone looking to connect with friends and like-minded folk (Facebook). Platforms, in other words, build *communities* and *markets* that users can access on demand.

(It's important to note that a company like Netflix, although it is often referred to as a "streaming platform," doesn't operate on a platform business model. It doesn't facilitate connections. It creates or licenses its own content for distribution, making it a traditional linear business with a fairly traditional supply chain. Therefore, not all digital-first businesses are platform businesses.)

As well as building a huge network, platforms create value by matching relevant users together, perhaps through recommendation engines. Platforms also ensure transactions and interactions take place in a safe, easy, and secure space, for example, by providing a payment mechanism, setting community rules and standards for users, and monitoring for offensive content.

Platform businesses aren't new. A shopping mall is effectively an old-school platform business because it connects retailers with consumers and facilitates a pleasant shopping environment. What's different about the new wave of powerful platform businesses is that the interactions and transactions are facilitated *online* – and, importantly, this means exchanges can be facilitated on a huge scale.

Examples of platform businesses

You've heard of the obvious platform businesses, like Facebook, Google, eBay, Twitter, Amazon, and the like. So let's take a whistle-stop tour through some platform businesses that you might not have heard of.

Winngie: A novel way to exchange money when abroad

Money transfer and foreign currency exchange platform Winngie allows travelers to find real people nearby to exchange money with, without banks and commission (which ties in with the trend of cutting out the middleman we looked at in Chapter 14). Aimed at foreign students, expats, businesspeople, and other international travelers, the platform also allows users to transfer money to family and friends back home.

Instacart: Connecting customers, grocery stores, and workers

Founded in 2012, Instacart builds on the channel digitization trend (see Chapter 10), where customers expect to buy anything online, including groceries. With the Instacart app, you select your favorite grocery store and the items you want to purchase, then an Instacart worker will go and buy those items for you and deliver them to your door in as little as one hour. Instacart allows customers across the US to shop online for groceries from a wide range of local stores, not just the huge supermarket chains, and to order from multiple stores at a time. And the platform allows smaller grocery stores to provide a delivery option without investing in their own e-commerce platform and delivery infrastructure.

Interestingly, Instacart has also created its own white-label enterprise product called Powered by Instacart, which allows shoppers to order groceries directly on the retailer's site, bypassing the Instacart site and giving grocery stores an easier way to connect directly with customers by leveraging Instacart's technology.

Instacart itself earns revenue through delivery fees, service fees, membership fees for Instacart Express (which provides unlimited free one-hour delivery), and marked-up prices on goods from certain retailers. And the workers who do the shopping earn a by-the-hour wage, and often a tip.

Github: The platform for software engineers

GitHub – which was acquired by Microsoft in 2018 for $7.5 billion – is essentially a collaboration platform for all things software, allowing software developers and other collaborators to manage their projects in one place. Users can store and edit their coding projects, collaborate with other developers, and track changes made to the project. Users can also purchase third-party tools as and when needed via GitHub's Marketplace (kind of like an app store), and stay up to date on best practices via educational materials and events. The company makes money through premium subscriptions for individuals and teams, and on fees when users buy third-party apps in the Marketplace.

GitHub has more than 50 million users, and has been adopted by 2.9 million organizations around the world who use the platform to manage their workflows.[1] The platform is so easy to use that it even attracts non-tech folks who want to collaborate on projects and track version control, such as authors working on books.

The Sharing Economy Is Here to Stay

The success of platform businesses like Uber and Airbnb shows that the sharing economy – in which people can access goods and services for short-term rentals – is thriving. And it's not just Western economies that are embracing the sharing economy. In India, for example, the sharing economy was on track to become a $2 billion industry in 2020.[2] The sharing economy is particularly popular in China, where 94 percent of people are willing to embrace shared goods and services.[3]

These days, it's possible to rent anything from a car to a house to a bike or a scooter for a short period of time, and there are many platform businesses out there that promise to facilitate these exchanges. Let's look at two of them.

Justpark: Matching drivers with parking spaces

Founded in London in 2006, JustPark reinvents parking by connecting people who have a spare driveway or allocated parking space with drivers who need somewhere to park. The app is so popular in the UK, it now helps more than 3.5 million drivers park at over 45,000 locations across the country.[4]

Zipcar: Moving from owning cars to sharing cars

Thanks to platforms like Zipcar, people living in cities or on college campuses have less and less need to own a car – rather, they can simply borrow one as and when needed. After all, public transport is great, but there are times when you just need a car – perhaps if you're collecting something heavy or going on a day tip. Borrowing a car for a short period every now and then is far cheaper than owning one, and is better for the environment (linking to the trend for conscious consumption; see Chapter 17).

Zipcar has been around since 2000, but has really taken off in recent years as the sharing economy has gathered speed. Today, Zipcar gives more than 1 million members access to over 12,000 vehicles in around 500 towns and cities across the world.[5] Members can access a car (or van) on demand, from around $7 an hour (depending on location), and gain easy access by simply tapping their app-based digital key against a reader located on the car's windshield.

I wanted to include this example because Zipcar is owned by car rental firm Avis Budget Group, which demonstrates that existing organizations can successfully add a platform business to their revenue stream.

Platforms Versus Blockchain

If platforms facilitate transactions and blockchain also facilitates transactions, you might be wondering what the difference is between the two. In very simple terms, platform businesses are, in essence, massive middlemen organizations. Many people have talked of Airbnb disrupting the travel industry by removing middlemen like travel agents, but in fact it's just replaced those previous middlemen with a new, more powerful middleman: Airbnb. Blockchain, on the other hand, allows individuals to connect (for example, trading Bitcoin) without a middleman involved.

To put it another way, platforms are a *business model*, but blockchain is a *technology*. It's an important distinction.

That said, blockchain technology is highly relevant to the platform economy because it poses an existential threat to the platform business model. If individuals can transact directly via a blockchain, what's the point of using a platform? This is why, as we saw in Chapter 14, some middlemen businesses are beginning to incorporate blockchain technology into their operations to add greater value for customers and keep them coming back for more. It makes sense, then, that the huge platform businesses we've talked about in this chapter could also benefit from blockchain technology.

Private, regulated blockchains could provide a way for platform businesses to leverage blockchain technology, while still adding value as a middleman. Blockchain originated as decentralized, distributed technology, with no one person or entity in charge of overseeing transactions or interactions. But with a private blockchain (such as those used in banking), the organization (in this case, the platform business) can apply its own rules to govern transactions in line with the platform's terms of usage, thereby continuing to build trust and add value for users.

In truth, I expect blockchain technology to both threaten and enhance the platform economy, depending on the extent to which platform businesses embrace blockchain's potential. Interestingly, we're also seeing the emergence of entirely new blockchain-based platform businesses, such as:

- Arcade City, a ride-hailing app that facilitates transactions through a blockchain system. Drivers can establish their own rates and build their own recurring customer base, while the blockchain logs interactions and transactions.

- Winding Tree, a blockchain-based travel marketplace that connects hotels, airlines, and tourism offices with travelers. The service makes travel cheaper for consumers and cuts the fees that hotels and airlines have to pay to traditional third-party middlemen. Lufthansa, Air France, and Air Canada are among the providers using Winding Tree.

- WAX Marketplace, a blockchain trading platform where gamers can buy and sell virtual accessories, such as gaming skins and weapons, and NFTs.

Tapping into the Crowd

Crowdsourcing is underpinned by the platform business model, so I couldn't talk about platforms without mentioning the power of the crowd. Broadly speaking, crowdsourcing can be used to source three things – ideas, skills, and services – making it a useful way to spark innovation and access talent, without investing in full-time hires. (Read more about finding talent in Chapter 20.) Crowdsourcing can therefore help businesses speed up the creative process and increase their options, while saving money.

How does it work? In very brief terms, you pose a question, task, or challenge to the "crowd" (which may be made up of consumers, entrepreneurs, specialists, startups, enthusiastic amateurs, or whomever) – usually via a third-party crowdsourcing platform business, or your own platform.

Let's explore some inspiring examples of leveraging crowdsourcing.

Crowdsourcing product ideas

Crowdsourced burgers? If this doesn't show that anything can be crowd-sourced, then I don't know what will. McDonald's has used crowdsourcing in the past to source new burger ideas (winners had their burger ideas released in stores), and encourage people to create their own McDonald's campaigns (such as viral videos) – garnering some free publicity and marketing content without spending a dime.

Elsewhere, LEGO has used its own LEGO Ideas crowdsourcing platform to build a community of nearly 1 million members that generate new product ideas.[6] Any user can submit a new LEGO design that other users can vote for, thereby testing demand. Product ideas with more than 10,000 votes get reviewed by LEGO, and if the design ends up going into production, the creator receives a royalty on sales. (One of the winning ideas is a Beatles Yellow Submarine LEGO set.) This approach is so clever because not only does LEGO get new product ideas for free, but users submitting their ideas also take it upon themselves to promote their idea, giving LEGO a handy brand boost.

Crowdsourcing skills and services

Need something designed? Across logos, apps, banding, packaging, wine labels, and more than 90 other design categories, the 99Designs crowd-sourcing platform can connect you with the right designer. Businesses and individuals can connect with designers around the world, and even get advice from a design expert. Simply submit a simple design brief (which only takes a few minutes), then you can either select a relevant designer or start a contest that's open to the entire design community (in which case multiple designers will submit their ideas and you pick your favorite). You pay at the end and ownership/copyright of the design is all yours.

Other cool examples of skills-based human crowd platforms include:

- uTest lets you crowdsource online usability testing for websites, games, apps, and services.

- Amazon's Mechanical Turk connects freelancers with "human intelligence tasks," such as data entry, data cleansing, and content creation.

PRACTICAL LESSONS

Whether you're a platform business or not, here are some key takeaways from this chapter:

- The platform business model is incredibly lucrative and powerful – many of the world's most valuable businesses are platform businesses.

- Remember that platform businesses are essentially giant middlemen, which means they may be impacted by the disintermediation trend (Chapter 14); in particular, blockchain technology has the potential to help consumers cut out the middleman. As such, we may see existing platform businesses leverage blockchain technology to offer greater value, plus new platform businesses emerge that are built entirely on blockchain.

- Platforms also underpin the sharing economy and crowdsourcing. With sharing platforms such as Uber and Airbnb, users have short-term, on-demand access to the goods and services they need. And with crowdsourcing platforms, businesses can connect with fresh ideas, skills, and services on an on-demand basis.

- Even if your business is a traditional linear business, consider how the platform business trend could improve – or potentially threaten – your business.

Now let's move from a very specific business model to a trend that can be applied across all sorts of businesses: immersive experiences.

Notes

1. The GitHub Business Model – How Does GitHub Make Money; Product-Mint; https://productmint.com/github-business-model-how-does-github-make-money/

2. Shared economy in India to be USD 2 billion industry by 2020-end; The Economic Times; https://economictimes.indiatimes.com/news/economy/indicators/shared-economy-in-india-to-be-usd-2-billion-industry-by-2020-end-maple-capital/articleshow/74337786.cms

3. Sharing economy is transforming Chinese society; China.org.cn; http://www.china.org.cn/opinion/2019-01/21/content_74392923.htm

4. JustPark; https://www.justpark.com/about/

5. Zipcar; https://www.zipcar.com/press/overview

6. Building Together: How LEGO leverages crowdsourcing to sustain both innovation and brand love; HBS Digital Initiative; https://digital.hbs.edu/platform-digit/submission/building-together-how-lego-leverages-crowdsourcing-to-sustain-both-innovation-and-brand-love/

CHAPTER 16
MORE IMMERSIVE EXPERIENCES

How Brands Are Wowing Customers with Memorable Experiences

Thanks to extended reality (XR) technologies like virtual reality (VR) and augmented reality (AR), brands can now impress their customers with engaging, immersive experiences. (In fact, I've written a whole book, called *Extended Reality in Practice*, about the use of XR across a wide range of industries.)

But this trend isn't just about virtual experiences – far from it. Today's consumers increasingly prioritize experiences over material goods, particularly among millennials, where 75 percent say they value experiences over things.[1] And this means brands that want to stay relevant must turn the customer journey – whether it is online or offline – into a thoughtful, memorable experience.

Introducing the Experience Economy

This overarching move toward experiences is known as the *experience economy*. The term was first coined in a 1998 *Harvard Business Review* article by Joseph Pine and James Gilmore, who used kids' birthday cakes as an example of economic progress.[2] First, parents would buy the ingredients and make a birthday cake from scratch. Then along came convenient, preprepared cake mix products, like those by Betty Crocker. Then came the service economy, where busy parents would order cakes from the local store or bakery (at ten times the price of a homemade or box cake mix). And now, many parents will gratefully outsource the whole birthday party to a restaurant or business that hosts events. For example, one of the birthday "experience" events that parents can now book is an activity at a bakery where party guests decorate their own cupcakes. This is the evolution of the experience economy – and, as Pine and Gilmore argued, it is quite distinct from the goods- and service-based economies that came before it. They went on to argue that, for the brands of the future, providing a good product or service would no longer be enough – brands would have to create memorable experiences as well.

Their prediction seems to be playing out before our eyes, as customers place more and more emphasis on the overall experience. According to a survey by Barclays, 81 percent of customers say value for money is important, but the experience provided by a brand is *just as important*. What's more, 42 percent are happy to pay extra for a more welcoming customer experience.[3]

Of course, there are whole sectors devoted to providing experiences (sports and entertainment spring to mind). But, as you'll see from the examples in this chapter, the focus on experiences is beginning to filter into other sectors, particularly retail. In other words, a customer entering a shop is no longer just looking to buy a product and leave – they want a memorable in-store experience while they're there. Which is why the flagship Topshop store on London's Oxford Street has DJs come and play on the ground floor, or why shopping malls frequently host pop-ups and activities for shoppers, or why Starbucks writes customers' names on their coffee cups. It's all about getting more people through the door, gaining customer loyalty – and, ideally, creating something that customers will want to share with their friends on social media.

With the continued rise of digital channels, this sort of tangible in-person experience is essential to attracting customers. Certainly, I buy as much as I can online – I can even order my groceries from Amazon and have them arrive at my door a couple of hours later – so I expect stores to give me a reason to come there in person.

Importantly, digital-first businesses are also capitalizing on this experience trend – whether it's by creating engaging virtual experiences or by adding tangible, in-person experiences to their offering. Think of Airbnb introducing Airbnb Experiences, which allows hosts to offer immersive local activities, like guided tours, cooking classes, or yoga. Even brands that are aggressively growing direct, online routes to customers, such as Nike, are also investing in physical flagship retail premises that offer a memorable in-person experience (see Chapter 14). Then there's the Amazon Go checkout-free stores, where customers can take what they want and Amazon automatically charges their account, thereby creating a smooth, highly integrated, and smart shopping experience.

Bottom line, whether you engage with your customers online, offline, or both, it's vital you rethink the value you're offering and ask yourselves, "How can we add even more value by turning this interaction into an experience?"

For brands like Adobe, this question is so important, they even employ a chief experience officer (CXO) to lead the customer and employee experience across the organization. Note that, ideally, the CXO's role should be to consider employee experience as well as customer experience, since one generally feeds into the other – happy employees tend to deliver a better customer experience.[4]

Now that we've got a good understanding of the experience economy, let's see what it looks like in practice.

Inspiring Examples of Tangible and Digital Experiences

Particularly for brick-and-mortar retailers, this question of "Why would people come here in person?" is key. Today's retailers need to be providing added value through engaging, enticing in-person experiences. Let's kick off with some inspiring examples of "experiential retail."

John Lewis: Fancy having the store to yourself?

High-end UK department store John Lewis made headlines a couple of years ago when it announced it was launching an after-hours private shopping service for high-roller customers. For those prepared to spend £10,000 in the store, staff would make themselves available after closing time to create a more exclusive shopping experience.[5] This is definitely not for everyone, but I can see how having the run of a department store after hours might be pretty cool.

Gucci: Taking experiential retail to a whole new level

The Gucci Garden in Florence, Italy, is a multilevel galleria situated within a 14th-century palazzo. As well as a retail space, the building houses a restaurant by Michelin-starred chef Massimo Bottura, and a two-floor brand experience that's more like a museum, with vintage Gucci displays and a 30-seat cinema. The experience is so impressive, Gucci charges people to enter (8 euros at the time of launch),[6] although half of each ticket sale goes to supporting restoration projects in Florence.

I should stress that the ground-floor retail space is free to enter; you only have to pay to see the two upper floors, which house the brand experience. For me, this is a pretty cool benchmark, where a brand creates such a great experience that people will pay for it.

Farfetch and Browns: Blending luxury retail and technology

Online luxury fashion retail platform Farfetch is the owner of luxury multi-brand boutique Browns. When the new Browns flagship store opened in London in April 2021, it unveiled what Farfetch refers to as the "store of the future."[7] This highly interactive retail space, which is designed to get customers to visit and stay longer, includes connected, interactive mirrors in changing rooms that display items in customers' wish lists, how the items can be styled, and complementary products.

And using the Browns app in-store mode, customers can share their wish list with staff, so they know which items are of interest. There are also QR codes next to products that bring up more information and similar stock. The store also houses a restaurant, courtyard, makeup and styling area, and a room with regularly rotating experiences (such as photography exhibitions). Combining technology, entertainment, hospitality, and personalized service, it's a store I'd genuinely be happy to spend time in.

Primark: Creating a theatrical retail experience

At the other end of the retail scale, we have budget fast fashion retailer Primark. When Primark opened its 12,000-square-meter store in Madrid, Spain, its goal was to create a "theatrical, cinematic" experience.[8] Beneath the store's impressive 30-meter-high dome are 11 huge, transparent LED screens that display audio and visuals and create a trippy holographic effect. The store also includes a "trend room," with screens that help shoppers learn about the latest trends and create their own look – which shows that incorporating even small screens into a store can help customers get more out of the shopping experience.

Vans: The House of Vans, London destination

Fashion, culture, BMX, skating, art, and music all come together in House of Vans, a 30,000-square-foot destination that includes a cinema, café, music venue, art gallery, and skatepark![9] Oh, and a shop. It's not just a place where you can buy the latest Vans products, it's a space where you come to hang out with friends.

Formula E Ghost Racing: Immersing sports fans

One of my favorite examples of immersive experiences comes from Formula E Ghost Racing. This mobile game, which is available to download on iOS and Android, allows Formula E racing fans to race against real drivers on the grid in real time.[10] The game features hyper-realistic scenery, and matches the same speed, positioning, and movement of the drivers on the track. All of this allows Ghost Racing to create an incredibly authentic racing experience – one that's much better than racing against an algorithm or your friends, or even watching a race on the TV. For me, this shows how the sports, entertainment, and gaming industries can make their experiences even more immersive.

Creating immersive experiences with AR and VR

Ghost Racing leads us nicely into some more tech-based experiences. Indeed, throughout this book, there are many examples of using technology to create an immersive experience – think of Warby Parker's AR tool for trying on glasses at home (Chapter 14), Wild Turkey's Alexa whiskey tasting (Chapter 10), Disney's Magic Bands (Chapter 10), and immersive education and training (Chapter 5).

In particular, AR and VR are providing exciting new ways for brands to create an immersive experience, whether virtual or real-world. For example, cosmetics brand MAC introduced AR mirrors into stores, allowing customers to instantly try out new makeup looks digitally.[11] Elsewhere, Chinese luxury lifestyle travel platform Zanadu has created a 360-degree VR experience in its cutting-edge Travel Experience Space in Shanghai.[12] The experience is designed to show off travel destinations and give an immersive flavor of trips and accommodations. Being the most immersive of the XR technologies, VR provides a unique way to transport customers to other worlds or experience the full capabilities of products and services.

In the Future, XR Could Create Even More Immersive Experiences

Let's dwell a little on the possibilities that XR technologies bring. XR is a rapidly evolving field, which means that in the not-too-distant future, organizations will be able to bring new levels of immersivity to their experiences, and create virtual experiences that feel very close to real-world ones.

Some of the technologies that will enable this leap in immersive experiences include:

- Smaller, lighter VR headsets incorporate built-in hand detection and eye tracking. Because hand detection allows VR users to control movements without clunky controllers, users can be more expressive and connect with their VR experience on a deeper level. And the inclusion of eye tracking technology helps to create a slicker, smoother experience, with less lag.

- New XR accessories help to deepen the experience, such as wearable robotic boots that provide the sensation of walking.

- Full-body haptic suits provide hyper-realistic sensations of touch. We already have things like haptic gloves, which simulate the feeling of touch through vibrations, but full-body suits take this to another level.

Looking even further ahead, we'll have neural VR technologies (basically, brain-computer interfaces) that hook up the brain directly to a VR experience. The basic idea of neural VR is that users will be able to manipulate objects and control movements in the virtual world through thoughts alone. In other words, the experiences of the future could harness brain waves to create a whole new level of immersion. If you think this sounds far-fetched, Boston-based startup Neurable is already working to develop an everyday brain-computer interface,[13] Elon Musk's Neuralink project is developing implants that will allow two-way communication between the human brain and an AI interface,[14] and Facebook is developing its own wearable brain-computer interface.[15] If such technology was integrated with XR technologies, it would revolutionize what it means to provide an immersive customer experience. This is years, potentially decades, away of course. But I wanted to provide a snapshot of what may lie ahead in this fast-evolving field.

PRACTICAL LESSONS

In the experience economy, consumers prioritize experiences over the ownership of goods. For organizations, this means:

- Whether you engage with your customers online, offline, or both, a key question to ask is, "How can we add even more value by turning this customer interaction into an experience?"

- Keep in mind that, as XR technology evolves, virtual experiences have the potential to become a lot more immersive and realistic.

- And don't forget about employee experience, since it tends to be intertwined with providing a great customer experience. Read more about the employee experience in Chapters 20 and 21.

As well as seeking experiences, consumers are also seeking to engage with brands that provide a more sustainable, eco-friendly offering. Read on to learn about the rise of conscious consumption.

Notes

1. New Data on Millennials Reveals What Draws Them to Events; Eventbrite; https://www.eventbrite.com/blog/millennials-event-trends-ds00/

2. Welcome to the Experience Economy; Harvard Business Review; https://hbr.org/amp/1998/07/welcome-to-the-experience-economy

3. The experience economy and what it means for your small business; Autopilot; https://journeys.autopilotapp.com/blog/experience-economy-small-business/

4. Why Every Company Needs a Chief Experience Officer; Harvard Business Review; https://hbr.org/2019/06/why-every-company-needs-a-chief-experience-officer

5. John Lewis launches after-hours private shopping service; Retail Gazette; https://www.retailgazette.co.uk/blog/2018/10/john-lewis-launches-hours-private-shopping-service/

6. Gucci Takes Experiential Retail to the Next Level; Forbes; https://www.forbes.com/sites/nicolafumo/2018/01/09/gucci-garden-florence/

7. Inside the new Browns; Farfetch's store of the future; Vogue Business; https://www.voguebusiness.com/consumers/inside-the-new-browns-london-flagship-farfetch-store-of-the-future

8. New Primark flagship store includes 11 LED screens; Design Week; https://www.designweek.co.uk/issues/19-25-october-2015/new-primark-flagship-store-includes-11-holographic-screens/

9. 9 case studies that prove experiential retail is the future; Storefront; https://www.thestorefront.com/mag/7-case-studies-prove-experiential-retail-future/

10. Race against the grid in real time as Virtually Live Ghost Racing launches; FIA Formula E; https://www.fiaformulae.com/en/news/2019/april/formulae-ghost-racing-launched

11. MAC Cosmetics Launches In-Store Augmented Reality Try-On Mirror Powered by ModiFace; Globe Newswire; https://www.globenewswire.com/news-release/2017/11/14/1228167/0/en/MAC-Cosmetics-Launches-In-Store-Augmented-Reality-Try-On-Mirror-Powered-by-ModiFace.html

12. The Future of Immersive Branding and Retail; AT&T Foundry; https://cdn2.hubspot.net/hubfs/508496/futuristreport/The%20Future%20of%20Immersive%20Branding%20and%20Retail.pdf

13. Neurable Raises $6 Million Series A to Build an "Everyday" Brain-Computer Interface; Forbes; https://www.forbes.com/sites/solrogers/2019/12/17/exclusive-neurable-raises-series-a-to-build-an-everyday-brain-computer-interface/

14. Elon Musk unveils updated Neuralink brain implant design and surgical robot; Dezeen; https://www.dezeen.com/2020/09/02/neuralink-elon-musk-brain-implant-technology/

15. Here's How Facebook's Brain-Computer Interface Development Is Progressing; IEEE Spectrum; https://spectrum.ieee.org/view-from-the-valley/consumer-electronics/portable-devices/heres-how-facebooks-braincomputer-interface-development-is-progressing

CHAPTER 17
CONSCIOUS CONSUMPTION

Consumer Demand for Sustainable, Responsible Products

Awareness of the climate crisis is rising very quickly (see Chapter 1), and with that comes a desire for more eco-friendly products. Certainly, in my family, we're keen to understand the impact of what we buy and are regularly asking questions such as, "Is this fair trade?" and "Was this farmed sustainably?" We're trying to be conscious consumers, in other words, seeking to understand the wider impact of our purchases and, wherever possible, choosing more sustainable, responsible alternatives. And as this trend shows, we're not alone.

The Rise of Conscious Consumption

Driven in part by movements such as Extinction Rebellion, and the work of environmental activist Greta Thunberg, we've reached a tipping point in environmental awareness. And this is impacting our buying decisions. Take "flygskam" or "flight shame" as an example. After the term was coined in Sweden in 2017, plane ticket sales began to fall in 2018, and train ticket sales began to climb.[1] So, rather than gaining status for opting *into* conscious consumption, there is now shame around not opting *out* of harmful consumerism. That's a clear sign that conscious consumption is going mainstream.

Eco-credentials, sustainability, responsible practices, and the like are now key considerations for consumers, alongside traditional factors such as price and value. Today, two out of three consumers are "belief-driven buyers,"[2] and more than two-thirds of consumers say they expect brands to stand up for social, cultural, and environmental issues.[3] To be clear, consumers still want fair prices and good deals – although three out of four millennials are willing to pay more for sustainable products[4] – but environmental and societal impact is now an added consideration. In particular, consumers want to know:

- Where a product is made

- How it's made

- What it's made from

Technology has played a key role here, since consumers can easily research these factors online before they decide to purchase.

For businesses, this means the notion of stakeholders is changing. Alongside customers, employees, investors, and so on, *society* itself is now a stakeholder – meaning organizations that act in the best interests of society, by providing responsibly made products, will be better equipped for the future. Businesses must therefore work to ensure their products are produced ethically, and from sustainable materials. They must also invest in more sustainable business operations (more on that in Chapter 18). And, of course, they must promote their eco-conscious approach to consumers (and, I'd argue, employees, investors, suppliers, and so on).

Regulators, as well as consumers, will also increasingly push organizations toward more eco-friendly practices and products. For example, I expect to see carbon emissions labels and food miles labels added to products in the not-too-distant future. With the majority of consumers being belief-driven, this sort of transparency will be a must in future.

But, for now, let's look at what this trend means in practice in the here and now – specifically, how conscious consumption has led to a plethora of eco-friendly, sustainable products.

Conscious Food Consumption

For me, the food industry is a perfect illustrator of this trend. I talked about the huge changes taking place in agriculture back in Chapter 6, but let's explore what this means in terms of specific products and brands.

Organic options

Organic food sales in the US hit $50 billion in 2019, up 4.6 percent from the previous year (outpacing the general food market growth rate of around 2 percent).[5] So, while organic is still a small part of the overall market, it is growing.

One example comes from family-owned US coffee-roasting company Grounds for Change, which provides fair trade and organic coffee from shade-grown beans, which in turn helps to prevent deforestation. Farmers receive a fair price for their coffee and work under fair conditions, and the coffee itself is certified carbon-free.[6] Among its other eco-credentials, Grounds for Change also uses renewable energy and donates a percentage of profits to environmental organizations.

While I love buying organic produce where possible, I accept that it just isn't possible for everyone to buy organic all the time, or feed a growing global population using purely organic methods. This means we need to make sure nonorganic food is as sustainable as possible.

Sustainable seafood

At the time of writing this, the *Seaspiracy* documentary had just been released, a key claim of which is that there's no such thing as sustainable fishing. Now, I do believe that if we all eat a more plant-based diet it will have a huge positive impact on our planet, but I also recognize that we're unlikely to see the entire world population go vegan anytime soon. So those of us who do eat fish (myself included) need to make the best buying decisions possible.

Supermarkets are increasingly aiding this journey by selling "responsibly sourced" seafood. UK supermarket chain Waitrose is among the retailers who are participating in the Ocean Disclosure Project, a voluntary project that publicly discloses wild-caught, farmed fish, and seafood sources. Waitrose's own listing shows that in 2019 more than 92 percent of its own-brand seafood was independently certified as responsibly sourced.[7] Other participating retailers include Asda, Aldi, Hannaford, Lidl, and Tesco.

Plant-based meats and dairy

I talked a lot about plant-based meats back in Chapter 6, but let me emphasize here the sheer breadth of plant-based meat options. Not only do we have companies such as Beyond Meat, Eat Just, and Impossible Foods, all of which are entirely built on selling plant-based options, but other household name brands are also getting in on the act. For example, the Incogmeato range by MorningStar is in fact a division of the Kellogg Company. Nestlé acquired Sweet Earth Foods in 2017 and now offers a range of plant-based meats including pizza, chik'n strips, and burritos. And Burger King, whose restaurants are pretty much a shrine to beef, has said its menus in the UK will be 50 percent plant-based by 2031.[8] Not only is this great news for vegetarians and vegans (well, those who are willing to buy from Burger King), it's a great way to help meat eaters enjoy more plant-based foods.

We even have animal-free dairy nowadays. Food company Perfect Day has invented "the world's first real milk proteins made without animals."[9] In other words, it provides the same texture, taste, and nutrition of dairy, but is produced through fermentation, not from cows. At the time of writing, the brand sells animal-free cheese, yogurt, and ice cream.

The palm oil backlash

Palm oil is found in so many products on the supermarket shelves, it's the most widely consumed vegetable oil on the planet, according to the World Wildlife Foundation (WWF).[10] This is bad news because the spread of palm oil plantations has led to the destruction of rainforests that are precious habitats for endangered species such as orangutans and tigers.

When my family and I went through our shelves, we were surprised how many products contained palm oil. For each one, we switched to an alternative that either doesn't contain palm oil or uses sustainable palm oil. Nutella is one product that contains sustainable palm oil, certified by the RSPO (Roundtable on Sustainable Palm Oil), which means the palm oil can be traced back to mills, ensuring it doesn't come from plantations that may contribute to deforestation. In fact, the WWF encourages consumers to buy products with sustainable palm oil, rather than give up palm oil altogether, which could harm the communities where it is grown. Good thing, because no one is going to convince my kids to give up Nutella!

But there are brands out there that shun palm oil altogether, and are certified as palm oil-free by POFCAP (International Palm Oil Free Certification Trademark). Meridian Foods, for example, doesn't use palm oil in its natural nut and seed butters; in fact, they contain nothing but nuts and seeds. The company also partners with International Animal Rescue to help rescue orangutans and plant trees (which, again, brings to mind the charitable credentials of direct-to-consumer brands; see Chapter 14).[11]

Eco-Friendly Examples from Other Industries

Looking beyond food, let's explore other products that may appeal to conscious consumers. You can also find many other examples of sustainable products in previous chapters, including sustainable cement (see Chapter 7) and eco mattresses (see Chapter 14).

Electric vehicles

We talked about the electrification of vehicles back in Chapter 8, but suffice to say that electric vehicles are now a mainstay of the automotive market, so much so that the Tesla Model 3 became the UK's third most popular new car in August 2019, as sales of electric vehicles doubled.[12] But critics say Tesla's decision to allow customers to pay with Bitcoin (see Chapter 14) has destroyed its eco-credentials, given the staggering energy use associated with Bitcoin mining (see Chapter 9). One critic compared Tesla's decision to PETA asking for donations in the form of fur coats.[13] This goes to show that companies must consider a holistic approach to sustainability.

Sustainable packaging

You'll find more about this topic in Chapter 18 (sustainable operations), but let's briefly explore how one company has drastically reduced the environmental impact of packaging.

One of the downsides of purchasing products online is the huge amount of packaging involved. I can't be the only one who's ordered a relatively small product from Amazon only to have it arrive in an enormous box filled with packaging. South Korean company Coupang's approach to packaging puts Amazon to shame.

Coupang is the largest e-commerce retailer and second largest publicly held company in South Korea[14] – it's the country's answer to Amazon. com, if you like. But, in my view, it's better. The company has eliminated the need for cardboard boxes and bubble wrap for 75 percent of deliveries, and its grocery service, Coupang Fresh, ships in reusable containers – customers simply leave the containers by their door when they're done and Coupang takes them away. Similarly, when a customer wants to return goods, they can leave them outside the door, with no need for a label or packaging. Believe me, if I could buy from Coupang here in the UK, I would.

Eco holidays

As well as buying responsible products from responsible companies, we can also holiday at responsible resorts. And if you think that means roughing it, forget it. Today, these eco resorts are distinctly high-end destinations in their own right.

For example, the Cala Luna Boutique Hotel & Villas in Costa Rica embeds sustainability into all aspects of its offering. Located on a semi-private wild beach that is a protected haven for sea turtles, the resort has one of the largest solar energy installations in Central America,[15] an organic garden that supplies the farm-to-table restaurant, plus biodegradable toiletries, and furniture that was made in-house.

Or there's Copal Tree Lodge in Belize, which is situated in preserved rainforest. This resort has a 3,000-acre organic farm, which supplies 70 percent of the food served in the lodge's restaurant (with the remaining produce being sourced from local suppliers).[16] There's an on-site rum distillery that makes rum from organic sugar, canopy water, and yeast from the farm. And the resort offers hands-on learning about organic chocolate and farming. Guests are also given aluminum water bottles to reduce waste.

Sustainable fashion

The fashion industry, particularly fast fashion, is a significant polluter, but many fashion brands are promoting sustainable fashion. Here are just a few examples:

- Allbirds is a brand that I'm particularly passionate about, partly because it makes incredibly comfortable shoes, but also because the company works hard to reduce carbon emissions in the creation of its products. Allbirds measures the emissions of everything from raw materials to their end of life, uses natural and recycled materials where possible, and offsets whatever's left – overall, making Allbirds a carbon-neutral business. But that's not enough; the company is on a mission to emit no carbon at all.[17]

- Reformation issues a quarterly sustainability report that helps the company track its progress toward becoming more environmentally friendly. It also tracks its environmental footprint, including the number of pounds of CO_2 emitted and gallons of water used in making products.[18] Plus, the company has been 100 percent carbon neutral since 2015.

- Even big brands like Adidas are trying to reduce the impact associated with their products. Adidas has partnered with Parley, an organization dedicated to ending the destruction of the oceans, to turn plastic pollution from the sea into shoes. Parley Ocean Plastic, which is created using upcycled marine plastic waste, is used in Adidas x Parley shoes in place of virgin plastic. When you consider that more than 5 trillion pieces of plastic litter our oceans,[19] we need more products like these.

Reducing plastic in cleaning and toiletry products

Look under your kitchen sink and around your bathroom and you'll probably see a lot of plastic bottles. What's more, tiny plastic beads in products such as toothpaste, face washes, and shower gels get washed down the drain and can enter our oceans, where they can harm marine life.[20] In our family, we've made a simple switch from bottled shower gels, shampoos, and face washes to soap and shampoo bars – which drastically cuts down the plastic we buy and flush down the drain.

Some companies are incorporating recycled plastic in their bottles, but it's not nearly enough. Proctor and Gamble, for example, has introduced Head & Shoulders bottles that are made with up to 25 percent recycled beach plastic.[21] But these big companies need to do much, much more. In my view, smaller companies are leading the charge in this field. Lush, which makes shampoo bars, is one example. Or there's Grove Collaborative, whose natural cleaning and personal care products are currently 100 percent plastic neutral, and will be completely plastic-free by 2025.[22]

Turning food waste into biodegradable plastics

Let me finish with an example that makes me much more hopeful for the future. Genecis, a student-run company spun out of the University of Toronto, takes PHAs (a type of hydroxy acid) from food waste destinated for landfill and converts it into high-performance biodegradable plastics. Genecis plastics have equivalent properties to traditional plastics, without the environmental cost. At the end of the product's useful life, the plastic can be composted within a month – and should it find its way into the ocean, it will degrade within one year.[23]

PRACTICAL LESSONS

In this chapter, we've learned:

- The majority of consumers are now belief-driven. And with rising awareness about the environment, that means consumers increasingly want to buy sustainable, eco-friendly, and responsible products.

- Across all kinds of sectors, companies are working to reduce plastic, reduce waste, track the environmental impact of their products, and reduce that impact.

- But reducing your environmental impact isn't enough. If you want to attract and retain customers, it's vital you promote your sustainability credentials to your audience.

Of course, offering more sustainable products is only part of the picture. Organizations must also look at making their everyday operations more sustainable. This leads us to the next part of this book – all about how businesses are run.

Notes

1. Year in a word: Flygskam; Financial Times; https://www.ft.com/content/5c635430-1dbc-11ea-97df-cc63de1d73f4

2. Conscious Consumerism; Raconteur; https://www.raconteur.net/infographics/conscious-consumerism/

3. Consumers Want Transparent & Authentic Companies That Care About Social and Environmental Issues; YouMatter; https://youmatter.world/en/consumers-expectations-transparent-companies-social-environment/

4. Conscious Consumerism: What Is It and How Can Businesses Promote It?; Daglar Cizmeci; https://daglar-cizmeci.com/conscious-consumerism/

5. Organic food sales hit $50 billion in 2019; IFT; https://www.ift.org/news-and-publications/news/2020/june/10/organic-food-sales-hit-$50-billion-in-2019

6. Grounds for Change; https://groundsforchange.com/

7. Waitrose & Partners Makes Seafood Sourcing Public on Ocean Disclosure Project; Sustainable Fisheries Partnership; https://www.sustainablefish.org/News/Waitrose-Partners-Makes-Seafood-Sourcing-Public-on-Ocean-Disclosure-Project

8. Burger King UK Says Its Menu Will Be 50% Plant-Based by the Year 2031; The Beet; https://thebeet.com/burger-king-uk-says-its-menu-will-be-50-plant-based-by-the-year-2031/

9. Perfect Day: https://perfectdayfoods.com/

10. Which Everyday Products Contain Palm Oil; WWF; https://www.worldwildlife.org/pages/which-everyday-products-contain-palm-oil

11. Why Meridian?; https://shop.meridianfoods.co.uk/pages/why-meridian

12. Tesla Model 3 was UK's third bestselling car in August; Guardian; https://www.theguardian.com/technology/2019/sep/05/tesla-model-3-was-uk-third-best-selling-car-in-august

13. You can now buy a Tesla with Bitcoin – at a staggering cost, critics warn; Fortune; https://fortune.com/2021/03/24/tesla-bitcoin-esg-environmental-cost/

14. Coupang Is the Amazon.com of South Korea, but Maybe Even Better. And Now You Can Buy the Stock; Barron's; https://www.barrons.com/articles/coupang-is-the-amazon-com-of-south-korea-but-maybe-even-better-51615590150

15. World's best eco-luxury resorts; Lonely Planet; https://www.lonelyplanet.com/articles/best-eco-luxury-resorts

16. Ibid.

17. Sustainability; Allbirds; https://www.allbirds.com/pages/sustainability

18. Sustainable practices; Reformation; https://www.thereformation.com/pages/sustainable-practices

19. Parley Ocean Plastic; Adidas; https://www.adidas.co.uk/sustainability-parley-ocean-plastic

20. Ban microbeads from all products washed down the drain, campaigners urge government; Independent; https://www.independent.co.uk/climate-change/news/ban-microbeads-microplastics-products-washed-down-drain-environmental-investigation-agency-fauna-flora-international-greenpeace-marine-conservation-society-a7569326.html

21. Head & Shoulders creates first recyclable shampoo bottle made with beach plastic; Manufacturing; https://www.manufacturingglobal.com/lean-manufacturing/head-and-shoulders-creates-first-recyclable-shampoo-bottle-made-beach-plastic

22. Sustainability; Grove Collaborative; https://www.grove.co/blog/sustainability

23. Genecis; https://genecis.co/

PART IV
RETHINKING HOW BUSINESSES ARE RUN

In the previous section, we focused purely on products and services, and how organizations are having to rethink their offering for the fourth industrial revolution.

Now we move away from products and services, to look at how organizations operate on a day-to-day basis. Building on what we've learned about product and service trends, technology trends, and the wider global shifts that are taking place, this part explores key operational trends – how businesses across all sectors are changing the way their business is run to suit our rapidly changing world.

Your own business will no doubt have to rethink its operations in a similar way, and I hope these chapters help. As always, there are plenty of real-world examples, from a wide range of sectors, to show what's possible.

CHAPTER 18
SUSTAINABLE AND RESILIENT OPERATIONS

Building a Stronger, More Responsible Company

Let's kick off this part with two key focus areas for business operations: resilience and sustainability.

Rethinking Resilience for the Fourth Industrial Revolution

I believe every chapter in this book is about building a more resilient business. After all, a critical part of resilience is being able to adapt and survive for the long term. Adapting your business for the fourth industrial revolution, in line with the business trends in this book, is absolutely a resilient thing to do.

What Does Resilience Mean in an Age of Regular Disruption?

I'm writing this in the spring of 2021, just as the UK emerges from its third lockdown. It's an interesting time to be writing about resilience! The year 2020 was hugely disruptive for society as a whole, with a worsening climate crisis and political and social unrest *on top of* a global pandemic. For businesses, it was a year that challenged the very concept of what it means to be "prepared."

With the global shifts I outlined in Chapter 1, and the dramatic tech advances from Chapter 2, I'd argue we're now entering an age where businesses will regularly face broad disruption of one kind or another. Indeed, a global survey by Deloitte revealed that 6 out of 10 business leaders believe we'll see either occasional or regular business disruption going forward, and three-quarters believed the climate crisis is of similar or greater magnitude than the pandemic.[1] Which makes resilience more important than ever. But how can organizations build resilience amidst potentially regular disruption?

According to Deloitte, companies that want to build resilience and overcome future challenges – both expected and unexpected – must cultivate five characteristics, all of which were found in resilient companies that successfully weathered the COVID-19 crisis.[2] These resilient organizations are:

1. **Prepared**: They successfully balance planning for short-term and long-term eventualities.

2. **Adaptable**: There is a particular focus on building a workforce of versatile, adaptable employees.

3. **Collaborative**: Improving collaboration and reducing silos across the organization speeds up decision-making and boosts innovation.

4. **Trustworthy**: Resilient organizations work hard to improve communication and transparency with key stakeholders, build trust, and lead with empathy.

5. **Responsible**: Successful organizations recognize that their responsibilities extend beyond the bottom line, and work hard to balance the needs of all stakeholders. (Although I'd argue responsibility also extends beyond stakeholders to the world around us.)

Cyber-resilience and the next pandemic

During the COVID-19 pandemic, organizations that were able to pivot to digital channels or accelerate their digital transformation were clearly better equipped to survive. But what if the next pandemic is a digital virus – one that takes down the internet, for example? If that were to happen, businesses with a physical infrastructure would be better equipped to survive, while those solely reliant on digital channels would face a major existential threat. Therefore, resilience in the fourth industrial revolution may include balancing digital with other channels, such as brick-and-mortar retail.

But even if a global digital virus doesn't hit, individual organizations are extremely vulnerable to cyberattacks, which can cripple operations, hit the bottom line, and destroy trust in the organization. And as we saw in Chapter 2, the severity of cyber breaches is increasing. This is why cyber-resilience is so important.

If cybersecurity is the practice of protecting your digital systems and assets (including data) from attack, cyber-resilience prepares the organization on what to do in the event of an attack. Cyber-resilience is all about maintaining key operations during an attack and getting the business fully operational as quickly as possible. These days, as the severity of attacks grows, you cannot have cybersecurity without cyber-resilience.

To build a more cyber-resilient business, organizations must:

- Train employees on cybersecurity and cyber-resilience, so that people in the organization understand the importance of cybersecurity and cyber-resilience and are better equipped to spot cybersecurity threats, such as phishing attempts. Part of this training should include what will happen in the event of an attack.

- Have robust cybersecurity technology and practices in place, including firewalls, data backups, and the like.

- Separate critical and noncritical systems, so that, should a noncritical system be breached, critical systems remain unaffected.

- Have an incident response plan that sets out:

  o The technology response – how you'll stop the attack, maintain business functions, repair systems, and so on. You may even want to practice running a mock attack and operating the business with restricted resources.

  o The communication approach – who you need to inform about the attack, including stakeholders, and potentially law enforcement and regulatory bodies.

  o The post-incident investigation procedures. Will you, for example, conduct an internal investigation into what went wrong or hire a third-party investigator?

If resilience (and cyber-resilience) is about making sure your business can continue to operate for the short and long term, then sustainability is of course a huge part of that. If we don't minimize the climate impact of doing business, then it's not just organizations that will suffer, but all of us.

Becoming a More Sustainable Business

Today, every business must look at its operations to minimize the environmental impact and eliminate or reduce the environmental costs of doing business.

Decarbonizing the supply chain

According to the World Economic Forum (WEF), eight supply chains account for more than 50 percent of global greenhouse gas emissions: food, construction, fashion, fast-moving consumer goods, electronics, automotive, professional services, and freight.[3] If companies in these sectors can address their supply chain emissions, they will create a bigger impact than solely focusing on their direct operations and power consumption. They can multiply their climate impact, in other words – with only a marginal increase on product costs, according to the WEF.

To address supply chain emissions, the WEF recommends nine major initiatives:

1. Build a comprehensive emissions baseline, and encourage suppliers to participate with actual data.

2. Set ambitious and holistic reduction targets, and report on progress.

3. Redesign products for sustainability.

4. Reconsider the (geographic) sourcing strategy.

5. Set ambitious procurement standards that integrate emissions metrics, and then track progress against these standards.

6. Work with suppliers to address their emissions.

7. Work together with peers to align sector targets and initiatives that maximize impact and level the playing field.

8. Use scale by driving up demand – for example, through "buyer groups" – to lower the cost of green solutions.

9. Develop internal governance mechanisms that align the incentives of decision-makers with emission targets.

While this is particularly relevant to the eight industries highlighted by the WEF, any business can work to decarbonize their supply chain by following these recommendations. If all businesses followed these steps, they could multiply their climate impact several times over and give global climate action an enormous boost. What an incredible thought.

How any business can become more eco-friendly

Looking beyond the supply chain, let's quickly explore some simple steps that any business can follow to build a more sustainable business:

- Understand your current impact. Once you understand where you're at now, you can take steps to improve the situation. You can start small by examining your energy usage and water intake, and work with energy and water providers to cut your usage.

- Switch to renewable energy. This is one of the most powerful ways your business can make a difference.

- Reduce waste, reuse, and recycle. From reducing energy waste to recycling materials like paper and plastic, there are many ways to reduce, reuse, and recycle across the organization.

- Audit the products, materials, and services you use and switch to sustainable alternatives. From the toilet paper in employee restrooms and the products used by cleaners, to your web hosting provider, shipping vendors, and software providers – there's often a carbon-neutral alternative out there.

- Switch to sustainable packaging for your products. Compostable packaging is ideal. Recyclable packaging is a bare minimum.

- Allow people to work remotely, where appropriate, because fewer people traveling for work means lower emissions. And where you do expect people to travel to work, offer them incentives to travel by bike or public transportation (bike loans, season ticket loans, subsidized fares, etc.).

The benefits of building a more sustainable business

As we saw in Chapter 17, consumers are increasingly concerned about the climate crisis and want to buy from responsible, sustainable businesses. Therefore, perhaps the biggest advantage of building a more sustainable business is increased brand recognition, which in turn helps to attract and retain customers.

Other benefits to consider include:

- Boost your employer brand. Promoting your sustainability credentials can help you attract and retain talent (more on this topic in Chapter 20).

- Reduce costs, in some areas. For example, reducing energy waste and water usage can add up to significant savings in the long term.

- Take advantage of tax incentives. Depending on where you are in the world, you may receive a tax credit for investing in renewable technologies.

Now let's turn these ideas into practice, and explore some of my favorite examples of sustainable business operations.

Sustainable Operations in Practice

There are so many interesting, inspiring examples I could have included in this chapter, and this selection of use cases is by no means exhaustive. More, it provides a taste of what's possible. Speaking of taste. . .

Tony's Chocolonely: Addressing environmental and social impact

I recently had my first taste of Dutch brand Tony Chocolonely's chocolate and let me tell you, it's delicious. But as well as providing great chocolate (some of which is vegan), Tony's is doing great things across its supply chain. The company works to make the cocoa industry fair trade and free from slavery and child labor. Meanwhile, from an environmental standpoint, Tony's doesn't use palm oil, and has introduced a number of measures to reduce and offset its climate impact. As an example, Tony's collaborates with nonprofit Justdiggit to restore and regreen dry lands in Africa, where the majority of cocoa beans are grown. It's no wonder Tony's has been crowned the Netherlands' most sustainable brand for four years in a row.[4]

For me, sustainability isn't just about businesses' environmental footprint, but also their social footprint. In other words, how we treat people matters. Tony's is a shining example of how businesses can work to calculate and reduce the true social costs of their products and services.

Patagonia: Sustainable clothing

In the sports and outdoor clothing sector, you might struggle to find a more substantiable brand than Patagonia. Through workshops, Patagonia teaches consumers how to repair their clothing (or the company will fix it for them) – whether it's Patagonia clothing or not. And the company is working toward being completely carbon neutral by 2025. As part of this, 100 percent of the company's electricity needs in the US are met with renewable electricity, and 64 percent of fabrics (at the time of writing) are made with recycled fabrics.[5]

In addition, 1 percent of the company's revenue goes to supporting environmental organizations, and its social responsibility programs ensure Patagonia products are produced under safe, fair, legal, and humane working conditions.

General Mills: Recycling waste

Several companies are rejecting the idea of sending their waste to landfill. Food company General Mills, for example, finds other uses for by-products, such as oat hulls, which are now used as fuel. Globally, the company reuses or recycles over 80 percent of its solid waste.[6]

Estrella: Making aluminum cans more sustainable

In 2021, the Estrella Damm brewery launched the world's first aluminum beverage cans to be certified by the Aluminium Stewardship Initiative, a scheme that guarantees high environmental, social, and ethical standards across the whole life cycle of aluminum. In addition, Damm works to raise awareness of recycling, has eliminated plastic rings from multi-packs, and instead uses 100 percent biodegradable cardboard – resulting in a reduction of over 260 tons of plastic per year.[7]

Mackmyra: Distilling whiskey the sustainable way

I mentioned Mackmyra's personalized whiskey offering back in Chapter 12, but the company also created what it calls the world's first "environmentally friendly distillery."[8] Named the Gravity Distillery, because it makes use of gravity at each stage of the process, the distillery uses barley from local farms (to reduce transport), heats water using bio-pellets, and returns wastewater back into the system.

Yum! Brands: Creating a clear pathway to reducing packaging waste

Yum! Brands is the company that owns KFC, Pizza Hut, and Taco Bell, and across these brands, Yum! is committed to reducing packaging waste via a number of milestones, including:[9]

- 2022: removing Styrofoam and expanded polystyrene from packaging at all KFC, Pizza Hut, and Taco bell locations around the world.

- 2025: making all consumer-facing packaging at Taco Bell recyclable, compostable, or reusable, and adding recycling and compost bins to restaurants.

- 2025: making all plastic-based consumer-facing packaging at KFC recoverable or reusable.

This shows how you don't have to tackle everything in one go. Rather, you can set out a series of measures and milestones that will make a big difference.

Orsted: Carbon-neutral energy generation

Orsted, ranked as the world's most sustainable energy company, is on track to become carbon neutral in its energy generation and operations by 2025, which will make it the first major energy company to transition from fossil fuels to net-zero emissions.[10] The company is focusing its sustainability on three themes: decarbonizing its supply chains, improving biodiversity management to work in balance with local ecosystems, and creating shared value with local communities.

Seven Bro7hers: One company's trash is another company's beer

Brewing company Seven Bro7hers has teamed up with Kellogg's to create sustainable beers made from cereal waste (or "upcycled cereal" as they call it).[11] Each beer is made from discarded grains created in Kellogg's cereal cooking process; in other words, grains that aren't quite up to scratch for our morning cereal are used to make beer. The range includes beers made from Corn Flakes, Rice Krispies, and Coco Pops – and with names like Throwaway IPA and Sling It Out Stout, it's clear that sustainability is core to the company's brand.

Hershey: Working to end deforestation

Through its Cocoa For Good initiative, Hershey is investing half a billion dollars by 2030 to create a more sustainable supply chain and end deforestation.[12] The company is a founding member of the Cocoa & Forest Initiative (CFI), and as part of its CFI forest protection plans in Ghana and Cote d'Ivoire, Hershey is distributing 900,000 trees to farms, distributing more than 2.5 million cocoa seedlings to farmers, and satellite mapping 50,000 farms. The satellite mapping will aid traceability and support a deforestation alert system.

The company is also investing in renewable energy, has set aggressive emissions targets, and has promised to make 100 percent of its plastic packaging recyclable, reusable, or compostable by 2030.[13]

Protix: Upgrading food waste to make insect protein

Maybe you've heard the hype about insect protein, and how we all should be learning to love eating insects, rather than other animals? The idea is sound, but the reality isn't very tempting to most meat eaters. So Protix took the idea and created sustainable insect protein, which is designed to be used as animal feed. (Protix supplies ingredients to the pet food, livestock, and aquaculture companies.)

Crucially, the company feeds its insects a mix of grain, fruit, and vegetable leftovers from local sources. The result is an insect-based animal feed that uses far less land and water than regular animal feed, such as soy (the production of which has led to huge deforestation). In fact, one ton of insect protein can be grown in just 14 days, using only 20 square meters.[14] And the company does this using high-tech solutions such as artificial intelligence, robotics, and genetic improvement.

PRACTICAL LESSONS

Let's recap with some practical lessons that any business can take away from this chapter:

- Everything in this book is about building resilience. But, in particular, businesses should look to cultivate the five traits of resilient organizations outlined by Deloitte.

- Sustainability and resilience are intrinsically linked. If we don't take care of our planet, we all suffer – including businesses.

- Every organization must therefore look at their supply chain and operations to minimize their environmental impact.

- Finally, don't overlook the importance of social impact. How businesses treat people across the supply chain matters.

I like the Protix insect protein example because it combines sustainability with other high-tech trends, such as automation. In the next chapter, we'll explore automation in more detail – specifically, how to find a balance between humans and intelligent machines.

Notes

1. Resilience in an age of disruption; World Economic Forum; https://www .weforum.org/agenda/2021/01/business-resilience-pandemic-disruption/

2. Building the resilient organization: 2021 Deloitte Global resilience report; https://www2.deloitte.com/global/en/insights/topics/strategy/characteristics-resilient-organizations.html

3. Net-Zero Challenge: The Supply Chain Opportunity; World Economic Forum; http://www3.weforum.org/docs/WEF_Net_Zero_Challenge_The_ Supply_Chain_Opportunity_2021.pdf

4. Tony's for the fourth time awarded as most sustainable brand in the Netherlands; Tony's; https://tonyschocolonely.com/nl/en/our-mission/news/ tonys-for-the-fourth-time-awarded-as-most-sustainable-brand-in-the-netherlands

5. Our footprint; Patagonia; https://www.patagonia.com/our-footprint/

6. Global responsibility; General Mills; https://globalresponsibility.generalmills .com/2016/PDF/general_mills-global_responsibility_2016_0072.pdf

7. Damm and Ball launch world's first Aluminium Stewardship Initiative certified beverage cans; PR Newswire; https://www.prnewswire. com/news-releases/damm-and-ball-launch-worlds-first-aluminium-stewardship-initiative-certified-beverage-cans-301254687.html

8. The first environmentally friendly distillery in the world; Mackmyra; https://mackmyra.co.uk/pages/gravity-distillery

9. Planet; Yum!; https://www.yum.com/wps/portal/yumbrands/Yumbrands/ citizenship-and-sustainability/planet

10. Sustainability; Orsted; https://orsted.com/en/sustainability

11. Sustainability beers; Seven Bro7hers; https://www.sevenbro7hers.com/ sustainabilitybeers/

12. Hershey increases its cocoa deforestation initiatives by investing in supply chain sustainability; Supply Chain; https://www.supplychaindigital.com/ supply-chain-2/hershey-increases-its-cocoa-deforestation-initiatives-investing-supply-chain-sustainability

13. Hershey Announces Bold 2030 Goals to Reduce Environmental Footprint and Address Climate Change; PR Newswire; https://www.prnewswire .com/news-releases/hershey-announces-bold-2030-goals-to-reduce-environmental-footprint-and-address-climate-change-301237166.html

14. Sustainable insect protein; Protix; https://protix.eu/for-our-planet/

CHAPTER 19
FINDING THE BALANCE BETWEEN HUMANS AND INTELLIGENT COBOTS

The Blended Workforces of the Future

As we saw in Chapter 2, we now have increasingly capable robots and artificial intelligence (AI) systems that can take on tasks that were previously done by humans. And with robots (or collaborative robots, cobots) and AI available on subscription – meaning that you can effectively hire robots or tap into AI as and when needed (see Chapter 13) – it's easier than ever for organizations to leverage intelligent machines.

This leaves employers with some key questions: how do we find the balance between intelligent machines and human intelligence? What roles should be given over to machines? Which roles are best suited to humans? To answer these questions, we first need to understand exactly what intelligent machines are capable of.

The Amazing Capabilities of AIs and Intelligent Robots

Particularly in traditional companies, business leaders often aren't up to speed on the sheer range of tasks that today's AIs and intelligent robots can take on. (In fact, I spend a lot of time educating executives in this area.) This knowledge is key to finding the right balance between humans and machines in your organization.

Some of the things AI and AI-enabled robots can do are pretty mind-blowing. For example, you might be surprised to know that AIs can:

- Read: Not only can AIs understand written text, but they can also extract meaning from it. For example, the SummarizeBot can digest content such as news articles, reports, websites, emails, and even legal documents and then give you the essential information.

- Write: Organizations such as the *New York Times,* Reuters and the *Washington Post* use AI to write articles, typically formulaic articles of the "who, what, where, when, and how" variety. But AIs can also generate more creative content; in Japan, a novel generated by AI almost won a literary award.[1]

- See: Back in Chapter 2, I mentioned that machine vision underpins facial recognition, and plays a key role in enabling self-driving cars to operate safely on the road. But machine vision can also be used for all sorts of uses, from monitoring machinery in a factory setting, to sorting cucumbers on a farm.[2]

- Hear: We know that AIs can already understand human speech extremely well (think Alexa and Siri), but they can also interpret other sounds. For example, the ShotSpotter AI policing tool can detect and locate gunshots, then alert the authorities.

- Speak: Many of us are used to having basic conversations with smart assistants like Alexa, but the Google Duplex assistant is capable of holding more complex conversations. The tool can make phone calls and book appointments on your behalf, using very conversational, natural language, and responding to the person on the other end of the call.

- Smell: Researchers have developed AI algorithms that can detect potential signs of illness or disease just by analyzing (smelling) a human's breath. The AI can detect chemicals called aldehydes that are associated with human illnesses and stress, including cancer and diabetes.[3]

- Touch: Remember the raspberry-picking robot I mentioned back in Chapter 6? It uses sensors and cameras to identify ripe raspberries before delicately picking them, which goes to show that some intelligent machines can be surprisingly dexterous.

- Move: AI propels all kinds of movement, from autonomous vehicles to Starship delivery robots and Ford's two-legged delivery robot (Chapter 6). In Tokyo, humanoid robot Alter 3 has even conducted an "android opera."[4]

- Understand emotions: AI can gather data from a person's facial expressions, body language, and the like and analyze it to determine what emotion is likely being expressed at that time.

- Create: Beyond writing an almost-award-winning novel, AIs can master a wide range of creative processes, including making visual art (see Sophia the Robot, Chapter 10), composing music, and writing poetry.

While some of these examples are very impressive, the AIs are, for the most part, taking one type of input (visual data, written data, or whatever) and generating a particular output, as programmed.

This means there is potential to automate all sort of tasks that follow this input-to-output model, such as scanning security video for suspicious behavior, moderating content online, answering simple customer enquiries, entering data, or maintaining bookkeeping records. Therefore, human jobs that are built on some sort of input-to-output scenario are very likely to be automated in the future. As Stanford professor Andrew Ng puts it, "If a typical person can do a mental task with less than one second of thought, we can probably automate it using AI either now or in the near future."[5]

Examples of Automation in Practice

Let's pause here and reflect on some real-world examples that illustrate just how far automation has come.

Ericsson's "Smart Factory of the Future"

Ericsson's 5G smart factory in Lewisville, Texas, provides an impressive vision of the future of manufacturing. Inside the factory – which opened in 2020 and produces the antenna systems that enable 4G and 5G mobile networks – assembly, packing, unpacking, and product handling is done autonomously. Meanwhile, autonomous drones patrol the factory to secure the site, day and night. In fact, robots do pretty much all of the manual labor, which Ericsson says accounts for between 50 and 80 percent of conventional factory activities.[6] Human employees instead focus their efforts on the business or training.

The factory is also built with sustainability in mind, as part of Ericsson's goal to be carbon neutral by 2030, and features solar panels, rainwater tanks, and free charging points for employees' electric cars. (Circle back to Chapter 18 for more on sustainable operations.)

JD.com: The fully automated warehouse

Online shopping giant JD.com has a huge warehouse in China manned by machines that carry out work that would normally be done by 180 workers.[7] There are automated conveyors that zip boxes around the facility, image scanners that check packages, and self-driving forklift trucks that bring packages to trucks for transportation. The facility can handle 9,000 orders per hour.

Ocado: More tech company than supermarket

UK online grocery retailer Ocado is another leader in fully automated warehouses. In Ocado's warehouses, robots navigate around facilities the size of several football fields, pick up bins, and deliver them to pick stations to complete customer orders. The traffic flow of robots is all managed by AI, as is the health and maintenance of the robots. In just five minutes, the robots can complete 50,000 orders.[8]

Apple's recycling rebot

Meet Daisy, Apple's recycling robot that can strip apart discarded iPhones so the parts can be reused. For example, Daisy recovers iPhone batteries so that the cobalt, a key battery material, can be combined with other materials and used to make brand-new batteries. Other recycled materials used in the production of Apple devices include tin and aluminum. Thanks to Daisy – which can disassemble 15 different iPhone models at the rate of 200 per hour – Apple helped divert more than 48,000 metric tons of electronic waste from landfills in 2018.[9]

Collaborative robots (cobots) that work alongside humans

The latest generation of robots are intended to work alongside humans, not replace them altogether. A far cry from the industrial robots of the past, which posed a danger to human workers, cobots can work flexibly in the same space as humans, learn tasks from humans, and recognize where humans are (to avoid colliding with them). In one example, the Animoto robot by Giga Automata has been designed to work together with humans.[10] Companies such as Ford and Amazon are already harnessing cobots in manufacturing and warehouse environments to get the best of humans and machines.[11]

The Future of Work: What Will Happen to All the Human Workers?

Thanks to AI, robotics, cobots, and other intelligent machines, we will see the work of humans affected in three key ways:

- Displacement of human jobs: Some jobs will be displaced by automation.

- Augmentation of human jobs: Even more will be altered or changed in some way by automation.

- Addition of new human jobs: Finally, new jobs will arise that previously did not exist.

Let's explore each area in turn.

Displacement of human jobs

According to the World Economic Forum's Future of Jobs Report 2020, the adoption of technology by organizations will transform jobs, tasks, and skills by 2025.[12] Forty-three percent of businesses surveyed for the report said they would be reducing their workforce due to technology integration. In fact, the WEF estimates that 85 million jobs may be displaced by automation by 2025, which is a staggering figure.

Naturally, this creates a lot of fear around the subject of automation (headlines that warn of robots coming for our jobs don't help). But while many jobs will be displaced, the WEF expects that more jobs will be augmented or added because of technology adoption. Indeed, those same businesses surveyed for the WEF report, said they hoped to internally redeploy nearly 50 percent of workers displaced. In other words, more employees will see their work change, rather than be laid off altogether.

Augmentation of human jobs

According to the WEF, by 2025, the time spent on current tasks at work by humans and machines will be equal. This means employers must find the perfect balance between those tasks done by humans and those done by machines. To put it another way, we need to ensure the work given to machines is best suited to machines, and the work given to humans is best suited to humans (so humans don't end up feeling like machines). For example, chatbots are great at answering simple customer queries, but they can't deal with complex questions so well, which means we still need humans in the loop. The benefit of balancing human workers and machines in this scenario is that humans spend less time on routine questions that are a waste of their capabilities; instead, they get to focus their time where they can really add value and improve the customer experience.

Co-creativity is a good example of blending humans and machines successfully. Professor Marcus du Sautoy, author of *The Creativity Code,* says that the role of AI is a "kind of catalyst to push our human creativity,"[13] and I couldn't agree more. Machine and human creativity can produce some exciting results – things that wouldn't be achieved if either were working alone. For example, musicians and producers are now collaborating with AI to produce music,[14] and, in a project with Google, award-winning choreographer Wayne McGregor has used AI to enhance choreography.[15]

Remember Stitch Fix from Chapter 13? It's the fashion subscription box that uses AI to pick out clothes that you'll love. But Stitch Fix doesn't just rely on AI to do this; it's the combination of data, AI algorithms, and human stylists that makes the service so impressive. Machines do the initial work of crunching through enormous amounts of data and evaluating the likelihood of a customer loving a particular style, based on the customer's information, preferences, and previous choices. Then a human stylist finalizes the selection and writes a personal note advising the client on how to style or accessorize various items.[16] For me, this is a fantastic example of getting the best out of both machines and humans.

This perfect symbiosis between intelligent machines and capable humans is referred to by automation pioneers Faethm as "responsible automation."[17] Faethm exists to ensure automation is done in a way that doesn't leave humans behind, and the company's approach involves breaking jobs down into task fractions to see what can and can't be automated. Done this way, automation – at least according to Faethm – doesn't have to result in job losses. Instead, humans transition to more rewarding tasks. It can even lead to the creation of new jobs within the workforce, which brings me to the next topic.

The addition of new human jobs

While the WEF estimates that 85 million jobs may be displaced, it also estimates that 97 million new roles may emerge – roles that are better adapted to the new division of labor between humans and machines.

These new roles are likely to rely on a slightly different set of skills and capabilities, compared to those skills that have traditionally been prioritized in the past. And this means employers have a responsibility to equip their workforces with the skills needed for the fourth industrial revolution. This ties in with the WEF report, in which employers expect to offer reskilling and upskilling to more than 70 percent of their employees by 2025.

Reskilling Employees for the Fourth Industrial Revolution

In this new blended workplace where labor is divided between humans and machines, certain skills will be prioritized over others. In particular, I expect to see greater emphasis on those "softer" skills – human qualities like creativity and critical thinking – that machines can't do so well. (At least, today's machines can't do so well.)

So tasks that can be easily automated will be. Meanwhile, the work left to humans will become altogether more, well, human. Employers therefore need to prepare their workforces for this shift in core skills, and upskill or reskill their people accordingly. Here are the skills I expect to become critical over the next few years:

- Critical thinking. Yes, AI is great at analyzing data, but the human ability to judge the quality of information (whether information is trustworthy) and remain open-minded will be very valuable in this data-rich world.

- Complex decision-making. While machines can extract valuable insights from data, ultimately it's the humans in the business who must make decisions based on that data. Therefore, organizations will need people who have good judgment, can make complex decisions, and can consider how those decisions will impact the organization and the people within it.

- Emotional intelligence and empathy. Today's machines just aren't able to compete with humans in terms of emotional intelligence and empathy.

- Creativity. AI is making inroads in creative work, but humans are still better at creativity. There's no substitute for the human ability to invent, imagine, and dream up a better future, although as the Stitch Fix example shows, human creativity can be enhanced by machines.

- Flexibility. With the startling pace of change, the half-life of skills is reducing, which means people need to be adaptable to change, and willing to commit to learning new skills throughout their careers. Being open to new ways of doing things will be highly valuable. Related to this are key skills like curiosity, openness, a growth mindset, and the ability to learn from mistakes.

- Cultural intelligence. As businesses operate across international borders, as remote workforces grow and businesses become more diverse (see Chapter 20), it's important that employees are sensitive to other cultures, languages, and political and religious beliefs.

- Ethics. New technological advances are likely to throw up new ethical dilemmas, so organizations will need people to help them address these issues.

- Leadership. With organizations adopting flatter structures, as opposed to the traditional hierarchical structures of old (more on this in Chapter 21), it will become increasingly important that people right across the company have the ability to inspire and bring out the best in others.

- Collaboration, communication, and teamwork. The human ability to communicate effectively with all sorts of people will be an essential skill in the fourth industrial revolution, especially as organizations transition to more remote working.

- Digital and data literacy. Alongside the softer skills mentioned, people need to be comfortable around and develop the skills to work alongside technology. And with data becoming a core business asset (see Chapter 2), organizations must train people on how to use data and extract business value from it.

PRACTICAL LESSONS

There's no doubt that automation will affect every industry, so business leaders must prepare their organizations – and their people – for the changing nature of work. In particular:

- The first step is to understand what can and can't be automated. The sheer range of tasks that intelligent machines can take on may surprise you.

- Then it's a case of understanding what this means for human jobs. Some jobs will be displaced, but more jobs will be augmented and new ones created.

- Responsible automation means identifying the tasks that are better suited to machines, so that they can be automated, leaving humans to do the more complex, rewarding work.

- In this blended work environment, where humans and machines collaborate – and as the shape of organizations changes (see Chapter 21) – skills such as empathy, creativity, leadership, and communication will become critical for success. It's absolutely vital that employers reskill their workforce accordingly.

Now let's focus more on the human side of things and look at another key trend for employers: how to find and keep talent.

Notes

1. Japanese AI Writes a Novel, Nearly Wins Literary Award; Big Think; https://bigthink.com/natalie-shoemaker/a-japanese-ai-wrote-a-novel-almost-wins-literary-award

2. How a Japanese cucumber farmer is using deep learning and TensorFlow; Google Cloud; https://cloud.google.com/blog/products/ai-machine-learning/how-a-japanese-cucumber-farmer-is-using-deep-learning-and-tensorflow

3. AI Designed with a "Sense of Smell" to Detect Illnesses from Human Breath; Evolving Science; https://www.evolving-science.com/intelligent-machines/ai-sense-smell-00783

4. New Opera Starring Humanoid Robot Alter 3 in the Works for Tokyo Theatre; Billboard; https://www.billboard.com/articles/news/international/8503764/new-opera-humanoid-robot-alter-3-tokyo-japan

5. What Artificial Intelligence Can and Can't Do Right Now; Harvard Business Review; https://hbr.org/2016/11/what-artificial-intelligence-can-and-cant-do-right-now

6. Our smart factory of the future: Let me show you around; Ericsson; https://www.ericsson.com/en/blog/2021/1/smart-factory-of-the-future

7. Chinese ecommerce giant shows off its first ever "robot warehouse"; Tech in Asia; https://www.techinasia.com/china-fully-automated-sorting-center-jd-ecommerce

8. The Amazing Ways Ocado Uses Artificial Intelligence and Tech to Transform the Grocery Industry; Forbes; https://www.forbes.com/sites/bernardmarr/2020/10/30/the-amazing-ways-ocado-uses-artificial-intelligence-and-tech-to-transform-the-grocery-industry/?sh=2bfc463e4797

9. Apple expands global recycling programmes; Apple; https://www.apple.com/uk/newsroom/2019/04/apple-expands-global-recycling-programs/

10. Giga Automata; http://gigaautomata.com/animoto/

11. The Future of Work: Are You Ready for Smart Cobots?; Bernard Marr; https://bernardmarr.com/default.asp?contentID=1555

12. The Future of Jobs Report 2020; World Economic Forum; http://www3.weforum.org/docs/WEF_Future_of_Jobs_2020.pdf

13. Can Machines and Artificial Intelligence Be Creative?; Forbes; https://www.forbes.com/sites/bernardmarr/2020/02/28/can-machines-and-artificial-intelligence-be-creative/?sh=685130364580

14. More Artists Are Writing Songs in the Key of AI; Wired; https://www.wired.com/story/music-written-by-artificial-intelligence/

15. Could Google Be the World's Next Great Choreographer?; Dance Magazine; https://www.dancemagazine.com/is-google-the-worlds-next-great-choreographer-2625652667.html

16. Algorithms Tour; Stitch Fix; https://algorithms-tour.stitchfix.com/

17. Responsible automation; Faethm; https://faethm.ai/

CHAPTER 20
FINDING AND KEEPING TALENT

The Shifting Talent Pool and Employee Experience

As we've already seen throughout this book, technology is enabling new ways of working, and this will impact both recruitment and the employee experience. Let's dive straight in with the changing nature of attracting talent.

Finding and Attracting Talent in the Fourth Industrial Revolution

Some major trends will affect how organizations recruit talent:

- In the wake of the COVID-19 pandemic, 84 percent of employers said they were set to rapidly digitize working processes and, in turn, expand remote working – with the potential to move 44 percent of their workforce to remote working.[1]

- More and more people are now "gig workers." In the US alone, more than one-third of workers (36 percent) participate in the gig economy, and more than 90 percent would consider freelancing.[2]

- Seventy-five percent of the workforce will be represented by millennials by 2030.[3] And millennials are very comfortable participating in the gig economy; almost half of all millennials use gig economy platforms to find work.[4]

The way we work is shifting, in other words, with more younger people entering the workforce, more gig workers, and more remote workers.

Tapping into a global talent pool

In their book *The Human Cloud: How Today's Changemakers Use Artificial Intelligence and the Freelance Economy to Transform Work* (which is well worth a read), Matthew Mottola and Matthew Coatney describe a new way of work in which AI (see Chapter 19) and the freelance economy combine to transform productivity.[5] They argue that traditional full-time employment will be a thing of the past, as organizations shift to hiring people on a contract basis – with those contractors working remotely.

This means the talent pool is now truly global. Your next hire could literally be located anywhere in the world. They could be a freelance contractor or a flexible gig worker, or a full-time employee who works remotely 100 percent of the time. They don't have to be in the same city as your business, or willing to move. You're no longer at the whim of local labor markets. (Read more about hybrid working, or blending on-site employees and remote workers, in Chapter 21.)

The advantages for employers are obvious. There's no doubt in my mind that this opening up of the talent pool is a positive shift, particularly in terms of diversity (more on that coming up), but it will require organizations to rethink their hiring strategies. According to Boston Consulting Group, employers may want to:[6]

- Assess their current workforce to evaluate the gaps for certain jobs, projects, and tasks.

- Upskill the existing workforce to take account of the new tasks and roles that are emerging. This should be done in addition to external hiring.

- Shift the focus from hiring for skill to "hiring for will." As we saw in Chapter 19, the half-life of skills is shrinking, so a willingness to learn new skills will be an increasingly important attribute in candidates, more so than specific education or qualifications. Hirers must therefore look at candidate criteria with an open mind, embracing self-taught candidates and those who embody a continual learning mindset, rather than those with specific qualifications, certification, or experience.

- Some employers may even choose to hire talent and add them to their "talent pool" before they even know which specific field of operations they are best suited to.

I would also add that employers must beef up their flexible working initiatives and allow more flexible working if they want to get the most out of the "human cloud."

Building an Inclusive Workforce

Employers increasingly have the ability to tap into a global pool of talent. Fantastic. The flip side, of course, is that workers can increasingly tap into a global pool of employers! This means employers must continue to work on their employer brand if they want to attract the best talent. For me, diversity and inclusion will be a key differentiating factor in this new, more global job market. As we saw in Chapter 1, organizations with inclusive cultures – where people feel valued, respected, and that they belong – are more likely to achieve better business outcomes, so the incentive is certainly there for employers.[7]

My hope is that more global competition for talent will prompt all employers to give diversity and inclusivity the attention it deserves. I now see more employers appointing people to be in charge of diversity and inclusion, which is a good sign. At Netflix, for example, Vernā Myers has been VP of inclusion strategy since 2018, and the company published its first inclusion report in 2021. Let's dwell a little on the report's findings to see how Netflix tackles inclusion.

Firstly, inclusion is one of the cultural values Netflix employees are asked about in surveys – through which the company found that it wasn't as inclusive as it thought. But, as the report sets out, Netflix has a plan to increase representation, and "cultivate a community of belonging and allyship."[8] Because, as the report says, diversity and inclusion "unlocks our ability to innovate, to be creative, to solve problems. It breaks up group think. It brings different lived experiences and perspectives to a problem, so that we're no longer solving them in old ways."

To drive inclusion, Netflix has what it called an "inclusion lens," where all employees are encouraged to ask questions like, who is being excluded? Whose voice is missing? But the company is also relying on recruiters and leaders to hire more inclusively. In particular:

- Netflix has built a training curriculum to help recruiters hire more inclusively, advise hiring managers, identify bias in the recruiting process, and source candidates in nontraditional ways.

- The company also runs a technical bootcamp with Norfolk State University, a historically black university, to create access for emerging talent.

- And, recognizing that people tend to hire people similar to themselves, Netflix's inclusion recruiting team helps managers break out of this mold and connect to networks outside of their own, by partnering with organizations like Ghetto Film School.

This is just a snapshot of what Netflix is doing to improve inclusion across the company, and I urge you to read the full Inclusion Report 2021. And, of course, having got talent through the door, Netflix wants to be the place where candidates stick around and build a rewarding career. This brings us to the second part of this chapter: the employee experience.

Improving the Employee Experience

Whether you're hiring employees or contractors, remote team members, or office-based workers, you want talent to stay with the organization. (After all, thanks to the gig economy, contract and project work, and companies embracing remote working, there's no shortage of options out there for unhappy employees looking to move on.) And if you want people to stay with the organization, you need to provide a great employee experience.

Employee experience is different than employee engagement, although a good employee experience obviously leads to higher engagement. Rather, the employee experience encompasses everything that occurs in the employee life cycle, from the recruitment process to the final day working for the company. Perhaps a more digestible way to consider the employee experience is via the following three areas:

- Organizational culture

- Technology

- Physical work environment

Let's briefly explore each area.

Having the Right Organizational Culture in Place

The organizational culture is what brings everyone together within a company – it epitomizes what it means to work for the organization. I could write a whole book on this topic alone, but for me some of the key cultural considerations for the future are:

- Inclusivity (which I've already mentioned).

- Lifelong learning. The successful organizations of the future will be those that cultivate a culture of lifelong learning. As we know, the digital age will require a constant upgrading of knowledge, which means companies must invest in internal development initiatives that ensure people have the skills needed to thrive in the fourth industrial revolution (circle back to Chapter 19 for skills). And this educational content will need to be delivered in a variety of formats to suit the more agile, flexible, and dispersed workforces of the future.

- Performance management. I believe the future of performance management is about making sure people understand their contribution to the organization's strategic objectives, giving them the responsibility and freedom to deliver that contribution – and then rewarding and celebrating success. (You can read more about this in Chapter 21.)

- Authenticity. This isn't just important for building connections and trust with customers; employees, too, want to connect with authentic brands and leaders. (Read more about this in Chapter 22.)

- Recruitment and onboarding. Typically, the first interaction people have with the organization (unless they have previously been a customer, supplier, etc.), the recruitment and onboarding processes provide a valuable way to acquaint employees with the organization's culture and get them excited to work for the company. A crappy recruitment experience will speak volumes.

Of course, maintaining your organizational culture when so many people work remotely can be a challenge, but you can read more about the organizing around hybrid working in the next chapter.

Having the right technology in place

If people don't have the tools they need to do their job, motivation will fall off a cliff. Therefore, this aspect is all about enabling people to do their jobs successfully – but also providing the technology that enables employees to work *how* they want, which increasingly will mean remotely (if only for some of the time). Therefore, organizations will rapidly need to embrace the tools that support remote working. As an example, one of my clients, a big tech company, is now doing digital-first meetings; this means even those people who are in the office join the meeting at their desk on Zoom, ensuring those people joining from home don't feel like they're missing out by not being "in the room."

In my experience, the technology people work with in companies often lags behind the tech they use at home. Or at least, that was generally the case before the pandemic – before companies drastically accelerated their adoption of new technologies. Now, most companies are routinely using tools like Slack and Zoom, and they even support people bringing their own devices into work, so the gap between what we routinely use at home and what we use at work is closing.

Having an attractive physical environment

Many of us spend eight hours or more at work, so of course the environment needs to be clean, safe, comfortable, enjoyable, and – hopefully – inspiring. These days, this isn't just about making sure the workplace itself is a good place to spend time; it's also about making sure those working from home are in the right environment. (I talk a bit more about this in Chapter 21.)

These three areas of the employee experience perhaps all sound like common sense, yet, as Deloitte points out, only 22 percent of executives feel their organizations do an excellent job of creating a great employee experience (despite 80 percent acknowledging that employee experience is either important or very important to business success).[9] Something is going wrong somewhere, and it must change. To succeed in the fourth industrial revolution, with all the challenges and opportunities around the global talent pool and hybrid working, having a great employee experience will be a necessity – as important, in my opinion, as providing a great customer experience.

PRACTICAL LESSONS

In this chapter, we've learned:

- The way we work is shifting, with more younger people entering the workforce, more gig workers, and more remote workers. Employers can now tap into a global talent pool.

- A willingness to learn new skills will be an increasingly important attribute in candidates. Rather than seeking specific qualifications, certification, or experience, employers must keep an open mind and embrace candidates who are passionate about continual learning.

- Diversity and inclusion will be a key differentiating factor in the global competition for talent, and organizations must help their recruiters to hire more inclusively.

- When it comes to retaining talent, the employee experience is key. Providing a great employee experience means having the right organizational culture, having the right technology in place, and having the right physical environment (including for those working remotely).

Closely linked to finding and retaining talent, in the next chapter I'll explore how businesses should organize themselves for success in the fourth industrial revolution.

Notes

1. The Future of Jobs Report 2020; World Economic Forum; http://www3 .weforum.org/docs/WEF_Future_of_Jobs_2020.pdf

2. Gig Economy Statistics: The New Normal in the Workplace; Fortunly; https://fortunly.com/statistics/gig-economy-statistics/

3. Employee Experience: Components, Importance & Strategies to Improve; Vantage Circle; https://blog.vantagecircle.com/employee-experience/

4. Gig Economy Statistics: The New Normal in the Workplace; Fortunly; https://fortunly.com/statistics/gig-economy-statistics/

5. *The Human Cloud: How Today's Changemakers Use Artificial Intelligence and the Freelance Economy to Transform Work*; Matthew Mottola and Matthew Coatney; https://www.humancloudbook.com/

6. The Future of Jobs in the Era of AI; BCG; https://www.bcg.com/ publications/2021/impact-of-new-technologies-on-jobs

7. The diversity and inclusion revolution; Deloitte; https://www2.deloitte .com/content/dam/insights/us/articles/4209_Diversity-and-inclusion-revolution/DI_Diversity-and-inclusion-revolution.pdf

8. Inclusion Takes Root at Netflix: Our First Report; Netflix; https://about.netflix.com/en/news/netflix-inclusion-report-2021

9. The employee experience: Culture, engagement and beyond; Deloitte; https://www2.deloitte.com/us/en/insights/focus/human-capital-trends/2017/improving-the-employee-experience-culture-engagement.html

CHAPTER 21
ORGANIZING TO WIN
Flatter, More Agile Organizations

This trend is all about organizing your business for success in the fourth industrial revolution. Whether you work for a startup, a giant multinational, or something in between, organizational structure is so embedded in the notion of work and business that we hardly notice it. But structure is important. It's what allows organizations – regardless of size – to run successfully. If you think about it, structure informs almost everything about the business, including its culture and values. So it makes sense that organizational structures should evolve and change, just as the nature of business and work itself is rapidly evolving.

From Hierarchical to Flatter, More Agile Organizational Structures

Traditionally, organizations have been very hierarchical and rigid in their structures. But that is changing, as leaders recognize the need for flatter, more agile structures that allow the business to quickly reorganize teams and respond to change. It is also, in part, a response to the changing nature of work, particularly the proliferation of freelance and remote workers.

The modern, flatter organization

No doubt you're already familiar with the traditional hierarchical business structure. You probably work in such a structure, or have done so in the past. It's essentially a top-down system, where each employee has a defined position on the "ladder," with very clearly defined roles and responsibilities. Perhaps a pyramid is a better description than a corporate ladder, since the CEO sits at the very top, then each layer below (heads of department, then line managers, then everyone else) gets wider, but less powerful.

This has worked well for generations. But now, in this age of rapid technological advancement and global workforces, things are beginning to change. We're seeing flatter organizational structures, which are more like flexible communities rather than a top-down pyramid structure. Of the various modern organizational structures, the flatter structure is the most widely adopted and, according to some experts (myself included), is the one that will grow the most.[1]

Key characteristics of flatter organizations include:

- **Collaboration.** In a flatter organizational structure, departmental boundaries are eliminated, and teams collaborate freely on projects that pursue the organization's strategic goals and solve the business's biggest challenges. (This may even involve pulling in external contractors or accessing the "human cloud" as and when needed; see Chapter 20.)

- **Autonomy.** Project teams work to specific requirements and goals, but they have the freedom to decide for themselves the best way to complete the project and deliver those goals. As a result, there is little or no middle management layer required to supervise employees; employees can interact directly with higher-up managers and executives.

- **Decision-making.** Employees have more decision-making power, and can proactively decide what needs doing and how, in order to achieve the organization's goals. (This ensures decisions happen faster – more on faster innovation coming up.) For more strategic decisions, managers and executives may collaborate with employees to make decisions, or at least solicit their feedback. Employees feel heard.

- **Communication.** Because there are fewer departmental boundaries, communication flows fast and free across the organization. Instant messaging apps are frequently used to ensure everyone in the business can communicate with everyone else.

- **Flexibility.** In the flatter organization, careers are flexible and dynamic. Remote work is common. And employees may even "float" from project to project, and team to team, choosing which projects to work on based on their skills and interests, rather than remain in one defined role.

A good example comes from multinational manufacturer Whirlpool, which eschews traditional job titles, instead grouping all employees according to one of four categories: leading self, leading others, leading function, and leading enterprise.[2] Everyone in the organization is viewed as someone who leads.

At Nike, teams are organized by product type, with subsidiary divisions such as Converse and Hurley. These divisions operate quite independently within the Nike brand – there's enough oversight to maintain Nike's consistent brand, but divisions have the flexibility to respond to their own customer demands.[3] Teams remain small and decisions are fast – which brings us onto a key advantage of flatter organizations: faster innovation.

The importance of speed and innovation

Speed is a really important component of flatter organizations, and with good reason. This book has hopefully given you a sense of the rapid pace of change under way. Organizations must learn to innovate faster if they want to compete in the fourth industrial revolution. For me, this means:

- **Embracing a "minimum viable product/service" (MVP) mindset.** Business leaders must accept that, in general, product and service life cycles are getting shorter and constant updates may be required to succeed. This is where MVP comes into play.

MVP essentially means developing a new product or service to the point where it has just enough features to be used by customers, who then provide feedback so that the product or service can continue to be improved.

- **Building customer feedback loops into the organization.** Customer feedback is an essential part of MVP, but even if you don't go down an MVP route, your business must listen to customers and ensure customers feel heard. This will be especially important as more tasks become automated (see Chapter 19). John Zerilli, author of *A Citizen's Guide to Artificial Intelligence*, talks about the "computer says no" mentality where decisions made by algorithms can hugely affect customers (think of a mortgage application, for example). If an algorithm says no, it's vital customers have another feedback route where they can be heard.

- **Not shying away from self-cannibalization.** Businesses must not be afraid to develop new products and services or set up new business units that are a direct threat to their most profitable products/services. Forward-thinking businesses recognize the need to self-cannibalize their own offering, rather than leave it to startups to do it for them.[4] Indeed, the big tech giants do this all the time (think of Apple's iPhone rendering iPods pretty much redundant), but so do other successful organizations; for example, when Proctor & Gamble launched Tide synthetic detergent in the 1940s, they knew it was a threat to their much-loved Ivory Soap.[5] But they also knew that if they didn't do it a competitor would!

- **Embedding a culture of "intrapreneurship" in the organization.** This concept takes the entrepreneurial process of turning ideas into actual innovations and transplants it within the corporate setting. In other words, employees are encouraged to come up with new ideas and pitch those to senior leaders. Research shows that intrapreneurship boosts both employee engagement and productivity.[6]

It can be difficult to achieve these characteristics in a traditional hierarchical structure, which is a big reason why the flatter organizational structure is better suited to the fourth industrial revolution.

Smaller, more dynamic teams – and the link to pizzas

As I've already mentioned, in a flatter organization, there are fewer boundaries, and teams organize themselves more organically, and this may include porous boundaries into the human cloud. Teams are also organized around value, meaning the focus shifts from measuring efficiency and output to creating customer *value* (more on managing performance coming up later). Work that does not create value is eliminated.

But, importantly, teams in flatter organizations are also smaller. Amazon refers to this as "two-pizza teams" – teams that can be fed by two pizzas. Amazon finds that collaboration is better in smaller teams, which further aids the company's ability to innovate and act fast.[7] It makes sense. Smaller teams spend less time on organizational stuff and more time doing what needs to be done. But what about the ability to scale up when needed, and add new product lines and services? At Amazon, these small teams work together and combine resources in order to achieve larger goals. Amazon calls this the "flywheel" approach – using scale to create an ever-increasing momentum that drives the company and basically makes it unstoppable.[8] It's certainly worked for Amazon.

Managing Performance in Flatter Organizations

What does this shift in structure mean for performance management? How can you get the best out of people in a flatter, more agile organizational structure with self-organizing teams and porous boundaries? Part of the answer lies in rethinking the employee experience (head back to Chapter 20 for more on this). But it also requires a rethink of how we define, measure, and manage performance.

The modern, more supportive way to manage performance

Traditional performance management tends to involve quite rigid control. In the hierarchical setup, goals are set at the top level, then cascade down into smaller and smaller goals, from one level to the next throughout the business. Employees' roles are broken down into specific tasks and the company monitors how well they do those tasks.

None of this works in the flatter organization. Instead, performance management in flatter organizations tends to involve:

- Setting top-level goals and key supporting goals simultaneously, with these goals focusing on *outcomes*, not output – meaning they tie in with the organization's overarching strategic priorities, rather than trying to control what individuals do on a granular level. This way, everyone feels they are working toward common goals, and teams and individuals understand how their work directly contributes to the organization's success. One goal-setting method that's gaining popularity is OKRs, or Objectives and Key Results, an approach favored by Google.[9] In very simple terms, the Objective part sets out what the organization wants to achieve, and the Key Result define what success looks like.

- Giving teams and individuals more autonomy on how they achieve desired results. So, having identified common goals, flatter organizations then give teams and individuals the freedom to work toward those goals and achieve the desired results in whatever way they think is best.

- Replacing the annual performance review with regular, two-way check-ins. Continual feedback – rather than an annual review – is becoming increasingly common, which is great because it allows employees to give and receive feedback much more frequently.

- Rewarding and celebrating success, by communicating how people's efforts have benefited the organization and helped deliver its strategic goals.

As an example, GE has ditched the annual review in favor of regular feedback – facilitated via its PD@GE app. Using the app, each employee can set a series of priorities and ask for feedback. They can also provide feedback, in real time, to others, and ask for an in-person conversation at any time.[10]

Adobe also ditched the annual review process because it took up too many hours, and created barriers to teamwork and innovation. Instead, Adobe switched to regular, ongoing performance discussions. As a result, the company saved 80,000 management hours.[11] What's more, voluntary turnover dropped by 30 percent and involuntary departures rose by 50 percent, meaning poor hires were being managed out more effectively.

So is this the end of KPIs?

I doubt it. This modern, more supportive approach to performance management is actually very data-driven. It just may require a rethink of *what* you measure. For example, you may want to set new metrics around communication that measure how well employees and managers communicate across the company.

KPIs certainly have a role to play in the new performance management landscape. Take OKRs, for example. OKRs help you define your organization's strategic goals and desired results. KPIs will help you measure performance against those goals. KPIs therefore remain an important part of performance management, but must be more closely tied to the organization's goals. In other words, there's no point measuring anything and everything just because you can.

The flexible, continual approach to performance management also fits well with the gig economy and remote workers (Chapter 20). There's simply no point trying to break down and control every little thing remote employees or freelancers do. Far better to engage them with the company's goals, give and receive regular feedback against project deliverables, then reward success so that remote employees and freelancers still feel connected to the organization's performance. And this brings us on to the next subject.

The New Hybrid Work Environment

We're entering a new work environment where more people will be working remotely (see Chapter 20) – including employees, freelancers, and those in the gig economy. Employers are increasingly recognizing this shift and embracing it. Pinterest, for example, paid $90 million in 2020 to get out of a lease on a new headquarters in San Francisco, citing a shift to more remote working.[12] And Oracle was able to relocate from California to Texas – taking advantage of lower taxes and costs – without losing California-based employees.[13] Software company GitLab takes this a step further and says it is the world's largest all-remote company, with over 1,300 employees located in 65 countries.[14]

What is hybrid working?

Hybrid working recognizes that going all-remote or remote-first – where employees' primary option is to work from home – may not be an option for all employers. Remote working just isn't possible for every job. (That said, when it comes to knowledge workers, all employers should be asking whether they absolutely need people in the office *every day*.) So, hybrid working steps in to bridge the gap between all-remote working and traditional office-based working. For this reason, I believe hybrid working will be more widely adopted than all-remote working.

Hybrid working basically means successfully blending on-site working and remote working to build a healthy and resilient organization. As well as giving employees more flexibility over where they work, this may also extend to *when* they work, recognizing that some people may be happier working outside regular office hours.

Does this signal the end of physical premises? Probably not. This is about blending the workplace with remote working, not eliminating the physical workplace altogether. After all, companies may still need a place to carry out face-to-face meetings with clients and teams (and many will always need premises for manufacturing, storage and logistics, and so on). It's just that the way office space is used will change, with people appearing on certain days or as and when required.

Overcoming the challenges of hybrid working

There are concerns – very valid concerns – over the impact that remote working has on areas such as training, onboarding, and the development of a cohesive company culture.

Everything I've outlined so far in this chapter – transitioning to a flatter organizational structure and rethinking performance management – will help to overcome these obstacles and better equip the organization for hybrid working. For example, focusing performance management on *outcomes* rather than output frees up employees and teams to decide for themselves how best to deliver results – and removes the need for line managers to closely oversee what people are doing. The continual feedback with employees will also be important for monitoring how people feel when they work remotely (for example, whether they feel connected to the rest of the team, stressed at having work intrude on their personal space, etc.).

Here are a few other ways in which organizations can overcome the challenges of hybrid working:

- Think about what needs to change in your office environment; for example, you may need to remove cubicles and individual workstations and replace them with more collaborative spaces.

- Embrace technology. Communication and collaboration tools like Slack, Zoom, and Facebook's Workplace are designed to facilitate cooperation and communication between remote teams. In the future, we may even see greater use of extended reality solutions to bring people together in a virtual space (see Chapter 2). And remember, harnessing technology also extends to passing the routine, day-to-day tasks that can be easily automated over to machines (see Chapter 19).

- Build personal connections. Face-to-face introductions, meet-and-greets, and team-building sessions will have a vital role to play in building rapport, friendship, and trust between team members (and managers). This may mean spending in-person time with new hires before they start working from home, or getting teams together every now and then. Then, when interactions move online, those bonds are already formed. That said, it's still important to make time for those casual workplace "watercooler" moments during digital meetings and calls – and encourage spontaneous calls and interactions online.

- Ensure remote employees are treated the same as on-site employees. Remember the company I mentioned in Chapter 20 that switched to digital first meetings (meaning even those in the office join the meeting on Zoom)? That's a perfect example of making sure those working from home don't feel like they're missing out.

- Evaluate the job performance of remote workers in exactly the same way as those who are office-based. And celebrate their success in the same way, too.

With steps like these, employers can balance the opportunities for innovative working practices with the everyday reality of getting business done.

PRACTICAL LESSONS

Here's what we've learned in this chapter:

- The flatter organizational structure is much better suited to success in the fourth industrial revolution, since it enables faster innovation, greater collaboration, and smaller, more agile teams.

- This has prompted a rethink of performance management. Instead of rigid goals and oversight, leaders set goals and desired results that tie in with the organization's strategic priorities. Individuals and teams then have the freedom to decide how best to contribute to those goals. The annual performance review is ditched in favor of continual feedback with employees.

- Hybrid working is, for many companies, a more achievable way forward than all-remote or remote-first working. But there will still be challenges to overcome around company culture, morale, communication, and so on. A flatter organizational structure and more agile performance management will help the organization harness hybrid working successfully, as will technology.

Now let's move from the organization's structure and performance to the very heart of the organization – in particular, what makes an organization authentic, and why authenticity matters in the fourth industrial revolution.

Notes

1. What is the right organization structure for the 21st century; Dropbox; https://blog.dropbox.com/topics/work-culture/21st-century-organization-structure

2. The future of work: Re-defining the workplace: Pacific Standard; https://psmag.com/economics/the-future-of-work-re-defining-the-workplace

3. Nike's Flat Organizational Structure; Bizfluent; https://bizfluent.com/facts-6887850-nike-s-flat-organizational-structure.html

4. The best companies aren't afraid to replace their most profitable products; IMD; https://www.imd.org/research-knowledge/articles/the-best-companies-afraid-to-replace-their-most-profitable-products/

5. Self-cannibalization in modern business; IMD; https://www.imd.org/bgs/insights/self-cannibalization-p-and-g-disruption/

6. Why You Should Become an "Intrapreneur"; Harvard Business Review; https://hbr.org/2020/03/why-you-should-become-an-intrapreneur

7. Two-Pizza Teams; Amazon; https://docs.aws.amazon.com/whitepapers/latest/introduction-devops-aws/two-pizza-teams.html

8. The two-pizza rule and the secret of Amazon's success; Guardian; https://www.theguardian.com/technology/2018/apr/24/the-two-pizza-rule-and-the-secret-of-amazons-success

9. Google's OKR Playbook; What Matters; https://www.whatmatters.com/resources/google-okr-playbook/

10. 5 Great Examples of Agile Organizations; Clear Review; https://www.clearreview.com/5-examples-of-agile-organisations/

11. Ibid.

12. Pinterest cancels huge SF office lease in unbuilt project, citing work-from-home shift; San Francisco Chronicle; https://www.sfchronicle.com/business/article/Pinterest-cancels-huge-SF-office-lease-in-unbuilt-15523170.php

13. Oracle Moves Headquarters to Texas, Joining Valley Exodus; Bloomberg; https://www.bloomberg.com/news/articles/2020-12-11/oracle-moves-headquarters-to-texas-joins-exodus-from-california

14. GitLab's Guide to All-Remote; GitLab; https://about.gitlab.com/company/culture/all-remote/guide/

CHAPTER 22
AUTHENTICITY

Why Brands and Leaders Need to Keep It Real

One theme that crops up throughout this book is customers seeking a more meaningful connection with brands. And as we saw in Chapter 20, employees also want to connect with the companies they work for. This need for connection has given rise to *authenticity* as a business trend in its own right.

Authenticity helps to foster human connections, because, as humans, we like to see brands (and business leaders, for that matter) display important human qualities like honesty, reliability, empathy, compassion, humility, and maybe even a bit of vulnerability and fear. We want brands (and leaders) to care about issues and stand for more than just turning a profit. Basically, we want to *trust* them.

Anatomy of an Authentic Business

Trust matters because, as consumer surveys demonstrate, we seem to be getting more skeptical – not just of organizations, but also the media, governments, and other institutions.[1] And in this environment, brands that have a reputation for being genuine immediately differentiate themselves from the pack. One study by research firm Stackla found that 86 percent of respondents across the US, UK, and Australia feel authenticity is a key factor when deciding what brands to support.[2]

But what is an authentic business?

It's kind of a woolly term, isn't it, authenticity? And it no doubt means different things to different people. But broadly speaking, authenticity is all about trust. And what attributes inspire trust?

Reliability

Consumers want to know they can count on a brand and its products. So products with a built-in obsolescence or companies that provide a less-than-great service are unlikely to spark trust. Consistency matters, then – which also means being a *consistently authentic* business. In other words, authenticity isn't a buzzword to focus on for the next year; it's something that must be baked into the business itself.

Respectfulness

By this I mean respect for people (including those involved in the making of products), cultures, and, crucially, our environment. Circle back to Chapter 18 for more on sustainable operations and Chapter 17 for conscious consumption.

Realness

Authenticity is about igniting and sustaining meaningful human connections. "Human" is a key word there – authentic brands shun corporate speak and talk to customers and employees as, well, humans. The corporate guard is dropped, in other words. And this allows vulnerability and humility to shine through – meaning authentic brands are able to fess up to their shortcomings and mistakes. This willingness to show that everything isn't perfect really helps to build trust. It shows the brand isn't trying to pull the wool over consumers' eyes, which, as the overall decline in trust shows, is something that many people suspect is happening. That brings us to the next attribute.

Transparency

We know that trust is essential if you want to have a long-term relationship with customers – especially in this age of subscription and servitization (Chapter 13), where the relationship relies on customers divulging their precious personal data. One thing that inspires trust is *transparency*.

Corporate transparency means being open and straight-up with customers, employees, and even competitors (see Chapter 24). So it's no surprise that the most trusted, authentic companies in the world are transparent in the way that they operate. They have transparent values and processes. They're also open about technology and how they use it.

Taking a Stance

With the majority of consumers being "belief-driven" (see Chapter 17), it makes sense that we want brands to believe in the same things we do. Authentic brands, then, often take a stance on issues – such as calling out racism or highlighting the climate crisis. Leaders, too, are increasingly expected to stand up for their beliefs (more on authentic leadership coming up).

One good example comes from Apple, which has taken an increasingly firm line on privacy, starting with blocking law enforcement from accessing people's iPhones.[3] More recently, Apple announced that it was rolling out a new privacy feature that would require apps in the App Store to get permission from users before tracking their data across other apps and websites.[4]

Similarly, while Facebook has much work to do around transparency and authenticity, it is good to see the social media giant taking a stand on misinformation. The company previously ran a Deepfake Detection Challenge, in which participants were invited to submit models for detecting deepfake videos, and in 2020 Facebook released the largest ever database of deepfakes to help AIs learn to spot them.[5]

Examples of authentic, trusted, and transparent brands

Let's briefly explore some brands that embody these notions of trustworthiness, realness, reliability, and transparency:

Adidas

Adidas is one company that often features in rankings of the most reputable, trusted brands. For one thing, the brand's footwear and sportswear is iconic and worn by some of the world's most admired athletes. But Adidas has also made great strides in sustainability and governance, and admitting what needs to change. Their partnership with Parley to make shoes out of recycled ocean plastic (see Chapter 17) is a big step forward.

LEGO

LEGO is another brand that's frequently among the most reputable – and according to RepTrak was the most trusted brand in the world in 2021 (for the second year running).[6] A part of what makes LEGO so trusted is that its core products have no built-in obsolescence. Look after your kids' LEGO and their kids will still be playing with it in a few decades' time. Thus, LEGO is loved by parents, grandparents, and children alike. In addition, the brand's move into "experiences," such as theme parks and movies, further embeds LEGO into the fabric of family life. Disney also features highly in rankings of trusted brands for the same reasons.

GitLab

In 2020, GitLab – the all-remote organization I mentioned in Chapter 21 – topped a list of the world's most transparent organizations.[7] Almost everything the company does is done in public, such as live-streaming bug fixes and patch updates.

Patagonia

At number three on the same transparency list as GitLab is Patagonia. The company is famously public about its supply chain (see Chapter 18), allowing customers to know where their purchases come from, and, in turn, to make better buying choices.

Netflix

Also in the same top 10 as GitLab and Patagonia is Netflix. I like that Netflix is honest about what works and what doesn't internally (I'm reminded here of the company's Inclusion Report from Chapter 20).

But Netflix also publishes, via its blog, lots of interesting behind-the-scenes technical content.

Authentic Leadership

Authentic organizations need authentic leaders. And just as with brands, authentic leaders are those that connect with people on a human level. Authentic leaders build trust. And because of that, they inspire loyalty in both employees and customers. As businesses face more regular disruption and change (driven by the societal and technology shifts explored in Part I), you could say they need authentic leaders now more than ever.[8]

What makes someone authentic?

Let's explore some of the attributes frequently associated with authentic leaders before moving on to some examples.

Leading with Empathy

The best leaders have that hard-to-define quality often referred to as "heart." They lead from the heart, as a human being, recognizing and responding to the humanness in others.

Being Honest

Authentic leaders inspire trust because they don't say things that they don't mean. They are honest, open, and transparent – and are comfortable discussing failures and mistakes, as well as successes.

Having a Strong Ethical and Moral Compass

Just as authentic brands take a stance, authentic leaders have strong values and are not afraid to publicly stand up for those values. But before you can take a stance, you must know who you are and what is important to you. This brings us to self-awareness.

Being Self-Aware

Authentic leaders know who they truly are. They're well aware of their weaknesses as well as their strengths, and openly share those weaknesses. As part of this, they reflect on their actions, decisions, and experiences – both good and bad – and learn from them.

Bringing Your Whole Self (Including on Social Media)

In the past, leaders often had different personas – one for work and one outside of work. But in today's age, it's really important to bring your "whole self" to work. Therefore, the public persona of an authentic leader reflects who they really are in private. They don't hide who they are; in fact, they often use public platforms such as social media to show who they are and what is important to them – rather than allowing corporate comms to speak for them.

This is a relatively new development, driven largely by social media. Traditionally, most leaders would have little or no public presence outside of corporate comms. But building an authentic digital footprint is now an essential way to connect with customers and employees alike.[9]

Examples of authentic leaders

Here are some of the authentic leaders I find inspiring.

Steve Jobs

Jobs is often held up as the shining example of an authentic leader, and with good reason. He spoke plainly and honestly, and he didn't gloss over his struggles and failures. At his commencement address at Stanford University in 2005, Job said, "Truth be told, this is the closest I've ever gotten to a college graduation." He then went on to describe his experience of college and why he dropped out.[10] Jobs wasn't always easy to be around. He was a notorious perfectionist – he's quoted as saying that "if something sucks, I tell people to their face"[11] – but he was certainly honest. And there's no doubt he inspired loyalty.

Oprah Winfrey

Serial entrepreneur and the first black female billionaire, Oprah (her surname is redundant, is it not?) epitomizes honesty, transparency, and self-awareness. Oprah has spoken openly about her traumatic childhood, experiences of sexual assault, and teenage pregnancy. She's not afraid to show her weaknesses and vulnerability, and has built a powerful empire around that authenticity.

Dan Schulman

CEO of PayPal Dan Schulman is a great example of a leader using social media to highlight issues and support social causes. For example, he has used his platforms to post about Black Lives Matter – and, importantly, followed up words with action (PayPal later pledged $530 million to support Black-owned businesses).[12] And he's a big proponent of purposeful organizations, saying, "The people who argue that profit and purpose are two separate things, I think don't really understand that they don't work against each other."[13] (Read more about purpose in Chapter 23.)

Michele Romanow

Co-founder and president of fintech lending firm Clearbanc, Michele Romanow is another leader using social media to show her true self. She posts compelling educational videos on Instagram about entrepreneurship and leadership, and during the pandemic, Romanow urged people to stay home and used her platform to raise awareness of fake news.

PRACTICAL LESSONS

In this chapter, we've learned:

- In an era of declining trust, authenticity is a way for businesses to differentiate themselves and build meaningful, lasting connections with audiences and employees alike.

- Core attributes of authentic businesses include transparency, trustworthiness, realness, and a willingness to stand up for important issues.

- Authentic businesses need authentic leaders, who lead with empathy, honesty, and self-awareness. Business leaders increasingly bring their whole self to work, and publicly show who they are and what they stand for – often via social media.

Caring about issues – and taking appropriate action – is something that's cropped up multiple times throughout this chapter. This leads us nicely on to the next trend: the purposeful business.

Notes

1. Why Brands Should Make Authenticity a Business Imperative; Forbes; https://www.forbes.com/sites/forbesbusinessdevelopmentcouncil/2019/06/20/why-brands-should-make-authenticity-a-business-imperative/?sh=4b7a477621fd

2. Survey Finds Consumers Crave Authenticity – And User-Generated Content Delivers; Social Media Today; https://www.socialmediatoday.com/news/survey-finds-consumers-crave-authenticity-and-user-generated-content-deli/511360/

3. Apple is reportedly closing a security loophole that will prevent police from accessing iPhones; Business Insider; https://www.businessinsider.com/apple-will-make-it-harder-for-police-to-access-locked-iphones-2018-6

4. "The current situation is urgent": In an exclusive interview with the Star, Apple CEO Tim Cook explains why his company is stepping up to protect privacy online; Toronto Star; https://www.thestar.com/business/2021/04/12/apple-ceo-tim-cook-on-privacy-permission-and-tracking-users.html

5. Facebook just released a database of 100,000 deepfakes to teach AI how to spot them; MIT Technology Review; https://www.technologyreview.com/2020/06/12/1003475/facebooks-deepfake-detection-challenge-neural-network-ai/

6. The 10 most trusted brands for 2021; CEO Magazine; https://www.theceo-magazine.com/business/management-leadership/trusted-brands-2021/

7. The 100 Most Transparent Companies of 2020; Org; https://theorg.com/insights/the-100-most-transparent-companies-of-2020

8. The Need for Authentic Leadership Is Greater Than Ever; TalentSoft; https://www.talentsoft.com/resource/the-need-for-authentic-leadership-is-greater-than-ever/

9. Why Leaders Shouldn't Be Silent on Social Media; LinkedIn; https://www.linkedin.com/pulse/why-leaders-shouldnt-silent-social-media-sarah-goodall/

10. "You've got to find what you love," Jobs says; Stanford News; https://news.stanford.edu/news/2005/june15/jobs-061505.html

11. Steve Jobs, an Example of Authentic Leadership; Penn State; https://sites.psu.edu/leadership/2020/06/25/steve-jobs-an-example-of-authentic-leadership/

12. PayPal Announces $530 Million Commitment to Support Black Businesses, Strengthen Minority Communities, and Fight Economic Inequality; PayPal; https://newsroom.paypal-corp.com/2020-06-11-PayPal-Announces-530-Million-Commitment-to-Support-Black-Businesses-Strengthen-Minority-Communities-and-Fight-Economic-Inequality

13. PayPal's CEO on why moral leadership makes clear capitalism needs an upgrade; Fortune; https://fortune.com/2020/09/08/dan-schulman-paypal-moral-leadership-stakeholder-capitalism/

CHAPTER 23
PURPOSEFUL BUSINESS
Why Does Your Business Exist?

This trend is all about expecting more than profits. It's about ensuring your organization exists to serve a meaningful purpose – a purpose that people can genuinely connect to – and not just serve up profits to shareholders.

Purpose defines *why the organization exists* (not what the organization is or what it does or for whom; therefore, purpose is different from mission and vision). Importantly, a strong purpose has the promise of transformation or striving for something better – whether a better world, a better way to do something, or whatever is important to your organization. In other words, purpose is about creating a positive impact, for individuals, for communities, for society, or for our planet.

Why Purpose Matters

Purpose matters because it matters to your customers. The groundbreaking Strength of Purpose study – which surveyed more than 8,000 consumers across eight markets – had people rate 75 brands on their strength of purpose. The results showed that having a clear, compelling purpose delivered serious business benefits. For example, when brands had a strong purpose, consumers were:[1]

- Four times more likely to buy from the brand
- Four times more likely to trust the brand
- Four and a half times more likely to recommend the brand to others
- Six times more likely to protect the brand in a challenging moment

What's more:

- Globally, 94 percent of consumers said the organizations they engage with have a strong purpose.

- 83 percent said companies should *only* earn a profit if they also have a positive impact.

- Purpose is especially important to younger consumers – 92 percent of Gen Z and millennials said they would support a purposeful brand, compared to 77 percent of baby boomers. Considering that millennials are estimated to make up 40 percent of all consumers,[2] this is not to be ignored. (As an aside, it also makes sense that purpose will be a key factor for employers wanting to attract millennial and Gen Z talent.)

Clearly, having a strong purpose is now a vital part of competing for customers (and talent) in today's markets. But purpose also delivers other clear business benefits. According to Deloitte, companies that authentically lead with purpose enjoy higher market share gains, grow three times faster than their competitors, and achieve higher customer and employee satisfaction.[3] Other analysis suggests that purposeful businesses outperform the stock market by 42 percent, while those without a sense of purpose underperform the market by 40 percent.[4]

The upshot is that companies must be recognized as a force for good if they want to succeed. This isn't at the expense of profit – rather, it signifies a shift to "profit with purpose." As the British Academy puts it, the purpose of business "is to solve the problems of people and planet profitably, and not profit from causing problems."[5]

Finding (And Living) Your Purpose

One obvious challenge is getting different people – customers, employees, managers – to rally around a single purpose. How can organizations do this and identify a meaningful purpose?

Start with the "why"

According to design and consulting firm IDEO, who have created a purpose framework called the Purpose Wheel, finding your purpose starts simply with the question "Why do we exist beyond profit?"[6] They propose answering this question in one of five ways, each of which is about creating a positive impact:

- We exist to enable potential (creating impact by inspiring greater possibilities).

- We exist to reduce friction (creating impact by simplifying and eliminating barriers).

- We exist to foster prosperity (creating impact by supporting the success of others).

- We exist to encourage exploration (creating impact by championing discovery).

- We exist to kindle happiness (creating impact by inciting joy).

Once you've identified your reason for existing, you can then move on to the *how* you intend to create your desired impact.

Of course, tools like the Purpose Wheel are helpful but you don't have to be that rigid when defining your purpose. An alternative way forward would be to simply connect your purpose – your reason for existing – to one or more of the key challenges I identified in Part I of this book. These are the biggest challenges facing society, businesses, individuals, and our planet, so if organizations can find a way to (profitably) solve these problems, so much the better.

Turning your purpose into action

Purpose doesn't mean paying lip service to issues. Successful companies translate their purpose into *action*. For me, this means:

- Clearly communicating your purpose both inside and outside the organization. This allows customers, employers, leaders, and managers to fully get behind the purpose – and hold the organization accountable when it doesn't deliver on its aspirations. This brings me to the next item.

- Living that purpose for the long term, at all levels of the business. Your purpose must permeate every facet of the company, including its internal processes, management, and the customer experience.[7] As part of this, I recommend measuring the organization's impact according to its purpose (for example, measuring environmental impact). In the future, we may even see more independent verification of such measures – meaning independent agencies and bodies will hold organizations accountable for delivering on their purpose.

Let me finish with a final warning about authenticity (see Chapter 22). It's really easy to get purpose wrong. Having an inauthentic purpose – one that has zero impact on the company's actions – is probably worse than having no purpose at all. So if you're going to do it, do it properly. This means it may take time to clearly identify an authentic purpose that you're prepared to commit to for the long term.

Compelling Examples of Purposeful Businesses

Let's explore some inspiring companies that are ahead of the purposeful business trend.

Novo Nordisk

I've worked with this Danish multinational pharmaceutical company – a world leader in diabetes care – for many years, and I've always been so impressed with them. Novo Nordisk's purpose is a simple one: to defeat diabetes.

The company says, "We will not allow the success of our company to be defined by the steady increase in the number of people living with serious chronic diseases, like type 2 diabetes and obesity. We take no pleasure in the suffering and hardships faced by people living with a chronic disease. In some countries, the financial burden of providing or getting access to medical care puts people at risk of serious health complications. We are committed to helping societies defeat diabetes, and our strategy is clear – accelerate prevention of type 2 diabetes and obesity, and provide access to affordable care for vulnerable patients in every country. Our success will be defined by the solutions we bring and the health and well-being of the people and communities benefiting from them."[8]

The company may not be a household name, but it certainly has a clearly defined, aspirational, and transformational goal (to defeat diabetes). Plus, it sets out how it intends to do that (accelerating diabetes prevention and providing affordable care) and for what benefit (for the benefit of patients living with chronic disease and obesity).

Setting a purpose like this is incredibly brave because, if you think about it, should Novo Nordisk manage to defeat diabetes, its reason for existing is gone. What a great example of profit with purpose.

The Body Shop

"We exist to fight for a fairer, more beautiful world," is The Body Shop's purpose. "We believe in the beauty of the planet and the good in people, but our world needs work. Nature is suffering at our hands, whole species are becoming extinct in our lifetimes, and our society remains desperately, deeply unfair and unequal. Our founder, Dame Anita Roddick, built The Body Shop to fight for what is good, and just, and beautiful. Today, this fight is still at the heart of everything we do."[9] As part of this fight, The Body Shop aims to help 40,000 economically vulnerable people around the world access work; ensure 100 percent of natural ingredients are traceable and sustainably sourced; and build 75 million square meters of bio-bridges (wildlife corridors) to help endangered species thrive.[10]

Timberland

When it comes to attracting and retaining talent, it makes sense that connecting your purpose to your employer brand is a good way to go. Outdoor apparel brand Timberland is a good example of an employer connecting employees' everyday work to a shared purpose. As part of its purpose to "inspire and equip the world to step outside, work together and make it better," Timberland encourages all employees to be "earth-keepers," meaning they don't have to leave their values at the door when they come to work. As senior manager of community engagement Atlanta McIlwraith says, "Being an earthkeeper is a whole philosophy and approach to how to we do business."[11] The company also connects its purpose to issues that impact the people who make Timberland products – for example, by partnering with Planet Water Foundation to install clean water towers in worker communities that lacked access to clean drinking water.

Dove

Through the Dove Self-Esteem Project, personal care brand Dove (part of Unilever) has taken up the cause of low body confidence and anxieties over appearance. The brand has helped teachers, parents, and mentors deliver self-esteem education to 20 million young people.[12] And, on an everyday level, Dove's "real beauty" advertising campaigns – which feature models with differing body shapes – have struck a real chord with women. In other words, Dove doesn't just exist to sell soap; it exists to improve the self-esteem of girls and women around the world.

Warby Parker

I've mentioned eyewear retailer Warby Parker a couple of times in this book, but they're also a great example of a purposeful business. Warby Parker was founded to "offer designer eyewear at a revolutionary price, while leading the way for socially conscious businesses."[13] Quite simply, the founders didn't understand why glasses had to cost so much, and they wanted to make eyewear more affordable. That's it. But the company also

gives back. Through the company's Buy a Pair, Give a Pair program, they have distributed 8 million pairs of glasses to people in need.[14]

The Cheeky Panda

Toilet paper manufacturer The Cheeky Panda was created to provide an alternative to regular, tree-based toilet tissue (for which 27,000 trees are cut down every day).[15] Instead, Cheeky Panda toilet tissue is made from bamboo – a plant that grows incredibly fast, without the need for fertilizers, making it more sustainable. What's more, as founder Chris Forbes says, "we realized that most regular tissue contains bleaching and chlorine that can cause irritation. By doing the right things well we have created a better product."[16] The company is also a certified B Corporation, FSC approved, and certified vegan and cruelty-free.

PRACTICAL LESSONS

I hope this chapter underscores the importance of giving your audience and employees something meaningful to connect to. Here are some key takeaways:

- Purpose is *why your organization exists*. A strong purpose has a clear aspirational, transformational slant – aiming to create a positive impact for the benefit of others. This doesn't replace the importance of profit; rather, it's about profitably making things better.

- Customers are more likely to purchase from, recommend, and protect a brand that they feel has a strong purpose. Purposeful businesses also demonstrate stronger financial performance than those without a strong purpose.

- Authenticity is key, so your purpose must translate into long-term action. You must *live your purpose*.

There's something collaborative about purpose that I love – this notion of people (including customers and employees) uniting around a shared goal. This leads us nicely on to our next trend: collaboration and integration between organizations.

Notes

1. Global Study Reveals Consumers Are Four to Six Times More Likely to Purchase, Protect and Champion Purpose-Driven Companies; Forbes; https://www.forbes.com/sites/afdhelaziz/2020/06/17/global-study-reveals-consumers-are-four-to-six-times-more-likely-to-purchase-protect-and-champion-purpose-driven-companies/?sh=1be67864435f

2. The future of business? Purpose, not just profit; World Economic Forum; https://www.weforum.org/agenda/2019/01/why-businesses-must-be-driven-by-purpose-as-well-as-profits/

3. Purpose is everything; Deloitte; https://www2.deloitte.com/us/en/insights/topics/marketing-and-sales-operations/global-marketing-trends/2020/purpose-driven-companies.html

4. Global Leadership Forecast; DDI; https://www.ddiworld.com/research/global-leadership-forecast-2018

5. Principles for Purposeful Business; British Academy; https://www.thebritishacademy.ac.uk/documents/223/future-of-the-corporation-principles-purposeful-business-executive-summary.pdf

6. Design an Organization's Purpose Statement with This Tool; IDEO; https://www.ideo.com/blog/design-an-organizations-purpose-statement-with-this-tool

7. 10 ways purposeful business will evolve in 2020; Fast Company; https://www.fastcompany.com/90450734/10-ways-purposeful-business-will-evolve-in-2020

8. Who we are; Novo Nordisk; https://www.novonordisk.com/about/who-we-are.html

9. Our brand purpose; The Body Shop; https://www.thebodyshop.com/en-gb/about-us/our-story/brand-purpose/a/a00003

10. Why do purpose-driven companies do better?; Peter Fisk; https://www.linkedin.com/pulse/why-do-purpose-driven-companies-better-peter-fisk/

11. What Does a Purpose-Driven Company Look Like?; Salesforce; https://www.salesforce.org/blog/what-does-a-purpose-driven-company-look-like/

12. Brand Purpose: The definitive guide; Brand Master Academy; https://brandmasteracademy.com/brand-purpose/

13. History; Warby Parker; https://www.warbyparker.com/history

14. Buy a Pair, Give a Pair; Warby Parker; https://www.warbyparker.com/buy-a-pair-give-a-pair

15. Our Story; The Cheeky Panda; https://us.cheekypanda.com/pages/our-story

16. The Cheeky Panda; Feel-Good Brands; https://feelgoodbrands.co.uk/the-brands-2020/the-cheeky-panda

CHAPTER 24
CO-OPETITION
AND INTEGRATION
A New Age of Integrated Collaboration

I was recently talking to a startup car company that makes solar cars. Except they don't exactly *make* anything themselves. The various parts of the manufacturing process are outsourced to other companies with expertise in those areas. It was a reminder that we live in a time where pretty much anything can be achieved by outsourcing.

This is possible because the global business world has never been so integrated. And that's good, because the need to work together to solve key business challenges (not to mention humanity's biggest challenges) is great. Indeed, in the future, it will become increasingly difficult to succeed without really close partnerships with other organizations.

Supply chain integration

Clearly, this vision of partnerships and cooperation requires a certain amount of system and process integration to work. Perhaps the most important area where we'll see greater integration is the supply chain – and closely linked to that comes data integration (more on that coming up). I believe some of the most successful organizations of the future will be those that can create an ecosystem of closely integrated companies across the supply chain.

Supply chains rely on the smooth flow not just of goods but of information. Supply chain integration therefore means that the various stakeholders' systems are able to seamlessly exchange information throughout the stages of procurement, production planning, and logistics. In other words, supply chain integration is the process of creating connectivity throughout the whole value chain, with the goals of improving production and response times, and reducing costs and waste.

With an integrated supply chain, every partner in the chain benefits. Key features and advantages include:

- Visibility: Complete transparency from supplier to customer is essential for making better business decisions. So an integrated supply chain is one that offers full visibility and real-time sharing of information.

- Paperless operations: Thanks to the software-as-a-service boom (see Chapter 13), even small businesses can access innovative IT solutions that enable this real-time sharing of information between supply chain partners.

- Flexibility: Most of us experienced some form of business disruption during the COVID-19 pandemic and, going forward, disruption may be a more regular occurrence (see Chapter 18). Integrated supply chains are by their nature better equipped to facilitate disruption management. Plus, they can allow organizations to react more quickly to new market opportunities.

- Advanced analytics: Integrated supply chains rely on highly accessible data. And this data enables advanced analytics that can help to, for example, identify areas of inefficiency, better forecast demand, and run digital simulations of potential events.

- Reduced waste: This connectivity also enables businesses to reduce or eliminate wasted time and materials, which, in turn, improves the bottom line.

A simple example comes from Procter & Gamble, which formed a partnership with Walmart to become an exclusive supplier of certain product lines. To achieve this, they had to integrate their backend information systems to ensure P&G could match stock as needed from store to store, rather than oversupplying and discounting (which was the previous arrangement). As a result of greater integration, both companies were able to increase their sales eightfold.[1]

When it comes to integrating your supply chain:

- You first need to identify your current level of integration, and the level of integration you want to achieve. The optimum level of integration is where all companies in the supply chain are sharing data and functioning almost as one to increase efficiencies and meet customer needs.

- You then need to carefully select supply chain partners that are willing to closely integrate the flow of information. Remember, integration adds value for all links in the chain.

- Only then can you begin to integrate functions and information, perhaps by using the same software, or by using tools that enable the flow of data between partners. This brings us to the next section.

Data Integration

The integration of data will be key to successful partnerships between companies, particularly in the supply chain. Let's explore some of the key technologies and trends related to data integration.

From me to we: The rise of multiparty systems

Multiparty systems are systems that seamlessly share data between organizations and individuals in order to boost efficiency and resilience. Blockchain is perhaps one of the best-known examples of a multiparty system since it enables frictionless payments between parties.

Multiparty systems really came into their own during the coronavirus crisis and a survey taken at the time found 90 percent of executives believed multiparty systems would enable them to be more resilient and create new value with partner organizations.[2] In the future, then, it's likely multiparty systems will play a more important role, and ultimately begin to blur the boundaries between organizations and even disparate industries.

APIs

An API, or application programming interface, is essentially a backend piece of machine-to-machine code that acts as an interpreter between programs. Your business is probably already using APIs; today, APIs facilitate everything from embedded videos in websites to the weather forecast on your car dashboard – and it's estimated that APIs perform 25 percent of all B2B interactions.[3] In the supply chain, APIs allow data to flow across the various partners at scale, sharing information such as the status of a specific order or the location of a shipment on a truck.

Electronic data interchange (EDI)

EDI is another machine-to-machine technology, this time allowing the exchange of business documents in a standard electronic format between business partners, over a secure connection. In other words, there's no need for manual emails; instead, documents automatically move from one party to another. A good example is a system that automatically sends purchase orders, invoices, and payment confirmations. Estimates suggest EDI can speed up business cycles by more than 60 percent, because transactions can take place in minutes (or even seconds).[4]

Machines as customers

For me, this is perhaps the biggest trend to watch in data integration – and perhaps the most challenging for the average business.

In the supply chain, we tend to think of humans as the customers. But, increasingly, machines are both gathering and *acting upon* data, effectively turning machines into customers. Take smart fridges as an example; in the future, these will not only identify the foods inside and tell you what you're running low on (see Chapter 11) – they'll be able to order items for you. A similar thing is already happening with Alexa devices. I can simply say, "Alexa, buy bread" and it'll be added to my cart. This is the start of machines entering the supply chain. It is the start of connected machines *becoming the market.*[5]

How will your business facilitate such machine-driven sales? If you're a retailer, for instance, and you haven't yet considered how to integrate smart assistants and connected machines into your supply chain, your business could be vulnerable in the near future. Because, mark my words, a competitor out there is already thinking about it.

To be clear, this trend could encompass a whole range of smart machines, not just digital assistants and household appliances. In theory, everything from cars to factory robots could be tasked with ordering items or services in future.

Co-Opetition: Co-Operating with Competitors

Increasingly, the sharing of information may not be limited to supply chain partners. Indeed, more and more organizations are choosing to share information and collaborate with their competitors to capitalize on market opportunities. Known as *co-opetition* – a mashup of cooperation and competition – this is another key trend in business integration.

It may seem counterintuitive, but a study out of Yale's School of Management suggests that sharing detailed info with competitors is a good idea under certain circumstances. In short, the study suggests that to extract more value and fully exploit opportunities, businesses sometimes need their competitors to recognize the opportunity as well.[6] A great example comes from Tesla allowing other firms to use its patented electric vehicle technologies, in order to further the development of the wider electric vehicle industry.[7] Another example is Samsung and Sony teaming up to share R&D costs for the design of flatscreen LED televisions in the early 2000s.[8] Let's explore some other examples in a little more detail.

Automotive alliances

As the Tesla example suggests, co-opetition is particularly prevalent in the automotive industry. It is the idea behind BMW and Daimler's €1 billion partnership to develop a suite of mobility services, including self-driving vehicles, ride-hailing, and pay-per-use cars.[9] And Ford and WV's agreement to investigate ways of collaborating on electric and autonomous vehicles.[10] And Honda's $2.8 billion investment in General Motors' self-driving unit.[11]

As we saw in Chapter 8, mobility is entering an era of huge transformation, with key trends being electrification, autonomous vehicles, and servitization. But developing new products and services in these areas is incredibly costly and complex, so it makes sense that joining forces can lower risk, spread the cost burden, boost innovation, and improve economies of scale. These manufacturers know that if they don't collaborate, they risk being overtaken by tech firms such as Uber and Waymo, which have endless tech expertise and seemingly bottomless pockets!

Vaccine development

The speed of vaccine development for COVID-19 was truly stunning. Producing a vaccine in less than a year – and with efficacy rates of more than 90 percent in some cases – was unthinkable before the pandemic, and could not have been achieved without co-opetition between scientists, pharma companies, and biotech companies. One example is the partnership between AstraZeneca and Oxford University. The pharma giant approached the university with a proposal to produce a low-cost vaccine, which neither party would profit from – and the result is a vaccine that, at around $4 per dose, costs a fraction of rivals' offerings.[12] Elsewhere, Pfizer partnered with biotech company BioNTech to use its mRNA technology – creating an entirely new type of vaccine.

And these partnerships clearly paid off, since both the Oxford/AstraZeneca and Pfizer/BioNTech vaccines are (at the time of writing) by far the most widely adopted vaccines on the market, being used in 166 and 101 countries, respectively.[13] In contrast, Merck, a top five global pharma company that produced the Ebola vaccine, decided to go it alone – and ended up abandoning trials after poor early results.[14]

Banking and tech

In Chapter 9, we saw how the tech world is increasingly encroaching on the turf of traditional banks and financial service providers. So when Google announced it would be launching digital bank accounts within the Google Pay app, it was perhaps surprising that eight banks in the US, including BBVA and BMO, agreed to partner with Google on the venture.[15] But, if you think about it, both sides benefit. The banks benefit from Google's front-end intuitive user experience and analytics expertise, while Google doesn't have to manage the financial side of these digital-first accounts. And, importantly, customers will benefit from built-in budgeting tools and financial insights, safe in the knowledge that their money is held in a federally regulated account.

PRACTICAL LESSONS

In this chapter, we've learned:

- The supply chains of the future will be increasingly integrated, with all partners in the chain seamlessly sharing information through digital systems. Data integration between partners will play a key role in supply chain integration.

- Companies must also think about machines entering the supply chain as customers. How will your business integrate machines into the supply chain and facilitate machine-driven orders?

- In some cases, collaborating and sharing information with competitors can deliver a competitive advantage, particularly when it comes to sharing the complexities and cost burdens of innovation, and improving economies of scale.

For our final trend in this book, let's look at the new forms of funding that are allowing companies of all kinds to access finance and grow their business.

Notes

1. Integrated Supply Chain Management: Horizontal and Vertical Integration; SmartSheet; https://www.smartsheet.com/integrated-supply-chain-management-vertical-and-horizontal

2. Technology Vision 2021; Accenture; https://www.accenture.com/gb-en/insights/technology/technology-trends-2021

3. How an API Economy Helps Supply Chains Deliver Strategic Value; Supply & Demand Chain Executive; https://www.sdcexec.com/sourcing-procurement/article/21160451/elemica-how-an-api-economy-helps-supply-chains-deliver-strategic-value

4. What is EDI (Electronic Data Interchange)?; Planergy; https://planergy.com/blog/electronic-data-interchange/

5. Ten Machines That Could Become Customers This Decade; Gartner; https://blogs.gartner.com/mark_raskino/2020/10/30/ten-machines-that-could-become-customers-in-this-decade/

6. When Should Companies Share Information with Competitors? Yale Insights; https://insights.som.yale.edu/insights/when-should-companies-share-information-with-competitors

7. All Our Patent Are Belong to You; Tesla; https://www.tesla.com/BLOG/ALL-OUR-PATENT-ARE-BELONG-YOU

8. Successful Co-opetition: Examples of collaboration between competitors; Stakeholder Agency; https://www.thestakeholderagency.co.nz/blog/successful-co-opetition-examples-of-collaborations-between-competitors

9. Why are more and more car companies teaming up?; BBC News; https://www.bbc.com/news/business-47376677

10. Ford and VW agree alliance to build vans and pickups; BBC News; https://www.bbc.com/news/business-46880937

11. Honda to invest $2.8 bn in GM's self-driving car unit; BBC News; https://www.bbc.com/news/business-45728169

12. Will COVID-19 Vaccine Success Inspire Future Coopetition?; Business Because; https://www.businessbecause.com/news/insights/7492/covid-19-vaccine-coopetition

13. Tracking Coronavirus Vaccinations Around the World; New York Times; https://www.nytimes.com/interactive/2021/world/covid-vaccinations-tracker.html

14. Will COVID-19 Vaccine Success Inspire Future Coopetition?; Business Because; https://www.businessbecause.com/news/insights/7492/covid-19-vaccine-coopetition

15. Google Pay to launch digital bank accounts in 2021; Google; https://9to5google.com/2020/08/03/google-pay-digital-bank-accounts/

CHAPTER 25
NEW FORMS OF FUNDING

The Democratization of
Business Funding

We all know businesses need money to grow. Traditionally, this money would come from a loan or selling equity stakes in the business – both of which involve having to get past gatekeepers, such as banks, brokers, and investment funds. This can make it difficult for some organizations to access funding. Creating an IPO, for example, is a complex and lengthy process.

But now, the ways in which companies can generate finance is changing. New platforms and mechanisms have sprung up to connect businesses with investors and donors. Many of these new methods are driven by the *decentralized finance* movement (in which financial services like borrowing and trading take place in a peer-to-peer network, via a public decentralized blockchain network).

This chapter outlines four trends that could influence how companies access finance in the future:

- Crowdfunding
- Initial coin offerings (ICOs)
- Tokenization
- Special purpose acquisition companies (SPACs)

Clearly, there are risks involved when you embrace any new financial mechanism (particularly for investors, it must be noted), so you need to understand exactly what you're getting into before you proceed. This chapter provides just brief overviews of these funding methods, so be sure to do your homework. That said, I do believe they offer exciting opportunities for organizations to raise funds and grow their business.

Tapping into the Crowd with Crowdfunding

Because it's been around for a while now, crowdfunding is probably the best known of the funding methods in this chapter. To date, more than $34 billion has been raised worldwide by crowdfunding.[1]

Crowdfunding basically involves raising money online for a specific goal or venture, via a crowdfunding platform that connects you with contributors. Crowdfunding is perhaps known as a way for individuals or creatives to raise money (indeed, movies such as *Veronica Mars* have been crowdfunded), but it's also a legitimate way for businesses – startups and established organizations – to raise funds.

Indiegogo and Kickstarter are well-known, all-round crowdfunding platforms (both with great track records). But many other platforms out there specialize in specific types of fundraising. For example, there's SeedInvest Technology, which is aimed at startups looking for funding; or Mightycause, which helps nonprofits and individuals raise money for causes; or Patreon, which helps artists and other creatives connect with patrons. In my view, PledgeCamp could be an interesting platform to watch, since it combines crowdfunding and blockchain. Designed to increase transparency and solve the trust issues associated with crowdfunding, PledgeCamp uses smart contracts and "backer insurance" to give donors more peace of mind.[2]

Successful crowdfunding campaigns have included the following:

- The Oculus VR headset came into being thanks to a crowdfunding campaign that raised $2.4 million in 30 days. The company

NEW FORMS OF FUNDING

was later acquired by Facebook for $2 billion, leaving initial crowdfunding backers miffed that they didn't benefit from the company's enormous success.[3]

- The Dash, wireless smart in-ear headphones that act partly like a fitness tracker, managed to raise more than $3.3 million from almost 16,000 backers across 50 days.[4]

- The Exploding Kittens game made Kickstarter history when it raised a whopping $8.7 million from 219,382 backers – making it the most-backed campaign of all time.[5]

Skipping the IPO Process: Initial Coin Offerings (ICOS)

You've heard of IPOs. Well, ICOs are the cryptocurrency equivalent. Instead of selling shares to investors, as you would with an IPO, ICOs involve raising funds from supporters, who, in turn, receive the blockchain equivalent of a share: a cryptocurrency token or "coin." An ICO is a bit like a crowdfunding campaign, then, except ICO backers potentially get a return on their investment (whereas crowdfunding supporters are effectively "donating" money). This is why ICOs are sometimes referred to as *crowdsales*. ICOs also differ from crowdfunding and IPOs because backers buy their tokens using digital currency.

ICOs are more popular with startups than established businesses, and particularly with blockchain startups. As an example, blockchain smartphone technology company Sirin Labs raised an astonishing $157.8 million from its ICO (more than $100 million of which was generated in the first 24 hours).[6] And that's not even the most successful ICO. Blockchainbased data storage company Filecoin netted $135 million in one hour, and ultimately raised $257 million.[7]

It's perhaps fair to say that the initial ICO "gold rush" is over, but, depending on your business, ICOs can still be an incredibly powerful way to raise money. There are downsides, however, especially for investors. That's because ICOs are largely unregulated (for now), and some have even turned out to be fraud.[8]

The Tokenization of Assets

Closely related to ICOs is the tokenization of assets. Here, assets are broken up into blockchain tokens, so people can invest in *part* of an asset – typically property or art, but in theory tokenization can be applied to any asset class. The basic idea is there are plenty of people out there who are happy to have a little piece of a big pie, so why not offer that to them? Therefore, tokenization allows investors to purchase tokens that potentially represent just a tiny, *tiny* percentage of the underlying asset.

How does tokenization differ from ICOs? Well, an ICO is a type of tokenization. But there are other types of offerings beyond ICOs, hence the broader term "tokenization." The main difference here is that tokens can be used to represent part of a real, tradable asset or security. (Indeed, such tokens are often referred to as "security tokens.") So the token could represent something like a share in a company, or part-ownership of a piece of real estate, a stake in a piece of fine art, participation in an investment fund, or even a commodity such as gold – crucially, the underlying asset is something that can be traded on a secondary market, giving investors greater piece of mind.[9]

Notable examples of tokenization so far come from the world of real estate, but that could change in future. For instance, a $30 million luxury condo development in Manhattan became the first major asset to be tokenized on the Ethereum blockchain.[10]

The obvious advantage of tokenization for organizations is it improves access to funding without having to go through traditional gatekeepers. (It could even transform the way businesses invest in assets in future.) And for investors, tokenization democratizes the world of investments; tokens are, in short, much more accessible than other types of investments. But there are some challenges to overcome. Regulatory alignment is a murky area, and if tokenization does become fully regulated, it could undermine some of the very advantages that draw people to it.

Creating a Special Purpose Acquisition Company (SPAC)

SPACs are nothing new, but they've certainly gained momentum in recent years. In 2020, SPACs raised $83 billion in funding across the whole of 2020, and $26 billion in January 2021 alone – and that's just in the US.[11] Therefore, there's huge hype around SPACs at the time of writing. Some people are saying the bubble is due to burst, but obviously no one knows what the future has in store.

But what is a SPAC? Also known as a "blank check company," a SPAC is a shell company that's formed specifically to raise money through an IPO in order to buy – and ultimately bring to market – a private company. These SPACS have no existing business operations at the time of their IPO, or even a stated acquisition target (there is usually an acquisition target in mind – it just isn't publicly stated). Therefore, it's a way of raising money without the paperwork and rigors of a traditional IPO.

Having raised the money needed, the SPAC then has two years to complete an acquisition (and if it doesn't, the money must be returned to investors). Then, once the merger is complete, the company is usually listed on a major stock exchange, potentially creating a huge upside for investors.

As an example, a SPAC formed by venture capitalist Chamath Palihapitiya bought a 49 percent stake in Virgin Galactic for $800 million, then took the company public in 2019.[12] (Palihapitiya later sold off his personal stake in the company for $200 million.)[13] Virgin Group itself is using SPACs to raise finance. In March 2021, Virgin formed its third SPAC, Virgin Group Acquisition III – led by Virgin Group's CEO and CIO – with a view to raise up to $500 million.[14]

What's interesting is SPAC investors have no idea which company they will ultimately be investing in – hence the name "blank check company." This is an obvious downside of SPACs. So what on earth draws investors to SPACs? It's usually the management team behind the SPAC, meaning

SPACs are typically formed by experienced executives with specific industry expertise.

It must be noted that because SPACs aren't subject to the same rigorous scrutiny that regular IPOs are, they do pose risks for investors. But that may change because SEC Chairman Jay Clayton has said the SEC is watching SPACs closely.[15] It'll be interesting to see what's in store for SPACs.

PRACTICAL LESSONS

In this chapter, we've learned:

- There's a lot happening in the business finance space, with new funding and investment mechanisms coming into play, so it's well worth staying up to date on the latest developments in this field.

- Thanks to trends like crowdfunding, ICOs, tokenization, and SPACs, access to funding is becoming easier – and fairer. Friction is also reduced, since there are typically no gatekeepers involved.

- That said, there are risks, particularly for investors. I expect we'll see regulation tighten up around nontraditional financing in the coming years.

That brings us to the end of the key trends around how businesses operate. In the next chapter, let's explore some final thoughts and takeaways for business leaders.

Notes

1. Best Crowdfunding Platforms; Investopedia; https://www.investopedia .com/best-crowdfunding-platforms-5079933

2. PledgeCamp: CBInsights; https://www.cbinsights.com/company/pledgecamp

3. The 10 Most Successful Crowdfunding Campaigns of All Time; Magistree; https://www.magistree.com/the-10-most-successful-crowdfunding-campaigns-of-all-time-part-1/

4. The Dash Wireless Headphones Raises Over $3.3 Million; Crowdfund Insider; https://www.crowdfundinsider.com/2014/04/34956-dash-wireless-headphones-raises-3-3-million/

5. Exploding Kittens Is the Most-Backed Project of All Time; Kickstarter; https://www.kickstarter.com/blog/exploding-kittens-is-the-most-backed-project-of-all-time

6. ICOs explained: 5 examples of successful coin offerings; Medium; https://medium.com/boosto/icos-explained-5-examples-of-successful-coin-offerings-2ddcb780ef58

7. ICOs explained: 5 examples of successful coin offerings; Medium; https://medium.com/boosto/icos-explained-5-examples-of-successful-coin-offerings-2ddcb780ef58

8. Spotlight on Initial Coin Offerings (ICOs); Securities and Exchange Commission; https://www.sec.gov/ICO

9. The tokenization of assets is disrupting the financial industry. Are you ready?; Deloitte; https://www2.deloitte.com/content/dam/Deloitte/lu/Documents/financial-services/lu-tokenization-of-assets-disrupting-financial-industry.pdf

10. A First for Manhattan: $30M Real Estate Property Tokenized with Blockchain; https://www.forbes.com/sites/rachelwolfson/2018/10/03/a-first-for-manhattan-30m-real-estate-property-tokenized-with-blockchain/?sh=b13e2e848957

11. The SPAC Bubble Is About to Burst; Harvard Business Review; https://hbr.org/2021/02/the-spac-bubble-is-about-to-burst

12. Special Purpose Acquisition Company (SPAC); Investopedia; https://www.investopedia.com/terms/s/spac.asp

13. Virgin Galactic Chairman Chamath Palihapitiya sells off remaining personal stake in the space company; TechCrunch; https://techcrunch.com/2021/03/05/virgin-galactic-chairman-chamath-palihapitiya-sells-off-remaining-personal-stake-in-the-space-company/

14. Virgin Group's third SPAC Virgin Group Acquisition III files for a $500 million IPO; Renaissance Capital; https://www.renaissancecapital.com/IPO-Center/News/79079/Virgin-Groups-third-SPAC-Virgin-Group-Acquisition-III-files-for-a-$500-mill

15. The SPAC Bubble Is About to Burst; Harvard Business Review; https://hbr.org/2021/02/the-spac-bubble-is-about-to-burst

PART V
WHERE TO GO
FROM HERE

We've covered dozens of trends throughout this book, from global shifts and technology mega-trends to industry-specific shifts and broader business trends.

No doubt you're wondering where to go from here. The "practical lessons" sections at the end of each chapter provide a useful summary that you can revisit as you consider each trend and its potential effect on your business. But I also wanted to leave you with some more general lessons and takeaways – things that I believe every business leader should keep in mind as they respond to these trends.

Read on to find out what they are.

CHAPTER 26
FINAL WORDS

Four Key Takeaways
for Business Leaders

I may have hooked you in with the promise of exciting trends, but it should be clear by now that this book is all about resilience. That's not to say the trends explored in this book aren't truly exciting and transformative. They are. But what ties all these trends together is the need for resilient, adaptable organizations – organizations that can cope with rapid change and are fit for the fourth industrial revolution. I hope this book has made you question how resilient your own organization is. I hope it sparks discussions on where your business is headed, what it offers, and how it operates.

Let me leave you with four key takeaways to keep in mind as you continue to digest what you've read. They are:

- This isn't a pick-and-mix buffet.
- Speed and adaptability are key.
- Remember the human side.
- And finally, let's invest in a future we actually want to live in.

This Isn't a Pick-and-Mix Buffet

For me, resilience means looking at all of these trends and making sure your business is ready. Certainly, the successful companies mentioned in this book – Apple, Amazon, Tesla, Microsoft, Nike, Disney, L'Oréal, and the like – are addressing many if not all of the trends discussed. What they're not doing is picking and choosing a few trends to focus all their efforts on and forgetting the rest.

Of course, depending on your industry, some of these trends will be a higher priority for your business than others. My point is, don't overlook the remaining trends or dismiss them as not relevant. Because, believe me, a competitor out there – maybe a cheeky new upstart – will step in to fill the gap.

Some of the biggest opportunities for your business may well lie at the intersection of trends. In other words, so many of the tech trends in this book are interlinked, which acts as rocket fuel for innovation, in turn driving many of the non-tech trends. For example, 5G will drive advances in VR hardware, which in turn will help businesses deliver more immersive experiences (and educators deliver more immersive content, etc.). AI will drive advances in gene editing, which in turn will transform agriculture and the food industry. AI will (literally) drive advances in autonomous vehicles, which will radically alter the automotive and transportation industry as we know it (particularly when combined with the servitization trend).

The most forward-thinking organizations out there are making sure they understand every business trend, are finding the links between them, and looking for the business opportunities that lie within those crossovers.

Speed and Adaptability Are Key

Resilient businesses are those that can adapt to change, quickly. Hopefully, this book has hammered home just how quickly things are changing. It can feel hard to keep up, and I say that as a futurist whose very job it is not just to keep up, but to look ahead! Yet the pace of change is only going to increase. So business leaders must make an effort to stay up to date, and build an organization that can adapt as needed (through a flatter, more agile structure, investing in the right skills for the 21st century, finding the ideal balance between humans and machines, etc.).

Ultimately, there will be mistakes as businesses respond to these trends, and these mistakes will be noticed. Tesla allowing customers to pay with Bitcoin springs to mind. For an electric car company, founded on the principle of making cars that are less harmful to the planet, allowing customers to pay with Bitcoin – with its huge energy and environmental cost – was surprising at best. And they caught a lot of flak for it. So what did Tesla do? They adapted again, announcing just as I was finishing this book that they would no longer accept Bitcoin due to environmental concerns.[1] Like Tesla, your business will need to remain adaptable.

I also believe that an important part of building an adaptable business means avoiding an overreliance on technology. If the next pandemic is a digital one (see Chapter 18), every business will no doubt be hit hard, but those businesses with multiple channels and routes to market (not just digital) will be better able to adapt.

Remember the Human Side

So many of the trends in this book are driven by technology, but we need to keep humans at the center of everything businesses do. This means it's essential to maintain a tight focus on customers and employees as you address these trends.

As you consider each trend, ask yourself:

- What does this trend mean in terms of my customers? How might it impact what they want, how we reach them, and so on? How will we build in customer feedback loops to make sure we're getting things right?

- How can we make sure we remain a human-centered organization, where humans are the most important asset? Will our organizational culture need to change? What is the right balance between humans and technology? How can we make sure our people have the skills they need to do their job, and adapt as roles change?

Let's Invest in a Future We Want to Live in

As leaders in our industries, we have an opportunity – an obligation, even – to tackle the world's biggest challenges and create a future that we actually want to live in. Part of this means building businesses that we're proud to work in, but it also means making the world a better place (profit with purpose, not profiting by causing harm).

For me, a good way forward is for leaders to consider the trends outlined in this book, understand them, and *act* on them – but also to blend this action with unmistakably human qualities like humility, curiosity, empathy, vulnerability, and creativity. If we hold on to our humanity, I believe we'll be much better placed to tackle the challenges facing our world and us, the people who live in it.

I'd like to finish by directing you to the United Nation's 17 Sustainable Development Goals. These goals not only capture the challenges we're facing, but how to address them – making it a really good starting point for business leaders and policymakers alike.[2]

Share Your Thoughts with Me

I'd love to hear what you think about these business trends. Much as I enjoy writing books, I'm most keen to establish a dialogue outside of these pages. So please do ask questions, share any of your own experiences with these trends, or get in touch if you need help preparing your organization for the fourth industrial revolution.

You can connect with me on the following platforms:

LinkedIn: Bernard Marr
Twitter: @bernardmarr
YouTube: Bernard Marr
Instagram: @bernardmarr
Facebook: facebook.com/BernardWMarr

Or head to my website at www.bernardmarr.com for more content and to join my weekly newsletter, in which I share the very latest information.

Notes

1. Tesla will no longer accept Bitcoin over climate concerns, says Musk; BBC News; https://www.bbc.com/news/business-57096305

2. 17 Sustainable Development Goals; United Nations; https://sdgs.un.org/goals

ACKNOWLEDGMENTS

I feel extremely lucky to work on future trends and topics that are innovative and fast moving and I feel privileged that I am able to work with companies and government organizations across all sectors and industries to help them prepare for future trends and create strategies that will enable them to succeed. This work allows me to learn every day, and a book like this wouldn't have been possible without it.

I would like to acknowledge the many people who have helped me get to where I am today – all the great individuals in the companies I have worked with who put their trust in me to help them and in return gave me so much new knowledge and experience. I must also thank everyone who has shared their thinking with me, either in person, on my podcast or in YouTube conversations, or in their blogposts, books, or any other formats. Thank you for generously sharing all the content I absorb every day! I am also lucky enough to personally know many of the key thinkers, futurists, and thought leaders in business and I hope you all know how much I value your inputs and our exchanges.

I would like to thank my editorial and publishing team for all your help and support. Taking any book from idea to publication is a team effort and I really appreciate your input and help – thank you, Annie Knight, Kelly Labrum, and Premkumar Narayanan.

My biggest acknowledgment goes to my wife, Claire, and our three children, Sophia, James, and Oliver, for giving me the inspiration, motivation, and space to do what I love: learning and sharing ideas that will make our world a better place.

ABOUT THE AUTHOR

Bernard Marr is a world-renowned futurist, influencer, and thought leader in the field of business and technology. He is the author of 20 best-selling books, writes a regular column for *Forbes*, and advises and coaches many of the world's best-known organizations. He has over 2 million social media followers and was ranked as one of the top 5 business influencers in the world by LinkedIn.

Bernard helps organizations and their management teams prepare for future trends and create the strategies to succeed. He has worked with or advised many of the world's best-known organizations, including Amazon, Microsoft, Google, Dell, IBM, Walmart, Shell, Cisco, HSBC, Toyota, Nokia, Vodafone, T-Mobile, the NHS, Walgreens Boots Alliance, the Home Office, the Ministry of Defence, NATO, and the United Nations, among many others.

Connect with Bernard on LinkedIn, Twitter (@bernardmarr), Facebook, Instagram, and YouTube to take part in an ongoing conversation, subscribe to Bernard's podcast, and head to www.bernardmarr.com for more information and hundreds of free articles, white papers, and e-books.

If you would like to talk to Bernard about any advisory work, speaking engagements, or influencer services, please contact him via email at hello@bernardmarr.com

Other books in his Wiley series include:

- *Extended Reality in Practice: 100+ Amazing Ways Virtual, Augmented and Mixed Reality Are Changing Business and Society*

ABOUT THE AUTHOR

- *Tech Trends in Practice: The 25 Technologies That Are Driving the 4th Industrial Revolution*

- *Artificial Intelligence in Practice: How 50 Successful Companies Used AI and Machine Learning to Solve Problems*

- *Big Data in Practice: How 45 Successful Companies Use Big Data Analytics to Deliver Extraordinary Results*

INDEX

A

Add-on subscriptions, 172–173
Adidas, 216, 274
Adobe, 201, 265
Aeroponics, 89
Agile organizations. *See*
  Organizations, agile
Aging, societal, 10–11, 17
Agriculture
  automation in, 86–87, 94, 239
  blockchain technology
    in, 88–89, 95
  environmental impacts of,
    85–86, 94, 95
  genetic engineering
    in, 90–91, 96
  notes on, 94–97
  practical lessons on, 93–94
  precision farming, 87–88, 95
  vertical farming, 89–90, 95
AI (artificial intelligence)
  capabilities of, 237–239
  China and, 7
  creativity and, 239, 243, 245
  data literacy and, 25, 29
  education and, 78, 80
  energy usage and, 52, 53
  financial services and,
    124, 127, 128

fourth industrial revolution
    and, 21, 22
  future of jobs and, 241–244,
    250, 256
  in healthcare, 62, 64, 66, 67
  products enhanced by, 145–149
  as a service (AIaaS), 168–169
  services enhanced by,
    149–153
  subscription model and, 171
  as technology mega-trend,
    29–31
Air pollution, deaths from,
    48. *See also* Greenhouse
    gas emissions
Air travel, 113, 116, 184, 195, 209
Airbnb, 183, 192, 194, 197, 201
Alcoholic beverages
  beer, 230, 232, 234
  gin, 172
  whiskey, 139–140, 162–163,
    204, 231
  wine, 161, 164
Alexa, 139, 141, 147, 148, 152,
    154, 204, 238, 295
Alibaba, 27, 42, 126, 168, 190
Allbirds, 215, 219
Alphabet, 115, 116, 120, 190
Aluminum cans, 230, 234

Amazon
  checkout-free stores, 201
  home security cameras,
    149, 172
  packaging, 214
  as platform business,
    190, 191, 197
  recommendation engine, 149
  resilience of, 311
  two-pizza teams at, 263, 269
Amazon Prime, 167, 174, 175
Amazon Web Services, 25, 168
Ant Group, 126, 129
Apple
  leadership at, 35, 276, 279
  as platform business, 190
  privacy and, 273, 278
  recycling robot at, 241
  resilience of, 311
  self-cannibalization at, 262
  solar energy and, 48
  as subscription business, 165,
    166, 167, 175
Apple Health app, 64
Apple News, 165, 167, 185
Apple Watch, 62, 153, 165
Application programming
    interface (API), 294, 298
Apps
  Arcade City app, 195
  BlueDot app, 64
  finance, 125, 129, 297, 299
  Gojek app, 136, 143
  Google Pay app, 297, 299
  healthcare, 61, 62, 64,
    135–136, 143
  importance of, 134, 136–137
  Instacart app, 191–192

JustPark app, 193, 198
language learning, 78–79
revolution in, 134–137, 143
Spin mobility app, 135
Starbucks app, 134,
  137–138, 143
super, 136
Vivino wine app, 161, 164
WeChat app, 136, 143
Artificial intelligence. See AI
  (artificial intelligence)
Artwork, 141, 143, 184, 239
Asprey, Dave, 65, 71
Attention span, 80, 83, 155
Augmented analytics, 29
Augmented reality (AR)
  in construction, 107
  cosmetics and, 204, 207
  defined, 31
  eyewear and, 180
  immersive experiences
    and, 199
  immersive learning and, 80
Authenticity
  brands that embody, 273–275
  defined, 272–273
  importance of, 254, 271
  leadership and, 275–277,
    278, 279
  notes on, 278–279
  practical lessons on, 277–278
  purpose and, 284, 287
  trust and, 271, 272, 277
Automation. See also AI (artificial
  intelligence); Robots
  in agriculture, 86–87, 94, 239
  examples of, 239–241
  human workers and, 237–248

in manufacturing, 101–102, 240
robotic process, 29, 169–170, 175
Automotive industry
  alliances, 295, 296, 298
  autonomous cars, 114–115, 146
  co-opetition in, 295
  electric cars, 5, 38, 49, 112, 119,
    120, 213–214
  mobility-as-a-service (MaaS)
    and, 117, 118
  parking app, 193, 198
  Tesla, 179–180, 213–214, 295,
    296, 311, 313, 315
  Zipcar, 193–194, 198

B
Banks
  blockchain technology and, 32,
    182, 183, 186
  business funding and, 301
  digital money and, 122,
    123, 124, 127
  finance apps versus, 125–126,
    134, 297
  as middlemen, 177, 191
  software bots and, 170
  WeBank, 126, 129
Barkbox, 180
Batteries, 5, 38, 43, 112, 241
Batty, Jonathan, 148
Beauty products
  direct-to-consumer, 182
  extended reality and, 204, 207
  personalized, 162
  plastic-free, 216
  purposeful business and, 285, 286
  subscriptions and, 172
Beer, sustainable, 230, 232, 234

BetterHelp app, 135
Beyond Meat, 91, 212
Biohacking, 65
Biology, synthetic, 35–37, 63
Bitcoin
  description of, 33, 123, 128
  environmental impact of,
    124, 129, 214, 218
  Tesla and, 124, 313, 315
Blacksocks, 171, 174
Blockchain technology
  banks and, 182, 183, 186
  in construction, 107
  defined, 32–33
  in energy sector, 53
  in farming, 88–89
  in financial services, 124
  in healthcare, 68
  middlemen service providers
    and, 182–184
  platforms versus, 194–195
  as technology mega-trend,
    32–34, 42
BlueDot app, 64
Body Shop, The, 285, 288
Bonaceto, Andrea, 141
Borlaug, Norman, 90, 95
Bottura, Massimo, 202
Buildings
  greener, 104–105
  modular and prefabricated,
    105–106
Burger King, 212, 218
Business funding methods
  crowdfunding, 301,
    302–303, 306
  initial coin offerings (ICOs),
    301, 303, 307

special purpose acquisition
companies (SPACs), 301,
305–306, 307, 308
tokenization of assets, 301,
304, 306, 307
Business leadership
authentic, 275–277, 278, 279
four key takeaways on, 311–315
importance of, 245
Business model
platform, 189–198
subscription, 165–175
Businesses, successful. *See also*
Organizations, agile
authenticity and, 271–279
purpose and, 281–289
resilience of, 223–226, 234
sustainability and, 226–233,
234, 235
ByteDance, 159

C
Cars
automotive alliances, 295,
296, 298
autonomous, 114–115, 146
electric, 5, 38, 49, 112, 119,
120, 213–214
mobility-as-a-service (MaaS)
and, 117, 118
parking, 193, 198
Tesla, 179–180, 213–214, 295,
296, 311, 313, 315
traffic flow, 27, 150, 154
Zipcar, 193–194, 198
Chatbots
domestic abuse and, 151–152
in healthcare, 61, 62

Cheeky Panda, 287, 289
Cheese, vegan, 93, 96
Chief experience officer (CXO),
201, 206
China
economic power of, 5, 7, 12
medical robots in, 66
polarization and, 9
population of, 10–11
rare earth materials
from, 5, 16, 49
sharing economy in, 193, 198
technology and, 7, 9
WeBank from, 126, 129
Chocolate, 229, 232, 234, 235
Circular economy, 104
Cities
concrete and steel for,
106–107
farming in, 89–90
greener buildings in,
104–105
growth of, 11, 17
Clayton, Jay, 306
Climate crisis, 4–6, 15, 16, 117,
209. *See also* Greenhouse
gas emissions
*Climate Disaster, How to
Avoid a*, 6
Clinique iD, 162
Clothing
digital-only, 140–141
immersive experiences
and, 202–203
intelligent fashion, 171
personalized browsing
for, 160–161
rentals, 171

socks, 171, 174
sportswear, 181–182
sustainable, 215–216, 230
Cloud computing, 25, 32, 168
Coatney, Matthew, 250, 256
Cobots, 102–103, 237. 241
Coffee
  Bulletproof, 65, 71
  Grounds for Change, 211, 218
  Starbucks, 134, 137–138,
    143, 200
Coffee machines, 147
Collaborative robots (cobots),
  102–103, 237, 241
Colonoscopy pill, 67, 71
Concrete and steel, 106–107, 110
Conscious consumption
  eco-friendly examples, 213–217
  food options and, 211–213
  notes on, 217–219
  practical lessons on, 217
  rise of, 209–210
Construction industry
  concrete and steel for,
    106–107, 110
  greener buildings, 104–105
  modular and off-site, 105–106
  technology adoption in, 107
Cook, Tim, 278
Co-opetition, 295–297, 298
Cornerstone4Care app, 62
Cornwall Local Energy
  Market, 52, 57
Cosmetics. See Beauty products
Coupang (e-commerce retailer),
  214, 218
Covid-19 crisis
  BlueDot app and, 64

China and, 7
construction industry and,
  104
digital transformation and,
  55, 133
healthcare systems and, 59
money and, 123
online learning and, 73, 78
polarization and, 9
remote working and, 13, 249
resilient companies
  and, 224, 225
technology tipping
  point and, 142
telemedicine and, 63–64
vaccine development
  and, 296–297
whiskey tastings and, 139
women and, 13
Creativity, 245, 246
CRISPR method, 36, 37, 42,
  90, 91
Crowdfunding, 301, 302–303, 306
Crowdsourcing, 189, 195–197
Cryptocurrency, 123–124. See
  also Bitcoin
Cultural intelligence, 245
Culture, organizational, 13–14,
  253–254, 257
Cultured meat, 92, 96
Customer feedback
  loops, 262, 313
Customers, machines as,
  294–295, 298
Customer-to-customer (C2C)
  economy, 189. See also
  Platform business model
Cyber-resilience, 225–226

D

Daimler, 113, 296
Dairy, animal-free, 91, 93, 212
Daisy, Apple's recycling
   robot, 241, 247
Damon, Matt, 159
Dark factories, 101–102
Dash headphones, 303, 307
Data breaches
   financial services and,
      122–123, 124
   in healthcare, 68, 69, 72
   largest breach, 28, 42
Data democratization, 29
Data integration, 293–297
Data lakes, 27
Data literacy, 28, 245
Data rivers, 27
Datafication, 27–29
Decarbonization of energy,
   48–50
Decentralized finance
   movement, 301
Deep learning, 30
Deliveroo, 184
Delivery robots, 116–117, 118
Democrats, 8
Demographics, 10–12, 15
Diabetes care, 62, 284–285
Digit delivery robot, 117
Digital trust, 32–34
Digital twins, 54, 67–68, 101
Digital wallet services,
   123, 125–127
Direct-to-consumer (DTC) trend
   description of, 177–182
   notes on, 186–187
   practical lessons on, 185–186

Disintermediation. *See* Direct-to-
   consumer trend
Disney
   direct-to-consumer strategy,
      178, 181, 186
   immersive experiences and, 204
   omnichannel experience at, 138
   resilience of, 311
   as trusted brand, 274
Distributed ledger technology,
   32, 33
Divergence, 8–10, 15
Diversity, 14, 18, 75, 251–252, 256
DNA
   editing, 30, 35–37, 90
   storage, 25–26, 27
   testing, 63
Dog doors, intelligent, 148
Dog treats, 180
Dollar Shave Club, 172, 177
Domestic abuse help, 151–152
Domino's, 139
DoorDash, 184
Dove Self-Esteem Project, 286
Driver, Minnie, 159
Drone use, 87, 107, 116
Drug delivery, 66
Du Sautoy, Marcus, 243
Duolingo language learning
   app, 78–79, 83

E

Eco resorts, 214–215, 218
Eco-friendly consump-
   tion, 209–219
Economic power, 6–8, 15
Economy, experience, 199–207
Economy, sharing, 192–194, 198

Edge computing, 25
Education
  bite-sized learning, 80, 82
  immersive learning, 80–81, 82
  job skills and, 74–77, 81
  lifelong learning, 76–77, 82, 253
  notes on, 82–83
  online learning, 73, 78
  personalized learning,
    77, 78–79, 82
  practical lessons on, 81–82
  project-based learning, 77, 79
  transformation needed in, 73
EHang, 116, 120
Electric cars
  batteries for, 38, 112
  conscious consumers
    and, 213–214
  mass adoption of, 112, 119
  rare earths and, 5, 49
Electric scooters, 112,
  117, 119, 135
Electronic Data Interchange
  (EDI), 294, 298
Empathy, 75, 244, 246, 275
Employee experience
  importance of, 252, 256
  organizational culture and,
    253–254, 257
  physical environment
    and, 253, 255
  technology and, 253, 254
  three ways to improve,
    252–253, 256
Employee recruitment,
  249–252, 254
Employment
  education and, 74–77, 81

future of, 241–244, 247
  reskilling for, 76–77, 81,
    244–246
Energy
  decarbonization of, 48–50
  decentralization of,
    48, 50–52, 57
  digitization of, 48, 53–54, 57
  notes on, 56–57
  practical lessons regarding, 55
  solar, 38–39, 48–49, 50, 56
  solutions, 6, 39–40
Ericsson's smart factory,
  240, 247
Estrella Damm brewery, 230, 234
Ethicist, AI, 75
Etsy, 189, 190
Exoskeletons, 66, 102, 109
Experience economy, 199–207
Exploding Kittens, 303, 307
Exponential growth, 22
Extended reality (XR)
  augmented reality (AR),
    31, 80, 107
  defined, 31
  in education, 80–81
  experience economy
    and, 199–205
  in healthcare, 64
  notes on, 206–207
  practical lessons on, 206
  as technology mega-
    trend, 31–32
  virtual reality (VR), 31, 64,
    80–81, 107, 199, 204, 205
Extended Reality in Practice,
  199, 319
Eyewear, 180, 204, 286–287, 289

F

Facebook
  brain-computer interface,
    205, 207
  deepfake detection
    and, 273, 278
  Oculus VR headset
    and, 302–303
  as platform business,
    189, 190, 191
  targeted ads and, 160, 164
  Workplace tool, 267
Factories
  dark, 101–102
  IoT sensors in, 100
  robots and cobots in, 102–103
  smart, 240, 247
Faethm automation pioneers,
    243, 248
Farfetch and Browns, 202–203, 207
Farming
  automation in, 86–87, 94
  blockchain technology
    in, 88–89, 95
  environmental impacts of,
    85–86, 94, 95
  genetic engineering in, 90–91, 96
  notes on, 94–97
  practical lessons on, 93–94
  precision, 87–88, 95
  vertical, 89–90, 95
Fashion
  digital-only, 140–141
  immersive experiences
    and, 202–203
  intelligent, 171
  personalized browsing for,
    160–161, 202

rentals, 171
  socks and underwear, 171, 174
  sportswear, 181–182
  sustainable, 215–216, 230
Filter bubble, 9
Financial services
  apps, 125, 129, 297, 299
  digital money, 121–124
  digital wallet services,
    123, 125–127
  notes on, 128–129
  personalized, 126–127
  practical lessons on, 127–128
Fish farming, 87, 94
Fisk, Peter, 288
Fitness apparel, 181–182, 216
Fitness products, 173, 175
Flatter organizations
  characteristics of, 259–261
  hybrid working and,
    265–268, 269
  notes on, 269–270
  performance management in,
    263–265, 268
  practical lessons on, 268–269
  speed and innovation
    in, 261–262
  two-pizza teams in, 263, 269
Flex feminine hygiene
    products, 170
Food consumption, conscious,
    211–213, 218
Food production, 5, 16, 91–93.
    See also Farming
Forbes, Chris, 287
Formula E Ghost Racing,
    203–204, 207
Fossil fuels, 6, 40, 47, 48, 111, 231

Fourth industrial revolution,
defined, 21–23, 40
Fox, Gary, 174
Funding methods
crowdfunding, 301, 302–303, 306
initial coin offerings (ICOs),
301, 303, 307
notes on, 306–308
practical lessons on, 306
special purpose acquisition
companies (SPACs), 301,
305–306, 307, 308
tokenization of assets, 301,
304, 306, 307

G
Gates, Bill, 6
GE, 53, 57, 100, 264
Gen Z, 13, 14, 15, 18, 282
Gender gap, 12–13, 18
Gene editing, 30, 35–37, 90
General Mills, 230, 234
Generis app, 135
Genetically modified foods
(GMOs), 36, 90–91
Ghost Racing, 203–204, 207
Gig workers, 249, 250, 255, 256
Giga Automata, 241, 247
Gilmore, James, 199, 200
Gin Club, Craft, 172
GitHub, 192, 198
GitLab, 266, 270, 274
Global shifts
climate crisis, 4–6, 15,
16, 117, 209
demographics, 10–12, 15
divergence, 8–10, 15
economic power, 6–8, 15

notes on, 15–19
practical lessons and, 14–15
workplace and culture, 12–14, 15
Global warming, 4, 6, 15,
48. *See also* Greenhouse
gas emissions
GMOs, 90–91
Gojek (super app), 136, 143
Google
choreography and, 248
goal-setting at, 264
personalized service
and, 158–159
as platform business, 190, 191
quantum computing and, 24
solar energy and, 48
Google Assistant, 141, 148, 152
Google Duplex Assistant, 238
Google Maps, 150, 154
Google Nest, 146, 173
Google Pay app, 297, 299
Grab (super app), 136
Green hydrogen, 39, 40
Green Mattress, My, 181
Greenhouse gas emissions
agriculture and, 85, 86, 87, 95
biggest sources of, 5, 118, 226
global warming and, 4, 6, 15, 48
manufacturing, construction,
and, 99, 106, 110
supply chains and, 226–227
transportation and, 111–112
zero-carbon solutions and, 6
Grooming products, 172, 216. *See
also* Beauty products
Grounds for Change, 211, 218
Gucci Garden, 202, 207
Gymshark, 181, 186

H

He Jiankui, 36, 42
Health insurance, 152–153, 154, 161
Health records, electronic, 64
Healthcare
  apps, 61, 62, 64, 135–136
  biohacking and, 30, 35–37, 65
  democratized, 61–62
  diabetes care, 62, 284–285
  digitized, 63–64
  notes on, 69–72
  personalized, 62–63, 69
  practical lessons on, 69
  preventative medicine, 59–61
  robots and nanobots in, 66–67, 71
  telemedicine, 63–64
  vaccine development, 296–297, 299
Healthcare professionals, shortage of, 59
Hershey, 232, 234, 235
Hirotec, 100, 108
Honda, 169, 296, 298
House of Vans, 203
Human jobs
  addition of, 243–244
  augmentation of, 241, 242–243
  displacement of, 102, 241, 242
Human-centered organizations, 313, 314
Hybrid work environment, 265–268, 269
Hydroponics, 90
Hyperloop travel, 113–114, 119, 120

I

IBM, 24, 32, 147, 169
Immersive learning, 80–81
Inclusion, 251–252, 253, 256, 257
Income inequality, 11–12, 18
India
  economy of, 7, 192–193, 198
  learning program in, 79
Industrial Internet of Things (IIoT), 100
Industrial revolution, fourth, 21–23, 40
Initial coin offerings (ICOs), 301, 303, 307
Insights tool, 127
Instacart app, 191–192
Insurance, health, 152–153, 154, 161
Insurwave, 183
International Thermonuclear Experimental Reactor (ITER), 39
Internet, splintering of, 9
Internet of Energy (IoE), 52
Internet of Medical Things (IoMT), 68
Internet of Things (IoT)
  defined, 21, 26
  energy usage and, 53
  industrial, 100
  number of, 41
  smarter products and, 145
Intrapreneurship, 262, 269

J

JD.com warehouse, 240
Jenner, Kylie, 181
Job performance, 253, 264, 268

Job skills
  education and, 74–77, 81
  future of work and,
    241–244, 247
  human qualities and, 244–246
Jobs, human
  addition of, 243–244
  augmentation of, 241, 242–243
  displacement of, 102, 241, 242
Jobs, Steve, 35, 276, 279
John Lewis department
  store, 202, 207
JustPark app, 193, 198

K
Kellogg's cereal, 232
Kelly, Kevin, 145
KickStarter, 302, 303
Klarna, 125

L
Labster, 81
Languages, learning, 74, 78–79, 83
Lawn mowers, robotic, 148
Leadership
  authentic, 275–277, 278, 279
  four key takeaways on, 311–315
  importance of, 245
Learning
  bite-sized, 80, 82
  immersive, 80–81, 82
  job skills and, 74–77, 81
  lifelong, 76–77, 82, 253
  online, 73, 78
  personalized, 77, 78–79, 82
  project-based, 77, 79
LEGO, 196, 198, 274
Lightbulbs, smart, 147

L'Oréal, 178, 182, 186, 311
Lufax, 126

M
MAC cosmetics, 204, 207
Machine learning, 30
Machine maintenance,
  100–101
Machine vision, 29
Mackmyra whisky, 162–163, 231
Manufacturing
  automation in, 101–102
  defined, 99
  digital twins and, 101, 108
  Industrial Internet of Things
    (IIoT), 100
  predictive maintenance
    in, 100–101
  robots and cobots in,
    102–103
  smart and sustainable
    products, 104
  3D printing and, 103, 105, 106
Maps, Google, 150, 154
Marr, Bernard, 175, 314–315,
  319–320
Marriage, 12
Mass personalization,
  157–158, 164
Mastercard, 124, 128
Masters, Tim, 181
Materials science, 38, 43
Mattresses, 180–181, 186
Mayflower Autonomous Ship,
  147–148, 154
McDonald's, 139, 196
McGregor, Wayne, 243
McIlwraith, Atlanta, 286

Meat
  environmental impact of, 85–86, 94
  new ways to create, 86, 91–93
  plant-based, 91–92, 96, 97, 212
Medical data breaches, 68, 69, 72
Medical robots and nanobots, 66–67, 71, 74
Medicine. *See also* Healthcare
  diabetes care, 62, 284–285
  preventative, 59–61
  telemedicine, 63–64
  vaccine development, 296–297, 299
Meeting notes, Ai-powered, 151
Megacities. *See* Cities
Micro-learning, 80
Micro-moments, 156–157, 164
Microsoft, 24, 25, 80, 169, 183, 192, 311
Microsoft Azure, 25, 168
Middlemen service providers
  blockchain threat to, 182–184
  direct-to-consumer (DTC) trend and, 177–182
Millennials, 13, 249, 282
Minimum viable product/service (MVP), 261–262
Mobility-as-a-service (MaaS), 117, 118
Modular and off-site construction, 105–106, 110
Money, digital. *See also* Bitcoin
  consequences of, 121–123
  defined, 123
  finance apps and, 125, 129
  financial services and, 123–124
  notes on, 128–129

  personalized service and, 126–127
  practical lessons on, 127–128
Moore's Law, 22, 23
Mottola, Matthew, 250, 256
Multiparty systems, 293–294
Murder mystery game, 170
Music industry
  android opera, 239, 247
  blockchain-based platforms and, 184, 187
Musk, Elon, 30, 114, 120, 205, 207, 315
My Green Mattress, 181
Myers, Verna, 251
MyQ Pet Portal, 148

N
Nanobots, in healthcare, 66–67, 71
Nano-learning, 80
Nanotechnology, 37–39, 66
Netflix
  inclusion at, 251–252, 257
  personalized approach of, 158, 159, 163, 164
  platform business model versus, 190
  as subscription model, 166
  as trusted brand, 274–275
Net-zero buildings, 105, 109
Newlight Technologies, 37, 42
News, personalized, 159–160, 185
Ng, Andrew, 239
Nike
  direct-to-consumer channel at, 182, 186
  personalization at, 162
  resilience of, 311